Managing Crisis and Man-made Disasters

Managing Crisis and Man-made Disasters

Dr. Alok Satsangi
&
Anshuman Sharma

RANDOM PUBLICATIONS
NEW DELHI (INDIA)

Managing Crisis and Man-made Disasters

ISBN 978-93-5111-492-5

Published in 2015 in India by

RANDOM PUBLICATIONS

4376-A/4B, Gali Murari Lal, Ansari Road
New Delhi-110 002
Phone : +9111-43580356, 011-23289044, 011-43142548
e-mail: sales@randompublications.com,
info@randompublications.com, randomexports@gmail.com

Reprinted 2018

Type Setting by : Friends Media, Delhi-110089
Digitally Printed at: Replika Press Pvt. Ltd.

Preface

Man made disasters are also known as anthropogenic disasters and they as a result of human intent, error or as a result of failed systems. These are broken down into several categories and while this is the case, there are some that cause more pronounced damage when compared to others. A good example is to look at man made disasters such as transportation. These are divided into different categories which include aviation, rail, road and space among others. Another type of disaster that falls in this category is nuclear bomb. When this occurs, it is often as a result of intent and the end results are even more catastrophic with a large percentage of those involved losing their lives or alternatively ending up with major defects or long term injuries. Other types of man made disasters which are just as catastrophic include chemical spill, arson and terrorism. There are also technological hazards which include power outages structural collapse, industrial hazards and fire.

The extent of damage caused by man made disasters varies greatly in accordance to geographical location and in this regard, the poorer countries are hardest hit when compared to the richer ones. This is attributed to the fact that the richer countries have what it take to respond with speed to calls of distress, and can implement the proper safety measures needed via remote control software from a distance to handle things safely and rapidly. Modern technology plays a very important part in the way you respond and prepare for distasters. On the other hand, the poorer countries have no resources or assets to respond with.

The present book provides practitioners, educators and students with a comprehensive overview of the players, processes and special issues involved in the management of man-made disasters and crises. It will be of immense help to all those contemplating to acquire expert knowledge of man-made disasters.

Author

Contents

1

Basics of Crisis Management

Crisis management is the process by which an organization deals with a major event that threatens to harm the organization, its stakeholders, or the general public. The study of crisis management originated with the large scale industrial and environmental disasters in the 1980s. Three elements are common to most definitions of crisis: (a) a threat to the organization, (b) the element of surprise, and (c) a short decision time. Venette argues that "crisis is a process of transformation where the old system can no longer be maintained." Therefore the fourth defining quality is the need for change. If change is not needed, the event could more accurately be described as a failure or incident.

In contrast to risk management, which involves assessing potential threats and finding the best ways to avoid those threats, crisis management involves dealing with threats before, during, and after they have occurred. It is a discipline within the broader context of management consisting of skills and techniques required to identify, assess, understand, and cope with a serious situation, especially from the moment it first occurs to the point that recovery procedures start.

Crisis management consists of:

- Methods used to respond to both the reality and perception of crises.
- Establishing metrics to define what scenarios constitute a crisis and should consequently trigger the necessary response mechanisms.
- Communication that occurs within the response phase of emergency management scenarios.

Crisis management methods of a business or an organization are called Crisis Management Plan.

Crisis management is occasionally referred to as incident management, although several industry specialists such as Peter Power argue that the term crisis management is more accurate.

A crisis mindset requires the ability to think of the worst-case scenario while simultaneously suggesting numerous solutions. Trial and error is an accepted discipline, as the first line of defense might not work. It is necessary to maintain a list of contingency plans and to be always on alert. Organizations and individuals should always be prepared with a rapid response plan to emergencies which would require analysis, drills and exercises.

The credibility and reputation of organizations is heavily influenced by the perception of their responses during crisis situations. The organization and communication involved in responding to a crisis in a timely fashion makes for a challenge in businesses. There must be open and consistent communication throughout the hierarchy to contribute to a successful crisis communication process.

The related terms emergency management and business continuity management focus respectively on the prompt but short lived "first aid" type of response (e.g. putting the fire out) and the longer term recovery and restoration phases (e.g. moving operations to another site). Crisis is also a facet of risk management, although it is probably untrue to say that Crisis Management represents a failure of Risk Management since it will never be possible to totally mitigate the chances of catastrophes occurring.

Types of Crisis

During the crisis management process, it is important to identify types of crises in that different crises necessitate the use of different crisis management strategies. Potential crises are enormous, but crises can be clustered.

Lerbinger categorized seven types of crises:

1. Natural disaster
2. Technological crises
3. Confrontation
4. Malevolence

5. Organizational Misdeeds
6. Workplace Violence
7. Rumours
8. Terrorist attacks/man-made disasters

Natural Crises

Natural crises, typically natural disasters considered as 'acts of God,' are such environmental phenomena as earthquakes, volcanic eruptions, tornadoes and hurricanes, floods, landslides, tsunamis, storms, and droughts that threaten life, property, and the environment itself.

Technological Crises

Technological crises are caused by human application of science and technology. Technological accidents inevitably occur when technology becomes complex and coupled and something goes wrong in the system as a whole. Some technological crises occur when human error causes disruptions. People tend to assign blame for a technological disaster because technology is subject to human manipulation whereas they do not hold anyone responsible for natural disaster. When an accident creates significant environmental damage, the crisis is categorized as megadamage. Samples include software failures, industrial accidents, and oil spills.

Confrontation Crises

Confrontation crises occur when discontented individuals and/or groups fight businesses, government, and various interest groups to win acceptance of their demands and expectations. The common type of confrontation crises is boycotts, and other types are picketing, sit-ins, ultimatums to those in authority, blockade or occupation of buildings, and resisting or disobeying police.

Crises of Malevolence

An organization faces a crisis of malevolence when opponents or miscreant individuals use criminal means or other extreme tactics for the purpose of expressing hostility or anger toward, or seeking gain from, a company, country, or economic system, perhaps with the aim of destabilizing or destroying it. Sample crises include product tampering, kidnapping, malicious rumors, terrorism, and espionage.

Crises of Organizational Misdeeds

Crises occur when management takes actions it knows will harm or place stakeholders at risk for harm without adequate precautions. Lerbinger specified three different types of crises of organizational misdeeds: crises of skewed management values, crises of deception, and crises of management misconduct.

Crises of Skewed Management Values

Crises of skewed management values are caused when managers favor short-term economic gain and neglect broader social values and stakeholders other than investors. This state of lopsided values is rooted in the classical business creed that focuses on the interests of stockholders and tends to disregard the interests of its other stakeholders such as customers, employees, and the community

Crises of Deception

Crises of deception occur when management conceals or misrepresents information about itself and its products in its dealing with consumers and others.

Crises of Management Misconduct

Some crises are caused not only by skewed values and deception but deliberate amorality and illegality.

Workplace Violence

Crises occur when an employee or former employee commits violence against other employees on organizational grounds.

Rumors

False information about an organization or its products creates crises hurting the organization's reputation. Sample is linking the organization to radical groups or stories that their products are contaminated.

Crisis Leadership

Erika Hayes James, an organizational psychologist at the University of Virginia's Darden Graduate School of Business, identifies two primary types of organizational crisis. James defines organizational crisis as "any emotionally charged situation that, once it becomes public, invites negative stakeholder reaction and thereby has the potential to threaten the financial well-being, reputation, or survival of the firm or some portion thereof."

1. Sudden crisis.
2. Smoldering crises

Sudden Crises

Sudden crises are circumstances that occur without warning and beyond an institution's control. Consequently, sudden crises are most often situations for which the institution and its leadership are not blamed.

Smoldering Crises

Smoldering crises differ from sudden crises in that they begin as minor internal issues that, due to manager's negligence, develop to crisis status. These are situations when leaders are blamed for the crisis and its subsequent effect on the institution in question.

James categorises five phases of crisis that require specific crisis leadership competencies. Each phase contains an obstacle that a leader must overcome to improve the structure and operations of an organization. James's case study on crisis in the financial services sector, for example, explores why crisis events erode public trust in leadership. James's research demonstrates how leadership competencies of integrity, positive intent, capability, mutual respect, and transparency impact the trust-building process.

1. Signal detection
2. Preparation and prevention
3. Containment and damage control
4. Business recovery
5. Learning

Signal detection

Si Sense-making: represents an attempt to create order and make sense, retrospectively, of what occurs. Perspective-taking: the ability to consider another person's or group's point of view.

Preparation and prevention

It is during this stage that crisis handlers begin preparing for or averting the crisis that had been foreshadowed in the signal detection stage.

Organizations such as the Red Cross's primary mission is to prepare for and prevent the escalation of crisis events. Walmart has been described as an emergency relief standard bearer after having witnessed the incredibly speedy and well-coordinated effort to get supplies to the Gulf Coast of the United States in anticipation of Hurricane Katrina.

Containment and damage control

Usually the most vivid stage, the goal of crisis containment and damage control is to limit the reputational, financial, safety, and other threats to firm survival. Crisis handlers work diligently during this stage to bring the crisis to an end as quickly as possible to limit the negative publicity to the organization, and move into the business recovery phase.

Business recovery

When crisis hits, organizations must be able to carry on with their business in the midst of the crisis while simultaneously planning for how they will recover from the damage the crisis caused. Crisis handlers not only engage in continuity planning (determining the people, financial, and technology resources needed to keep the organization running), but will also actively pursue organizational resilience.

Learning

In the wake of a crisis, organizational decision makers adopt a learning orientation and use prior experience to develop new routines and behaviors that ultimately change the way the organization operates. The best leaders recognize this and are purposeful and skillful in finding the learning opportunities inherent in every crisis situation.

Models and Theories Associated with Crisis Management

Crisis Management Model

Successfully defusing a crisis requires an understanding of how to handle a crisis – before they occur. Gonzalez-Herrero and Pratt found the different phases of Crisis Management.

There are 3 phases in any Crisis Management are as below

1. The diagnosis of the impending trouble or the danger signals.
2. Choosing appropriate Turnaround Strategy.
3. Implementation of the change process and its monitoring.

Management Crisis Planning

No corporation looks forward to facing a situation that causes a significant disruption to their business, especially one that stimulates extensive media coverage. Public scrutiny can result in a negative financial, political, legal and government impact. Crisis management planning deals with providing the best response to a crisis.

Contingency Planning

Preparing contingency plans in advance, as part of a crisis management plan, is the first step to ensuring an organization is appropriately prepared for a crisis. Crisis management teams can rehearse a crisis plan by developing a simulated scenario to use as a drill. The plan should clearly stipulate that the only people to speak publicly about the crisis are the designated persons, such as the company spokesperson or crisis team members. The first hours after a crisis breaks are the most crucial, so working with speed and efficiency is important, and the plan should indicate how quickly each function should be performed. When preparing to offer a statement externally as well as internally, information should be accurate. Providing incorrect or manipulated information has a tendency to backfire and will greatly exacerbate the situation. The contingency plan should contain information and guidance that will help decision makers to consider not only the short-term consequences, but the long-term effects of every decision.

Business Continuity Planning

When a crisis will undoubtedly cause a significant disruption to an organization, a business continuity plan can help minimize the disruption. First, one must identify the critical functions and processes that are necessary to keep the organization running. Then each critical function and or/process must have its own contingency plan in the event that one of the functions/processes ceases or fails. Testing these contingency plans by rehearsing the required actions in a simulation will allow for all involved to become more sensitive and aware of the possibility of a crisis. As a result, in the event of an actual crisis, the team members will act more quickly and effectively.

Structural-functional Systems Theory

Providing information to an organization in a time of crisis is critical to effective crisis management. Structural-functional systems theory addresses the intricacies of information networks and levels of command making up organizational communication. The structural-functional theory identifies information flow in organizations as "networks" made up of members and "links". Information in organizations flow in patterns called networks.

Diffusion of Innovation Theory

Another theory that can be applied to the sharing of information is Diffusion of Innovation Theory. Developed by Everett Rogers, the theory describes how innovation is disseminated and communicated through certain channels over a period of time. Diffusion of innovation in communication occurs when an individual communicates a new idea to one or several others. At its most elementary form, the process involves: (1) an innovation, (2) an individual or other unit of adoption that has knowledge of or experience with using the innovation, (3) another individual or other unit that does not yet have knowledge of the innovation, and (4) a communication channel connecting the two units. A communication channel is the means by which messages get from one individual to another.

Role of Apologies in Crisis Management

There has been debate about the role of apologies in crisis management, and some argue that apology opens an organization up for possible legal consequences. "However some evidence indicates that compensation and sympathy, two less expensive strategies, are as effective as an apology in shaping people's perceptions of the organization taking responsibility for the crisis because these strategies focus on the victims' needs. The sympathy response expresses concern for victims while compensation offers victims something to offset the suffering."

Leadership Competencies

James identifies five leadership competencies which facilitate organizational restructuring during and after a crisis.

1. Building an environment of trust
2. Reforming the organization's mindset
3. Identifying obvious and obscure vulnerabilities of the organization
4. Making wise and rapid decisions as well as taking courageous action
5. Learning from crisis to effect change.

Crisis leadership research concludes that leadership action in crisis reflects the competency of an organization, because the test of crisis demonstrates how well the institution's leadership structure serves the organization's goals and withstands crisis. Developing effective human resources is vital when building organizational capabilities through crisis management executive leadership.

Unequal Human Capital Theory

James postulates that organizational crisis can result from discrimination lawsuits. James's theory of unequal human capital and social position derives from economic theories of human and social capital concluding that minority employees receive fewer organizational rewards than those with access to executive management. In a recent study of managers in a Fortune 500 company, race was found to be a predictor of promotion opportunity or lack thereof. Thus, discrimination lawsuits can invite negative stakeholder reaction, damage the company's reputation, and threaten corporate survival.

Social Media and Crisis Management

Social media has accelerated the speed that information about a crisis can spread. The viral affect of social networks such as Twitter means that stakeholders can break news faster than traditional media - making managing a crisis harder. This can be mitigated by having the right training and policy in place as well as the right social media monitoring tools to detect signs of a crisis breaking. Social media also gives crisis management teams access to real-time information about how a crisis is impacting stakeholder sentiment and the issues that are of most concern to them.

The crisis management mantra of Lanny Davis, former counsellor to Bill Clinton is to "Tell it Early, Tell it All, Tell it Yourself". A strategy employed at the Clinton White House 1996 – 1998, to any breaking

Organisations should have a planned approach to releasing information to the media in the event of a crisis. A media reaction plan should include a company media representative as part of the Crisis Management Team (CMT). Since there is always a degree of unpredictability during a crisis, it is best that all CMT members understand how to deal with the media and be prepared to do so, should they be thrust into such a situation.

In 2010 Procter & Gamble Co called reports that its new Pampers with Dry Max caused rashes and other skin irritations "completely false" as it aimed to contain a public relations threat to its biggest diaper innovation in 25 years. A Facebook group called "Pampers bring back the OLD CRUISERS/SWADDLERS" rose to over 4,500 members. Pampers denied the allegation and stated that only two complaints had been received for every one million diapers sold. Pampers quickly reached out to people expressing their concerns via social media, Pampers even held a summit with four influential "mommy bloggers," to help dispel the rumour. Pampers acted quickly and decisively to an emerging crisis, before competitors and critics alike could fuel the fire further.

Examples of Successful Crisis Management

Tylenol

In the fall of 1982, a murderer added 65 milligrams of cyanide to some Tylenol capsules on store shelves, killing seven people, including three in one family. Johnson & Johnson recalled and destroyed 31 million capsules at a cost of $100 million. The affable CEO, James Burke, appeared in television ads and at news conferences informing consumers of the company's actions. Tamper-resistant packaging was rapidly introduced, and Tylenol sales swiftly bounced back to near pre-crisis levels.

When another bottle of tainted Tylenol was discovered in a store, it took only a matter of minutes for the manufacturer to issue a nationwide warning that people should not use the medication in its capsule form.

Odwalla Foods

When Odwalla's apple juice was thought to be the cause of an outbreak of E. coli infection, the company lost a third of its market value. In October 1996, an outbreak of E. coli bacteria in Washington state, California, Colorado and British Columbia was traced to unpasteurized apple juice manufactured by natural juice maker Odwalla Inc. Forty-nine cases were reported, including the death of a small child. Within 24 hours, Odwalla conferred with the FDA and Washington state health officials; established a schedule of daily press briefings; sent out press releases which announced the recall; expressed remorse, concern and apology, and took responsibility for anyone harmed by their products; detailed symptoms of E. coli poisoning; and explained what consumers should do with any affected products. Odwalla then developed - through the help of consultants - effective thermal processes that would not harm the products' flavors when production resumed. All of these steps were communicated through close relations with the media and through full-page newspaper ads.

Mattel

Mattel Inc., the toy maker, has been plagued with more than 28 product recalls and in Summer of 2007, amongst problems with exports from China, faced two product recalls in two weeks. The company "did everything it could to get its message out, earning high marks from consumers and retailers. Though upset by the situation, they were appreciative of the company's response. At Mattel, just after the 7 a.m. recall announcement by federal officials, a public relations staff of 16 was set to call reporters at the 40 biggest media outlets. They told each to check their e-mail for a news release outlining the recalls, invited them to a teleconference call with executives and scheduled TV appearances or phone conversations with Mattel's chief executive. The Mattel CEO Robert Eckert did 14 TV interviews on a Tuesday in August and about 20 calls with individual reporters. By the week's end, Mattel had responded to more than 300 media inquiries in the U.S. alone."

Pepsi

The Pepsi Corporation faced a crisis in 1993 which started with claims of syringes being found in cans of diet Pepsi. Pepsi urged stores not to remove the product from shelves while it had the cans and the situation investigated. This led to an arrest, which Pepsi made public and then followed with their first video news release, showing the production process to demonstrate that such tampering was impossible within their factories. A second video news release displayed the man arrested. A third video news release showed surveillance from a convenience store where a woman was caught replicating the tampering incident. The company simultaneously publicly worked with the FDA during the crisis.

The corporation was completely open with the public throughout, and every employee of Pepsi was kept aware of the details. This made public communications effective throughout the crisis. After the crisis had been resolved, the corporation ran a series of special campaigns designed to thank the public for standing by the corporation, along with coupons for further compensation. This case served as a design for how to handle other crisis situations.

Examples of Unsuccessful Crisis Management

Bhopal

The Bhopal disaster in which poor communication before, during, and after the crisis cost thousands of lives, illustrates the importance of incorporating cross-cultural communication in crisis management plans. According to American University's Trade Environmental Database Case Studies (1997), local residents were not sure how to react to warnings of potential threats from the Union Carbide plant. Operating manuals printed only in English is an extreme example of mismanagement but indicative of systemic barriers to information diffusion. According to Union Carbide's own chronology of the incident (2006), a day after the crisis Union Carbide's upper management arrived in India but was unable to assist in the relief efforts because they were placed under house arrest by the Indian government. Symbolic intervention can be counter productive; a crisis management strategy can help upper management make more calculated decisions in how they should respond to disaster scenarios. The Bhopal incident illustrates the difficulty in consistently applying management standards to multi-national operations and the blame shifting that often results from the lack of a clear management plan.

Ford and Firestone Tire and Rubber Company

The Ford-Firestone Tire and Rubber Company dispute transpired in August 2000. In response to claims that their 15-inch Wilderness AT, radial ATX and ATX II tire treads were separating from the tire core—leading to grisly, spectacular crashes—Bridgestone/Firestone recalled 6.5 million tires. These tires were mostly used on the Ford Explorer, the world's top-selling sport utility vehicle (SUV). The two companies committed three major blunders early on, say crisis experts. First, they blamed consumers for not inflating their tires properly. Then they blamed each other for faulty tires and faulty vehicle design. Then they said very little about what they were doing to solve a problem that had caused more than 100 deaths—until they got called to Washington to testify before Congress.

Exxon

On March 24, 1989, a tanker belonging to the Exxon Corporation ran aground in the Prince William Sound in Alaska. The Exxon Valdez spilled millions of gallons of crude oil into the waters off Valdez, killing thousands of fish, fowl, and sea otters. Hundreds of miles of coastline were polluted and salmon spawning runs disrupted; numerous fishermen, especially Native Americans, lost their livelihoods. Exxon, by contrast, did not react quickly in terms of dealing with the media and the public; the CEO, Lawrence Rawl, did not become an active part of the public relations effort and actually shunned public involvement; the company had neither a communication plan nor a communication team in place to handle the event—in fact, the company did not appoint a public relations manager to its management team until 1993, 4 years after the incident; Exxon established its media center in Valdez, a location too small and too remote to handle the onslaught of media attention; and the company acted defensively in its response to its publics, even laying blame, at times, on other groups such as the Coast Guard. These responses also happened within days of the incident.

Impact of Catastrophes on Shareholder Value

One of the foremost recognized studies conducted on the impact of a catastrophe on the stock value of an organization was completed by Dr Rory Knight and Dr Deborah Pretty (1996, Templeton College, University of Oxford - commissioned by the Sedgewick Group). This study undertook a detailed analysis of the stock price (post impact) of organizations that had experienced catastrophes. The study identified organizations that recovered and even exceeded pre-catastrophe stock price, (Recoverers), and those that did not recover on stock price, (Non-recoverers). The average cumulative impact on shareholder value for the recoverers was 5% plus on their original stock value. So the net impact on shareholder value by this stage was actually positive. The non-recoverers remained more or less unchanged between days 5 and 50 after the catastrophe, but suffered a net negative cumulative impact of almost 15% on their stock price up to one year afterwards.

One of the key conclusions of this study is that "Effective management of the consequences of catastrophes would appear to be a more significant factor than whether catastrophe insurance hedges the economic impact of the catastrophe".

While there are technical elements to this report it is highly recommended to those who wish to engage their senior management in the value of crisis management.

Crisis as Opportunity

To address such shareholder impact, management must move from a mindset that manages crisis to one that generates crisis leadership. Research shows that organizational contributory factors affect the tendency of executives to adopt an effective "crisis as opportunity" mindset. Since pressure is both a precipitator and consequence of crisis, leaders who perform well under pressure can effectively guide the organization through such crisis.

James contends that most executives focus on communications and public relations as a reactive strategy. While the company's reputation with shareholders, financial well-being, and survival are all at stake, potential damage to reputation can result from the actual management of the crisis issue. Additionally, companies may stagnate as their risk management group identifies whether a crisis is sufficiently "statistically significant". Crisis leadership, on the other hand, immediately addresses both the damage and implications for the company's present and future conditions, as well as opportunities for improvement.

Public Sector Crisis Management

Corporate America is not the only community that is vulnerable to the perils of a crisis. Whether a school shooting, a public health crisis or a terrorist attack that leaves the public seeking comfort in the calm, steady leadership of an elected official, no sector of society is immune to crisis. In response to that reality, crisis management policies, strategies and practices have been developed and adapted across multiple disciplines.

Schools and Crisis Management

In the wake of the Columbine High School Massacre, the September 11 attacks in 2001, and shootings on college campuses including the Virginia Tech massacre, educational institutions at all levels are now focused on crisis management.

A national study conducted by the University of Arkansas for Medical Sciences (UAMS) and Arkansas Children's Hospital Research Institute (ACHRI) has shown that many public school districts have important deficiencies in their emergency and disaster plans (The School Violence Resource Center, 2003). In response the Resource Center has organized a comprehensive set of resources to aid schools is the development of crisis management plans.

Crisis management plans cover a wide variety of incidents including bomb threats, child abuse, natural disasters, suicide, drug abuse and gang activities – just to list a few. In a similar fashion the plans aim to address all audiences in need of information including parents, the media and law enforcement officials.

Government and Crisis Management

Historically, government at all levels – local, state, and national – has played a large role in crisis management. Indeed, many political philosophers have considered this to be one of the primary roles of government. Emergency services, such as fire and police departments at the local level, and the United States National Guard at the federal level, often play integral roles in crisis situations.

To help coordinate communication during the response phase of a crisis, the U.S. Federal Emergency Management Agency (FEMA) within the Department of Homeland Security administers the National Response Plan (NRP). This plan is intended to integrate public and private response by providing a common language and outlining a chain-of-command when multiple parties are mobilized. It is based on the premise that incidences should be handled at the lowest organizational level possible. The NRP recognizes the private sector as a key partner in domestic incident management, particularly in the area of critical infrastructure protection and restoration.

The NRP is a companion to the National Incidence Management System that acts as a more general template for incident management regardless of cause, size, or complexity.

FEMA offers free web-based training on the National Response Plan through the Emergency Management Institute.

Common Alerting Protocol (CAP) is a relatively recent mechanism that facilitates crisis communication across different mediums and systems. CAP helps create a consistent emergency alert format to reach geographically and linguistically diverse audiences through both audio and visual mediums.

Elected Officials and Crisis Management

Historically, politics and crisis go hand-in-hand. In describing crisis, President Abraham Lincoln said, "We live in the midst of alarms, anxiety beclouds the future; we expect some new disaster with each newspaper we read."

Crisis management has become a defining feature of contemporary governance. In times of crisis, communities and members of organizations expect their public leaders to minimize the impact of the crisis at hand, while critics and bureaucratic competitors try to seize the moment to blame incumbent rulers and their policies. In this extreme environment, policy makers must somehow establish a sense of normality, and foster collective learning from the crisis experience.

In the face of crisis, leaders must deal with the strategic challenges they face, the political risks and opportunities they encounter, the errors they make, the pitfalls they need to avoid, and the paths away from crisis they may pursue. The necessity for management is even more significant with the advent of a 24-hour news cycle and an increasingly internet-savvy audience with ever-changing technology at its fingertips.

Public leaders have a special responsibility to help safeguard society from the adverse consequences of crisis. Experts in crisis management note that leaders who take this responsibility seriously would have to concern themselves with all crisis phases: the incubation stage, the onset, and the aftermath. Crisis leadership then involves five critical tasks: sense making, decision making, meaning making, terminating, and learning.

A brief description of the five facets of crisis leadership includes:

1. Sense making may be considered as the classical situation assessment step in decision making.
2. Decision making is both the act of coming to a decision as the implementation of that decision.
3. Meaning making refers to crisis management as political communication.
4. Terminating a crisis is only possible if the public leader correctly handles the accountability question.
5. Learning, refers to the actual learning from a crisis is limited. The authors note, a crisis often opens a window of opportunity for reform for better or for worse.

References

Barton, L. (2007). *Crisis leadership now: A real-world guide to preparing for threats, disaster, sabotage, and scandal.* New York, NY: McGraw-Hill.

Borodzicz, Edward P. (2005). *Risk, Crisis and Security Management.* West Sussex, England: John Wiley and Sons Ltd.

Dezenhall, E.; Weber, J. (2007). *Damage control: Why everything you know about crisis management is wrong*. Portfolio Hardcover.

Erickson, Paul A. (2006). *Emergency Response Planning for Corporate and Municipal Managers* (2nd ed.). Burlington, MA: Elsevier, Inc..

Mitroff, Ian I.; Gus Anagnos (2000). *Managing Crises Before They Happen: What Every Executive Needs to Know About Crisis Management*. New York: AMACOM.

Smith, Larry; Dan Millar, PhD (2002). *Crisis Management and Communication; How to Gain and Maintain Control* (2nd ed.). San Francisco, CA: International Association of Business Communicators.

Ulmer, R. R.; Sellnow, T. L., & Seeger, M. W. (2006). *Effective crisis communication: Moving from crisis to opportunity*. Thousand Oaks, CA: Sage Publications.

2

Phases of Emergency Management

Emergency management is the generic name of an interdisciplinary field dealing with the strategic organizational management processes used to protect critical assets of an organization from hazard risks that can cause events like disasters or catastrophes and to ensure the resiliency of the organization within their planned lifetime.

Emergencies, Disasters, and Catastrophes are not gradients, they are separate, distinct problems that require distinct strategies of response. Disasters are events distinguished from everyday emergencies by four factors: Organizations are forced into more and different kinds of interactions than normal; Organizations lose some of their normal autonomy; Performance standards change, and; More coordinated public sector/private sector relationships are required.

Catastrophes are distinct from disasters in that: Most or all of the community built structure is heavily impacted; Local officials are unable to undertake their usual work roles; Most, if not all, of the everyday community functions are sharply and simultaneously interrupted, and; Help from nearby communities cannot be provided.

Assets are categorized as either living things, non-living things, cultural or economic. Hazards are categorized by their cause, either natural or human-made. The entire strategic management process is divided into four fields to aid in identification of the processes. The four fields normally deal with risk reduction, preparing resources to respond to the hazard, responding to the actual damage caused by the hazard and limiting further damage (e.g., emergency evacuation, quarantine, mass decontamination, etc.), and returning as close as possible to the state before the hazard incident. The field occurs in both the public and private sector, sharing the same processes, but with different focuses.

There may be various types of threats to organizations in their day to day operations. These threats may not be visible in their initial stages but may hamper the whole growth strategies and put organizations into losses in a very short span of time. In the case of serious area-wide events, first responders will prioritize public institutions. Therefore, in order to respond to sudden, unwanted events, organizations need a holistic and integrated planning, aiming not only at minimizing and avoiding escalation, but also at providing the capability to adapt and to strengthen.

An emergency is an unplanned event with the capability to endanger life, disrupt operations, cause environmental damage and affect reputation, and which requires a significant and comprehensive response. Although emergency plans may be integrated in wider crisis or business continuity plans, their main focus is placed in dealing with localized events and immediate response to incidents/emergencies, natural, or man-made, having in mind the need to preserve life and safety of employees, assets and the public.

Phases and Professional Activities

The nature of management depends on local, economic and social conditions. Some disaster relief experts, such as Fred Cuny, have stated that in a sense the only real disasters are economic. Cuny stated that the cycle of Emergency Management must include long-term work on infrastructure, public awareness, and even human justice issues. The process of Emergency Management involves four phases: mitigation, preparedness, response, and recovery.

Recently the Department of Homeland Security and FEMA have adopted the terms "resilience" and "prevention" as part of the paradigm of EM. The latter term was mandated by PKEMA 2006 as statute enacted in October 2006 and made effective March 31, 2007. The two terms definitions do not fit easily as separate phases. Resilience, describes the goal of the four phases: an ability to recover from or adjust easily to misfortune or change.

Comprehensive Emergency Management: To be effective, Emergency Management requires an integrated approach that pays attention to all phases and types of emergencies, whether natural or man-made, organization and availability of resources. This concept is a security risk management method that uses the all-hazards approach which when applied enhances organizational resilience. This approach consists of four components:

Mitigation

Mitigation efforts are attempts to prevent hazards from developing into disasters altogether or to reduce the effects of disasters. Mitigation is the effort to reduce loss of life and property by lessening the impact of disasters. This is achieved through risk analysis, which results in information that provides a foundation for mitigation activities that reduce risk, and flood insurance that protects financial investment,. The mitigation phase differs from the other phases in that it focuses on long-term measures for reducing or eliminating risk. The implementation of mitigation strategies is a part of the recovery process if applied after a disaster occurs.

Mitigation measures can be structural or non-structural. Structural measures use technological solutions like flood levees and building retrofitting for earthquakes. Non-structural measures include legislation, land-use planning and insurance.

Mitigation is the most cost-efficient method for reducing the effect of hazards although not always the most suitable. Mitigation includes providing regulations regarding evacuation, sanctions against those who refuse to obey the regulations (such as mandatory evacuations), and communication of risks to the public. Some structural mitigation measures may harm the ecosystem.

A precursor to mitigation is the identification of risks. Physical risk assessment refers to identifying and evaluating hazards. The hazard-specific risk combines a hazard's probability and effects. The equation below states that the hazard multiplied by the populations' vulnerability to that hazard produces a risk Catastrophe modeling. The higher the risk, the more urgent that the vulnerabilities to the hazard are targeted by mitigation and preparedness. If, however, there is no vulnerability then there will be no risk, e.g. an earthquake occurring in a desert where nobody lives.

Preparedness

Preparedness is how we change behavior to limit the impact of disaster events on people. Preparedness is a continuous cycle of planning, managing, organizing, training, equipping, exercising, creating, evaluating, monitoring and improving activities to ensure effective coordination and the enhancement of capabilities of concerned organizations to prevent, protect against, respond to, recover from, create resources and mitigate the effects of natural disasters, acts of terrorism, and other man-made disasters.

In the preparedness phase, emergency managers develop plans of action carefully to manage and counter their risks and take action to build the necessary capabilities needed to implement such plans. Common preparedness measures include:

— communication plans with easily understandable terminology and methods.
— proper maintenance and training of emergency services, including mass human resources such as community emergency response teams.
— development and exercise of emergency population warning methods combined with emergency shelters and evacuation plans.
— implement and maintain an emergency communication system that can help identify the nature of an emergency and provide instructions when needed.
— stockpiling, inventory, streamline foods supplies, and maintain other disaster supplies and equipment.
— The Federal Emergency Management Agency (FEMA), recommends the following for a disaster preparedness kit: one gallon of water per person per day for three days, non-perishable food for each person for three days, battery powered or hand crank radio and extra batteries, flashlights for each person and extra batteries, first aid kit, whistle, filter mask or a cotton t-shirt for each person, moist towlettes, garbage bags, and plastic ties, wrench or pliers, manual can opener, plastic sheeting and duct tape, important family documents, daily prescription medicine, other things include diapers/formula for babies and special need items. Typically a three day supply of food and water is the minimum recommendation, having a larger supply means longer survival (Federal Emergency Management Agency [FEMA), n.d.). Small comfort items can be added like a few toys for children, a candy bar, or a book/comic to read. These small items that do not take up much space can come in handy to increase moods during survival time.

— develop organizations of trained volunteers among civilian populations. Professional emergency workers are rapidly overwhelmed in mass emergencies so trained, organized, responsible volunteers are extremely valuable. Organizations like Community Emergency Response Teams and the Red Cross are ready sources of trained volunteers. The latter's emergency management system has gotten high ratings from both California, and the Federal Emergency Management Agency (FEMA).

Another aspect of preparedness is casualty prediction, the study of how many deaths or injuries to expect for a given kind of event. This gives planners an idea of what resources need to be in place to respond to a particular kind of event.

Emergency Managers in the planning phase should be flexible, and all encompassing – carefully recognizing the risks and exposures of their respective regions and employing unconventional, and atypical means of support. Depending on the region – municipal, or private sector emergency services can rapidly be depleted and heavily taxed. Non-governmental organizations that offer desired resources, i.e., transportation of displaced home-owners to be conducted by local school district buses, evacuation of flood victims to be performed by mutual aide agreements between fire departments and rescue squads, should be identified early in planning stages, and practiced with regularity.

Response

The response phase includes the mobilization of the necessary emergency services and first responders in the disaster area. This is likely to include a first wave of core emergency services, such as firefighters, police and ambulance crews. When conducted as a military operation, it is termed Disaster Relief Operation (DRO) and can be a follow-up to a Non-combatant evacuation operation (NEO). They may be supported by a number of secondary emergency services, such as specialist rescue teams.

A well rehearsed emergency plan developed as part of the preparedness phase enables efficient coordination of rescue. Where required, search and rescue efforts commence at an early stage. Depending on injuries sustained by the victim, outside temperature, and victim access to air and water, the vast majority of those affected by a disaster will die within 72 hours after impact.

Organizational response to any significant disaster – natural or terrorist-borne – is based on existing emergency management organizational systems and processes: the Federal Response Plan (FRP) and the Incident Command System (ICS). These systems are solidified through the principles of Unified Command (UC) and Mutual Aid (MA)

There is a need for both discipline (structure, doctrine, process) and agility (creativity, improvisation, adaptability) in responding to a disaster. There is also the need to onboard and build an effective leadership team quickly to coordinate and manage efforts as they grow beyond first responders. The leader and team must formulate and implement a disciplined, iterative set of response plans, allowing initial coordinated responses that are vaguely right, adapting to new information and changes in circumstances as they arise.

Recovery

The aim of the recovery phase is to restore the affected area to its previous state. It differs from the response phase in its focus; recovery efforts are concerned with issues and decisions that must be made after immediate needs are addressed. Recovery efforts are primarily concerned with actions that involve rebuilding destroyed property, re-employment, and the repair of other essential infrastructure.

Efforts should be made to "build back better", aiming to reduce the pre-disaster risks inherent in the community and infrastructure. An important aspect of effective recovery efforts is taking advantage of a 'window of opportunity' for the implementation of mitigative measures that might otherwise be unpopular. Citizens of the affected area are more likely to accept more mitigative changes when a recent disaster is in fresh memory.

In the United States, the National Response Plan dictates how the resources provided by the Homeland Security Act of 2002 will be used in recovery efforts. It is the Federal government that often provides the most technical and financial assistance for recovery efforts in the United States.

Command and Control

In order to achieve effectiveness and efficiency managing emergencies, a hierarchical management structure is required. Due to the latest disruptions occurred in the past decade, several countries have established laws and industry standards to regulate the emergency organization. It is generally accepted that the emergency management organization should consists of two main teams; the emergency management team (EMT) and the emergency response team (ERT). The emergency management team is made up of senior personnel and normally chaired by the highest ranking official, in the role of emergency director. Ideally business recovery representatives should be members of the EMT, thus enabling the transition from response to recovery and continuity operations. The emergency management team is responsible for the oversight and coordination of activities during all the phases of the emergency. The emergency management team may operate from an Emergency Operations Centre (EOC), where all the actions required for response and recovery to incidents are coordinated and monitored. An important requirement in dealing with emergencies is the need to be aware of specific government regulations and a close coordination of activities with local emergency services.

The emergency response team consists of trained employees namely from security, safety, engineering etc., with specific duties, equipment and training, with the task of responding to emergencies.

Phases and Personal Activities

Mitigation

Personal mitigation is mainly about knowing and avoiding unnecessary risks. This includes an assessment of possible risks to personal/family health and to personal property.

In a flood plain, in areas of subsidence or landslides, home owners may not be aware of a property being exposed to a hazard until it strikes. However, specialists can be hired to conduct risk identification and assessment surveys. Purchase of insurance covering the most prominent identified risks is a common measure.

Personal structural mitigation in earthquake prone areas includes installation of an Earthquake Valve to instantly shut off the natural gas supply to a property, seismic retrofits of property and the securing of items inside a building to enhance household seismic safety. The latter may include the mounting of furniture, refrigerators, water heaters and breakables to the walls, and the addition of cabinet latches. In flood prone areas houses can be built on poles/stilts, as in much of southern Asia. In areas prone to prolonged electricity black-outs installation of a generator would be an example of an optimal structural mitigation measure. The construction of storm cellars and fallout shelters are further examples of personal mitigative actions.

Mitigation involves Structural and Non-structural measures taken to limit the impact of disasters. Structural mitigation are actions that change the characteristics of a building or its surrounding, examples include shelters, windows shutters, clearing forest around the house. Non-structural mitigation on personal level mainly takes the form of insurance or simply moving house to a safer area.

Preparedness

Personal preparedness focuses on preparing equipment and procedures for use when a disaster occurs, i.e., planning. Preparedness measures can take many forms including the construction of shelters, implementation of an emergency communication system, installation of warning devices, creation of back-up life-line services (e.g., power, water, sewage), and rehearsing evacuation plans.

Two simple measures can help prepare the individual for sitting out the event or evacuating, as necessary. For evacuation, a disaster supplies kit may be prepared and for sheltering purposes a stockpile of supplies may be created. The preparation of a survival kit such as a "72-hour kit", is often advocated by authorities. These kits may include food, medicine, flashlights, candles and money. Also, putting valuable items in safe area is also recommended.

Response

The response phase of an emergency may commence with search and rescue but in all cases the focus will quickly turn to fulfilling the basic humanitarian needs of the affected population. This assistance may be provided by national or international agencies and organisations. Effective coordination of disaster assistance is often crucial, particularly when many organizations respond and local emergency management agency (LEMA) capacity has been exceeded by the demand or diminished by the disaster itself.

On a personal level the response can take the shape either of a shelter in place or an evacuation. In a shelter-in-place scenario, a family would be prepared to fend for themselves in their home for many days without any form of outside support. In an evacuation, a family leaves the area by automobile or other mode of transportation, taking with them the maximum amount of supplies they can carry, possibly including a tent for shelter. If mechanical transportation is not available, evacuation on foot would ideally include carrying at least three days of supplies and rain-tight bedding, a tarpaulin and a bedroll of blankets being the minimum.

Recovery

The recovery phase starts after the immediate threat to human life has subsided. During reconstruction it is recommended to consider the location or construction material of the property.

The most extreme home confinement scenarios include war, famine and severe epidemics and may last a year or more. Then recovery will take place inside the home. Planners for these events usually buy bulk foods and appropriate storage and preparation equipment, and eat the food as part of normal life. A simple balanced diet can be constructed from vitamin pills, whole-meal wheat, beans, dried milk, corn, and cooking oil. One should add vegetables, fruits, spices and meats, both prepared and fresh-gardened, when possible.

Emergency Management as a profession

Emergency managers are trained in a wide variety of disciplines that support them throughout the emergency life-cycle. Professional emergency managers can focus on government and community preparedness (Continuity of Operations/Continuity of Government Planning), or private business preparedness (Business Continuity Management Planning). Training is provided by local, state, federal and private organizations and ranges from public information and media relations to high-level incident command and tactical skills such as studying a terrorist bombing site or controlling an emergency scene.

In the past, the field of emergency management has been populated mostly by people with a military or first responder background. Currently, the population in the field has become more diverse, with many experts coming from a variety of backgrounds without military or first responder history. Educational opportunities are increasing for those seeking undergraduate and graduate degrees in emergency management or a related field. There are over 180 schools in the US with emergency management-related programs, but only one doctoral program specifically in emergency management.

Professional certifications such as Certified Emergency Manager (CEM) and Certified Business Continuity Professional (CBCP) are becoming more common as the need for high professional standards is recognized by the emergency management community, especially in the United States. Professional emergency management organizations should also be utilized by professional in this field. These organizations allow for professional networking and the sharing of information related to emergency management. The National Emergency Management Association and the International Association of Emergency Managers are two examples of these professional organizations.

Principles of Emergency Management

In 2007, Dr. Wayne Blanchard of FEMA's Emergency Management Higher Education Project, at the direction of Dr. Cortez Lawrence, Superintendent of FEMA's Emergency Management Institute, convened a working group of emergency management practitioners and academics to consider principles of emergency management. This project was prompted by the realization that while numerous books, articles and papers referred to "principles of emergency management," nowhere in the vast array of literature on the subject was there an agreed-upon definition of what these principles were. The group agreed on eight principles that will be used to guide the development of a doctrine of emergency management. The summary provided below lists these eight principles and provides a brief description of each.

Principles: Emergency management must be:

— *Comprehensive* – emergency managers consider and take into account all hazards, all phases, all stakeholders and all impacts relevant to disasters.

— *Progressive* – emergency managers anticipate future disasters and take preventive and preparatory measures to build disaster-resistant and disaster-resilient communities.

— *Risk-driven* – emergency managers use sound risk management principles (hazard identification, risk analysis, and impact analysis) in assigning priorities and resources.

— *Integrated* – emergency managers ensure unity of effort among all levels of government and all elements of a community.

- Collaborative – emergency managers create and sustain broad and sincere relationships among individuals and organizations to encourage trust, advocate a team atmosphere, build consensus, and facilitate communication.
- *Coordinated* – emergency managers synchronize the activities of all relevant stakeholders to achieve a common purpose.
- *Flexible* – emergency managers use creative and innovative approaches in solving disaster challenges.
- *Professional* – emergency managers value a science and knowledge-based approach; based on education, training, experience, ethical practice, public stewardship and continuous improvement.

Tools

In recent years the continuity feature of emergency management has resulted in a new concept, Emergency Management Information Systems (EMIS). For continuity and interoperability between emergency management stakeholders, EMIS supports the emergency management process by providing an infrastructure that integrates emergency plans at all levels of government and non-government involvement and by utilizing the management of all related resources (including human and other resources) for all four phases of emergencies. In the healthcare field, hospitals utilize HICS (Hospital Incident Command System) which provides structure and organization in a clearly defined chain of command with set responsibilities for each division.

International organizations of Emergency Management

International Association of Emergency Managers

The International Association of Emergency Managers (IAEM) is a non-profit educational organization dedicated to promoting the goals of saving lives and protecting property during emergencies and disasters. The mission of IAEM is to serve its members by providing information, networking and professional opportunities, and to advance the emergency management profession.

It currently has seven Councils around the World: Asia, Canada, Europa, International, Oceania, Student and USA.

The Air Force Emergency Management Association (www.af-em.org, www.3e9x1.com, and www.afema.org), affiliated by membership with the IAEM, provides emergency management information and networking for US Air Force Emergency Managers.

International Recovery Platform

The International Recovery Platform (IRP) was conceived at the World Conference on Disaster Reduction (WCDR) in Kobe, Hyogo, Japan in January 2005. As a thematic platform of the International Strategy for Disaster Reduction (ISDR) system, IRP is a key pillar for the implementation of the Hyogo Framework for Action (HFA) 2005–2015: Building the Resilience of Nations and Communities to Disasters, a global plan for disaster risk reduction for the decade adopted by 168 governments at the WCDR.

The key role of IRP is to identify gaps and constraints experienced in post disaster recovery and to serve as a catalyst for the development of tools, resources, and capacity for resilient recovery. IRP aims to be an international source of knowledge on good recovery practice.

Red Cross/Red Crescent

National Red Cross/Red Crescent societies often have pivotal roles in responding to emergencies. Additionally, the International Federation of Red Cross and Red Crescent Societies (IFRC, or "The Federation") may deploy assessment teams, e.g. Field Assessment and Coordination Team – (FACT) to the affected country if requested by the national Red Cross or Red Crescent Society. After having assessed the needs Emergency Response Units (ERUs) may be deployed to the affected country or region. They are specialized in the response component of the emergency management framework.

United Nations

Within the United Nations system responsibility for emergency response rests with the Resident Coordinator within the affected country. However, in practice international response will be coordinated, if requested by the affected country's government, by the UN Office for the Coordination of Humanitarian Affairs (UN-OCHA), by deploying a UN Disaster Assessment and Coordination (UNDAC) team.

World Bank

Since 1980, the World Bank has approved more than 500 operations related to disaster management, amounting to more than US$40 billion. These include post-disaster reconstruction projects, as well as projects with components aimed at preventing and mitigating disaster impacts, in countries such as Argentina, Bangladesh, Colombia, Haiti, India, Mexico, Turkey and Vietnam to name only a few.

Common areas of focus for prevention and mitigation projects include forest fire prevention measures, such as early warning measures and education campaigns to discourage farmers from slash and burn agriculture that ignites forest fires; early-warning systems for hurricanes; flood prevention mechanisms, ranging from shore protection and terracing in rural areas to adaptation of production; and earthquake-prone construction.

In a joint venture with Columbia University under the umbrella of the ProVention Consortium the World Bank has established a Global Risk Analysis of Natural Disaster Hotspots.

In June 2006, the World Bank established the Global Facility for Disaster Reduction and Recovery (GFDRR), a longer term partnership with other aid donors to reduce disaster losses by mainstreaming disaster risk reduction in development, in support of the Hyogo Framework of Action. The facility helps developing countries fund development projects and programs that enhance local capacities for disaster prevention and emergency preparedness.

European Union

Since 2001, the EU adopted Community Mechanism for Civil Protection, which started to play a significant role on the global scene. Mechanism's main role is to facilitate co-operation in civil protection assistance interventions in the event of major emergencies which may require urgent response actions. This applies also to situations where there may be an imminent threat of such major emergencies.

The heart of the Mechanism is the Monitoring and Information Centre. It is part of Directorate-General for Humanitarian Aid & Civil Protection of the European Commission and accessible 24 hours a day. It gives countries access to a platform, to a one-stop-shop of civil protection means available amongst the all the participating states. Any country inside or outside the Union affected by a major disaster can make an appeal for assistance through the MIC. It acts as a communication hub at headquarters level between participating states, the affected country and despatched field experts. It also provides useful and updated information on the actual status of an ongoing emergency.

National Organizations

Australia

Natural disasters are part of life in Australia. Drought occurs on average every 3 out of 10 years and associated heatwaves have killed more Australians than any other type of natural disaster in the 20th century.

Australia's emergency management processes embrace the concept of the prepared community. The principal government agency in achieving this is Emergency Management Australia.

Canada

Public Safety Canada is Canada's national emergency management agency. Each province is required to have legislation in place for dealing with emergencies, as well as establish their own emergency management agencies, typically called an "Emergency Measures Organization" (EMO), which functions as the primary liaison with the municipal and federal level.

Public Safety Canada coordinates and supports the efforts of federal organizations ensuring national security and the safety of Canadians. They also work with other levels of government, first responders, community groups, the private sector (operators of critical infrastructure) and other nations.

Public Safety Canada's work is based on a wide range of policies and legislation through the Public Safety and Emergency Preparedness Act which defines the powers, duties and functions of PS are outlined. Other acts are specific to fields such as corrections, emergency management, law enforcement, and national security.

Germany

In Germany the Federal Government controls the German Katastrophenschutz (disaster relief) and Zivilschutz (civil protection) programs. The local units of German fire department and the Technisches Hilfswerk (Federal Agency for Technical Relief, THW) are part of these programs.& The German Armed Forces (Bundeswehr), the German Federal Police and the 16 state police forces (Länderpolizei) all have been deployed for disaster relief operations.

Besides the German Red Cross, humanitarian help is dispensed by the Johanniter-Unfallhilfe, the German equivalent of the St. John Ambulance, the Malteser-Hilfsdienst, the Arbeiter-Samariter-Bund, and other private Organization, to cite the largest relief organisation that are equipped for large-scale emergencies. As of 2006, there is a joint course at the University of Bonn leading to the degree "Master in Disaster Prevention and Risk Governance"

India

The role of emergency management in India falls to National Disaster Management Authority of India, a government agency subordinate to the Ministry of Home Affairs. In recent years there has been a shift in emphasis from response and recovery to strategic risk management and reduction, and from a government-centered approach to decentralized community participation. The Ministry of Science and Technology.headed by Dr Karan Rawat, supports an internal agency that facilitates research by bringing the academic knowledge and expertise of earth scientists to emergency management.

A group representing a public/private has recently been formed by the Government of India. It is funded primarily by a large India-based computer company and aimed at improving the general response of communities to emergencies, in addition to those incidents which might be described as disasters. Some of the groups' early efforts involve the provision of emergency management training for first responders (a first in India), the creation of a single emergency telephone number, and the establishment of standards for EMS staff, equipment, and training. It operates in three states, though efforts are being made in making this a nation-wide effective group.

Aniruddha's Academy of Disaster Management (AADM) is a Non-Profit Organization in Mumbai, India with 'Disaster Management' as its principal objective. The basic aim of AADM is to save life and property in the event of a disaster, be it natural or manmade. It has successfully trained 60,000 citizens, the Disaster Management Volunteers (DMVs) to handle various disasters and disaster situations effectively. The AADM has build up a volunteer base that assists the Government authorities during the disaster relief and rehabilitation work.

The Netherlands

In the Netherlands the Ministry of the Interior and Kingdom Relations is responsible for emergency preparedness en emergency management on national level and operates a national crisis centre (NCC) The country is divided in 25 safety regions (veiligheidsregio) Each safety region is covered by three services:- police,fire and ambulance All regions operate according to the Coordinated Regional Incident Management system Other services such as the Ministry of Defence water board(s) Rijkswaterstaat etc. can have an active role in the emergency management process.

New Zealand

In New Zealand, responsibility for emergency management moves from local to national depending on the nature of the emergency or risk reduction programme. A severe storm may be manageable within a particular area, whereas a national public education campaign will be directed by central government. Within each region, local governments are unified into 16 Civil Defence Emergency Management Groups (CDEMGs).

Every CDEMG is responsible for ensuring that local emergency management is robust as possible. As local arrangements are overwhelmed by an emergency, pre-existing mutual-support arrangements are activated. As warranted, central government has the authority to coordinate the response through the National Crisis Management Centre (NCMC), operated by the Ministry of Civil Defence & Emergency Management (MCDEM). These structures are defined by regulation, and best explained in The Guide to the National Civil Defence Emergency Management Plan 2006, roughly equivalent to the U.S. Federal Emergency Management Agency's National Response Framework.

Pakistan

Disaster management in Pakistan basically revolves around flood disasters with a primary focus on rescue and relief. After each disaster episode the government incurs considerable expenditure directed at rescue, relief and rehabilitation. Within disaster management bodies in Pakistan, there is a dearth of knowledge and information about hazard identification, risk assessment and management, and linkages between livelihoods and disaster preparedness. Disaster management policy responses are not generally influenced by methods and tools for cost-effective and sustainable interventions. There are no long-term, inclusive and coherent institutional arrangements to address disaster issues with a long-term vision. Disasters are viewed in isolation from the processes of mainstream development and poverty alleviation planning. For example, disaster management, development planning and environmental management institutions operate in isolation and integrated planning between these sectors is almost lacking. Absence of a central authority for integrated disaster management and lack of coordination within and between disaster related organizations is responsible for effective and efficient disaster management in the country. State-level disaster preparedness and mitigation measures are heavily tilted towards structural aspects and undermine non-structural elements such as the knowledge and capacities of local people, and the related livelihood protection issues.

Russia

In Russia the Ministry of Emergency Situations (EMERCOM) is engaged in fire fighting, Civil Defense, Search and Rescue, including rescue services after natural and human-made disasters.

United Kingdom

The United Kingdom adjusted its focus on emergency management following the 2000 UK fuel protests, severe flooding in the same year and the 2001 United Kingdom foot-and-mouth crisis. This resulted in the creation of the Civil Contingencies Act 2004 (CCA) which defined some organisations as Category 1 and 2 Responders. These responders have responsibilities under the legislation regarding emergency preparedness and response. The CCA is managed by the Civil Contingencies Secretariat through Regional Resilience Forums and at the local authority level.

Disaster Management training is generally conducted at the local level by the organisations involved in any response. This is consolidated through professional courses that can be undertaken at the Emergency Planning College. Furthermore diplomas, undergraduate and postgraduate qualifications can be gained throughout the country – the first course of this type was carried out by Coventry University in 1994. The Institute of Emergency Management is a charity, established in 1996, providing consulting services for the government, media and commercial sectors.

One of the largest emergency exercises in the UK was carried out on 20 May 2007 near Belfast, Northern Ireland, and involved the scenario of a plane crash landing at Belfast International Airport. Staff from five hospitals and three airports participated in the drill, and almost 150 international observers assessed its effectiveness.

United States

Disaster and catastrophe planning in the United States has utilized the functional All-Hazards approach for over 20 years, in which emergency managers develop processes (such as communication & warning or sheltering) rather than developing single-hazard/threat focused plans (e.g., a tornado plan). Processes then are mapped to the hazards/threats, with the emergency manager looking for gaps, overlaps, and conflicts between processes.

This has the advantage of creating a plan more resilient to novel events (because all common processes are defined), encourages planning done by the process owners who are the subject matter experts (e.g., the traffic management plan written by public works director, rather than the emergency manager), and focuses on processes (which are real, can be measured, ranked in importance, and are under our control). This key planning distinction often comes in conflict with non-emergency management regulatory bodies which require development of hazard/threat specific plans, such as development of specific H1N1 flu plans and terrorism-specific plans.

In the United States, all disastrous events are initially considered as local, with a local authorities usually a law enforcement agency (LEA) having charge. Law enforcement agencies, typically have situational responsibility as disasters may lead to the normal tenants for lawful instruction (infrastructure, signage, etc.) being destroyed or in need of extraneous enforcement. Most disasters do not exceed the capacity of the local jurisdiction or the capacity that they have put in place to compensate such as memorandum of understandings with adjacent localities. However, if the event becomes overwhelming to local government, state emergency management (the primary government structure of the United States) becomes the controlling emergency management agency. Under the Department of Homeland Security (DHS), the Federal Emergency Management Agency (FEMA) is lead federal agency for emergency management and supports, but does not override, state authority. The United States and its territories are covered by one of ten regions for FEMA's emergency management purposes.

If, during mitigation it is determined that a disaster or emergency is terror related or if declared an "Incident of National Significance", the Secretary of Homeland Security will initiate the National Response Framework (NRF). Under this plan the involvement of federal resources will be made possible, integrating in with the local, county, state, or tribal entities. Management will continue to be handled at the lowest possible level utilizing the National Incident Management System (NIMS).

The Citizen Corps is an organization of volunteer service programs, administered locally and coordinated nationally by DHS, which seek to mitigate disaster and prepare the population for emergency response through public education, training, and outreach. Community Emergency Response Teams are a Citizen Corps program focused on disaster preparedness and teaching basic disaster response skills. These volunteer teams are utilized to provide emergency support when disaster overwhelms the conventional emergency services.

The US Congress established the Center for Excellence in Disaster Management and Humanitarian Assistance (COE) as the principal agency to promote disaster preparedness and societal resiliency in the Asia-Pacific region. As part of its mandate, COE facilitates education and training in disaster preparedness, consequence management and health security to develop domestic, foreign and international capability and capacity.

Most secondary or long-term disaster response is carried out by volunteer organizations. In the US, the Red Cross is chartered by Congress to coordinate disaster response services. For large events, religious organizations are able to mount volunteers quickly. The largest partners are the Salvation Army and Southern Baptists. The Salvation Army is usually primary for emergency lodging/shelter and direct feeding, chaplaincy and rebuild services; the Baptists' 82,000+ volunteers do bulk food preparation (90% of the meals in a major disaster) for Salvation Army distribution and homeowner services such as debris and downed limb removal, mold abatement, hot showers and laundry, child care and chaplaincy. Similar services are also provided by Methodist Relief Services, the Lutherans, and Samaritan's Purse.

Unaffiliated volunteers can be counted on to show up at most large disasters. To prevent abuse by criminals and for the safety of the volunteers, procedures have been implemented within most response agencies to manage and effectively use these 'SUVs' (Spontaneous Unaffiliated Volunteers).

References

Alexander, David (2002). *Principles of Emergency planning and Management.* Harpenden: Terra Publishing.

Cuny, Fred C. (1983). *Disasters and Development.* Oxford: Oxford University Press.

Drabek, Thomas E. (1986). *Human System Responses to Disaster.* New York: Springer-Verlag. p. 21.

Haddow, George D.; Jane A Bullock (2003). *Introduction to emergency management.* Amsterdam: Butterworth-Heinemann.

Quarantelli, E.L.. "Emergencies, Disasters, and Catastrophes are Different Phenomena". *Preliminary Papers.* University of Delaware Disaster Research Center. Retrieved September 26, 2011.

3

Types of Anthropogenic Hazards

Anthropogenic hazards or human-made hazards can come to fruition in the form of a human-made disaster. In this case, "anthropogenic" means threats having an element of human intent, negligence, or error; or involving a failure of a human-made system. It results in huge loss of life and property. It further affects a person's mental, physical and social well-being. This is opposed to natural disasters resulting from natural hazards.

Sociological Hazards

Crime

Crime is a breach of the law for which some governing authority (via the legal systems) can ultimately prescribe a conviction which will carry some form of penalty, such as imprisonment or a fine. At least in the view of the legislators, the criminal act will cause harm to other people. Each legal jurisdiction may define crime differently. While every crime violates the law, not every violation of the law counts as a crime: for example, breaches of contract and of other private law may rank as "offenses" or as "infractions". Modern societies generally regard crimes as offenses against the public or the state, distinguished from torts.

Arson

Arson is the criminal intent of setting a fire with intent to cause damage. The definition of arson was originally limited to setting fire to buildings, but was later expanded to include other objects, such as bridges, vehicles, and private property. Arson is the greatest recorded cause of fire. Some human-induced fires are accidental: failing machinery such as a kitchen stove is a major cause of accidental fires.

Civil Disorder

Civil disorder is a broad term that is typically used by law enforcement to describe forms of disturbance. Although civil disorder does not necessarily escalate to a disaster in all cases, the event may escalate into general chaos. Rioting has many causes, from antipathy over low minimum wages to racial segregation. Examples of well-known civil disorders and riots are the Poll Tax Riots in the United Kingdom in 1990; the 1992 Los Angeles riots in which 53 people died; the 2008 Greek riots after a 15-year-old boy was fatally shot by police; and the 2010 Thai political protests in Bangkok during which 91 people died.

Terrorism

Terrorism is a controversial term with varied definitions. One definition means a violent action targeting civilians exclusively. Another definition is the use or threatened use of violence for the purpose of creating fear in order to achieve a political, religious, or ideological goal. Under the second definition, the targets of terrorist acts can be anyone, including civilians, government officials, military personnel, or people serving the interests of governments.

Definitions of terrorism may also vary geographically. In Australia, the Security Legislation Amendment (Terrorism) Act 2002, defines terrorism as "an action to advance a political, religious or ideological cause and with the intention of coercing the government or intimidating the public", while the United States Department of State operationally describes it as "premeditated, politically-motivated violence perpetrated against non-combatant targets by sub national groups or clandestine agents, usually intended to influence an audience".

War

War is a conflict between relatively large groups of people, which involves physical force inflicted by the use of weapons. Warfare has destroyed entire cultures, countries, economies and inflicted great suffering on humanity. Other terms for war can include armed conflict, hostilities, and police action.

Acts of war are normally excluded from insurance contracts and sometimes from disaster planning.

Technological Hazards

Industrial Hazards

Industrial disasters occur in a commercial context, such as mining accidents. They often have an environmental impact. The Bhopal disaster is the world's worst industrial disaster to date, and the Chernobyl disaster is regarded the worst nuclear accident in history. Hazards may have longer-term and more dispersed effects, such as dioxin and DDT poisoning.

Structural Collapse

Structural collapses are often caused by engineering failures. Bridge failures may be caused in several ways, such as under-design (as in the Tay Bridge disaster), by corrosion attack (such as in the Silver Bridge collapse), or by aerodynamic flutter of the deck (as in Galloping Gertie, the original Tacoma Narrows Bridge). Failure of dams was not infrequent during the Victorian era, such as the Dale Dyke dam failure in Sheffield, England in the 1860s, causing the Great Sheffield Flood. Other failures include balcony collapses or building collapses such as that of the World Trade Center.

Power Outage

A power outage is an interruption of normal sources of electrical power. Short-term power outages (up to a few hours) are common and have minor adverse effect, since most businesses and health facilities are prepared to deal with them. Extended power outages, however, can disrupt personal and business activities as well as medical and rescue services, leading to business losses and medical emergencies. Extended loss of power can lead to civil disorder, as in the New York City blackout of 1977. Only very rarely do power outages escalate to disaster proportions, however, they often accompany other types of disasters, such as hurricanes and floods, which hampers relief efforts.

Electromagnetic pulses and voltage spikes from whatever cause can also damage electricity infrastructure and electrical devices.

Recent notable power outages include the 2005 Java–Bali Blackout which affected 100 million people, 2012 August India Blackout which affected 600 million and the 2009 Brazil and Paraguay blackout which affected 60 million people.

Fire

Bush fires, forest fires, and mine fires are generally started by lightning, but also by human negligence or arson. They can burn thousands of square kilometers. If a fire intensifies enough to produce its own winds and "weather", it will form into a firestorm. A good example of a mine fire is the one near Centralia, Pennsylvania. Started in 1962, it ruined the town and continues to burn today. Some of the biggest city-related fires are The Great Chicago Fire, The Peshtigo Fire (both of 1871) and the Great Fire of London in 1666.

Casualties resulting from fires, regardless of their source or initial cause, can be aggravated by inadequate emergency preparedness. Such hazards as a lack of accessible emergency exits, poorly marked escape routes, or improperly maintained fire extinguishers or sprinkler systems may result in many more deaths and injuries than might occur with such protections.

Hazardous Materials

Radiation Contamination

When nuclear weapons are detonated or nuclear containment systems are otherwise compromised, airborne radioactive particles (nuclear fallout) can scatter and irradiate large areas. Not only is it deadly, but it also has a long-term effect on the next generation for those who are contaminated. Ionizing radiation is hazardous to living things, and in such a case much of the affected area could be unsafe for human habitation. During World War II, United States troops dropped atomic bombs on the Japanese cities of Hiroshima and Nagasaki. As a result, the radiation fallout contaminated the cities' water supplies, food sources, and half of the populations of each city were stricken with disease. The Soviet republics of Ukraine and Belarus are part of a scenario like this after a reactor at the Chernobyl nuclear power plant suffered a meltdown in 1986. To this day, several small towns and the city of Chernobyl remain abandoned and uninhabitable due to fallout. In the 1970s, a similar threat scared millions of Americans when a failure occurred at the Three Mile Island Nuclear Power Plant in Pennsylvania. The incident was fortunately resolved, and the area retained little contamination. A number of military accidents involving nuclear weapons have also resulted in radioactive contamination, for example the 1966 Palomares B-52 crash and the 1968 Thule Air Base B-52 crash.

CBRNs

CBRN is a catch-all initialism for chemical, biological, radiological, and nuclear. The term is used to describe a non-conventional terror threat that, if used by a nation, would be considered use of a weapon of mass destruction. This term is used primarily in the United Kingdom. Planning for the possibility of a CBRN event may be appropriate for certain high-risk or high-value facilities and governments. Examples include Saddam Hussein's Halabja poison gas attack, the Sarin gas attack on the Tokyo subway and the preceding test runs in Matsumoto, Japan 100 kilometers outside of Tokyo, and Lord Amherst giving smallpox laden blankets to Native Americans.

Transportation

Aviation

An aviation incident is an occurrence other than an accident, associated with the operation of an aircraft, which affects or could affect the safety of operations, passengers, or pilots. The category of the vehicle can range from a helicopter, an airliner, or a space shuttle. The world's worst airliner disaster is the Tenerife crash of 1977, when miscommunications between and amongst air traffic control and an aircrew caused two fully laden jets to collide on the runway, killing 583 people.

Rail

A railroad disaster is an occurrence associated with the operation of a passenger train which results in substantial loss of life. Usually accidents with freight (goods) trains are not considered disasters, unless they cause substantial loss of life or property. One of the most devastating rail disasters occurred in 2004 in Sri Lanka when 1,700 people died in the Sri Lanka tsunami-rail disaster. Other notable rail disasters are the 1989 Ufa accident in Russia which killed 574, and the 1917 Modane train accident in France which killed 540.

Road

Traffic collisions are the leading cause of death, and road-based pollution creates a substantial health hazard, especially in major conurbations.

Space

Space travel presents significant hazards, mostly to the direct participants (astronauts or cosmonauts and ground support personnel), but also carry the potential of disaster to the public at large. Accidents related to space travel have killed 22 astronauts and cosmonauts, and a larger number of people on the ground.

Accidents can occur on the ground during launch, preparation, or in flight, due to equipment malfunction or the naturally hostile environment of space itself. An additional risk is posed by (unmanned) low-orbiting satellites whose orbits eventually decay due to friction with the extremely thin atmosphere. If they are large enough, massive pieces travelling at great speed can fall to the Earth before burning up, with the potential to do damage.

The worst space disaster to date occurred on February 15, 1996 in Sichuan, China, when a Long March 3B rocket, carrying the Intelsat 708 telecommunications satellite, suffered a guidance system failure two seconds after liftoff and crashed into a nearby village. The Chinese government officially reported six deaths and 57 injuries, but some U.S. estimates run as high as 200 deaths.

The second worst disaster was the Nedelin catastrophe which occurred in the Soviet Union on October 24, 1960, when an R-16 intercontinental ballistic missile exploded on the launch pad, killing around 120 (best estimate) military ground support personnel. The Soviet government refused to acknowledge the incident until 1989, then claiming only 78 deaths.

One of the worst manned space accidents involved the Space Shuttle Challenger which disintegrated in 1986, claiming all seven lives on board. The shuttle disintegrated 73 seconds after taking off from the launch pad in Cape Canaveral, Florida.

Another example is the Space Shuttle Columbia, which disintegrated during a landing attempt over Texas in 2003, with a loss of all seven astronauts on board. The debris field extended from New Mexico to Mississippi.

Sea travel

Ships can sink, capsize or crash in disasters. Perhaps the most infamous sinking was that of the Titanic which hit an iceberg and sank, resulting in one of the worst maritime disasters in history. Other notable incidents include the capsizing of the Costa Concordia, which killed at least 32 people; and is the largest passenger ship to sink, and the sinking of the MV Doña Paz, which claimed the lives of up to 4,375 people, making it the worst peacetime maritime disaster in history.

Costs of Man-made Disasters

Some man-made disasters have been particularly notable for the high costs associated with responding to and recovering from them, including:

- Deepwater Horizon oil spill, 2010: Between $60 and $100 billion.
- September 11 attacks, 2001: $20.7 billion;
- Chernobyl disaster, 1986: $15 billion estimated cost of direct loss. It is estimated that the damages could accumulate to €235 billion for Ukraine and €201 billion for Belarus in the thirty years following the accident;
- Three Mile Island, 1979: $1 billion;
- Exxon Valdez oil spill, 1989: The clean-up of oil spill cost an estimated $2.5 billion; recovery for settlements, $1.1 billion; and the economical loss (fisheries, tourism, etc.) suffered due to the damage to thc Alaskan ecosystem was estimated at $2.8 billion;
- AZF chemical plant explosion, 2001: €1.8 billion

The costs of disasters varies considerably depending on a range of factors, such as the geographical location where they occur. When a disaster occurs in a densely populated area in a wealthy country, the financial damage might be huge, but when a comparable disaster occurs in a densely populated area in a poorer country, the actual financial damage might be relatively small, in part due to a lack of insurance. For example, the 2004 Indian Ocean earthquake and tsunami (although obviously not man-made) with a death toll of over 230,000 people, cost $15 billion, whereas the Deepwater Horizon oil spill, in which 11 people died, the damages were six-fold.

References

Alexander D. (2002). *Principles of Emergency planning and Management. Harpended*: Terra publishing.

Barton A.H. (1969). *Communities in Disaster. A Sociological Analysis of Collective Stress Situations.* SI: Ward Lock

Beck, U. (2006). *Risk Society, towards a new modernity.* Buenos Aires, Paidos

Kahneman, D. y Tversky, A. (1984). "Choices, Values and frames". *American Psychologist* 39 (4): 341-350.

Mileti, D. and Fitzpatrick, C. (1992). "The causal sequence of Risk communication in the Parkfield Earthquake Prediction experiment". *Risk Analysis*. Vol. 12: 393-400.

Phillips, B. D. (2005). "Disaster as a Discipline: The Status of Emergency Management Education in the US". *International Journal of Mass-Emergencies and Disasters*. Vol. 23 (1): 111-140.

4

Management of Chemical Disasters

The terms "chemical disaster" refer to an event resulting in the release of a substance or substances hazardous to human health and/or the environment in the short or long term. Such events include fires, explosions, leakages or releases of toxic or hazardous materials that can cause people illness, injury, disability or death.

While chemical disasters may occur whenever toxic materials are stored, transported or used, the most severe disasters are industrial disasters, involving major chemical manufacturing and storage facilities. The most significant chemical disasters in recorded history was the 1984 Bhopal disaster in India, in which more than 3,000 people were killed after a highly toxic vapour, (methyl isocyanate), was released at a Union Carbide pesticides factory.

Efforts to prevent disasters range from improved safety systems to fundamental changes in chemical use and manufacture, referred to as primary prevention or inherent safety.

In the United States, concern about chemical disasters after the Bhopal disaster led to the passage of the 1986 Emergency Planning and Community Right-to-Know Act. The EPCRA requires local emergency planning efforts throughout the country, including emergency notifications. The law also requires companies to make publicly available information about their storage of toxic chemicals. Based on such information, citizens can identify the vulnerable zones in which severe toxic releases could cause harm or death.

In 1990, the Chemical Safety and Hazard Investigation Board was established by Congress, though the CSB did not become operational until 1998. The Board's mission is to determine the root causes of chemical disasters and issue safety recommendations to prevent future Safety Performance Indicators. It also organizes workshops on a number of issues related to preparing for, preventing, and responding to chemical disasters.

In the European Union, incidents such as the Flixborough disaster and the Seveso disaster led to legislation such as the Seveso Directive and Seveso planning and provide for safety reports to local authorities. Many countries have organisations that can assist with substance risk assessment and emergency planning that is required by a wide variety of legislation.

Handling large quantities of Hazardous Chemicals (HAZCHEMs) in installations, isolated storages, and during transportation, poses the grave risk of a sudden release of copious quantities of toxicants in the environment. There are about 1666 MAH units in India, handling a large number of chemicals as raw materials, in processes, products, and wastes, with flammable, explosive, corrosive, toxic and noxious properties. Any accident involving these may have an adverse impact on both the community and the environment.

Large quantities of chemicals are also stored/ processed in industries that are located in densely populated areas. Inappropriate and haphazard construction and the lack of awareness and preparedness on the part of the community further enhance their vulnerability. The potential of heavy losses and adverse consequences on the environment due to a chemical accident calls for further improvement of safety measures in all processes/procedures and the adoption of appropriate methods for handling HAZCHEMs.

The Bhopal Gas Disaster in December 1984 brought into sharp focus the unprecedented potential of HAZCHEM like Methyl Isocyanate in terms of loss of life, health, injury and the long-term effects on the population and environment. It created compelling evidence to approach DM and chemical safety holistically. The era of restructuring with the induction of new HAZCHEM control systems and procedures all over the world in the wake of the Bhopal disaster also resulted in the strengthening of institutional mechanisms at local, district, state and central levels for the management of chemical disasters in India. The consolidation of these institutional mechanisms and the mobilisation of corporate support for the preparation and implementation of emergency plans is an integral part of these Guidelines.

Causes of Chemical Disasters

Chemical accidents may originate in:

i) Manufacturing and formulation installations including during commissioning and process operations; maintenance and disposal.

ii) Material handling and storage in manufacturing facilities, and isolated storages; warehouses and godowns including tank farms in ports and docks and fuel depots.

iii) Transportation (road, rail, air, water, and pipelines).

Chemical disasters, in general, may result from:

i) Fire.

ii) Explosion.

iii) Toxic release.

iv) Poisoning.

v) Combinations of the above.

Chemical disasters may occur due to process deviations concerning the chemistry of the process, pressure, temperature and other identified parameters with regard to the state of the substance i.e., solid, liquid or gas, proximity to other toxic substances and the probability of a runaway reaction due to the incidental mixing of two or more HAZCHEMs with dissimilar properties. In addition, it may be due to hardware failure, resulting in large-scale spills of toxic substances (in any form) due to loss of containment, or an explosion. Further, Boiling Liquid Expanding Vapour Explosion (BLEVE) may occur due to sparks, shocks or frictional forces on the chemicals during transportation.

The effects can be further compounded by the micro-meteorology of the area, wind speed and direction, rate of precipitation, toxicity/quantity of chemical released, population in the reach of release, probability of formation of lethal mixtures (fuel-air or other mixtures) and other industrial activities being performed in closer vicinity.

It is very important to understand that the state of the chemical substance (solid, liquid or gas) contributes substantially to the gravity of the accident and affects control measures. Chemicals in solid form may have devastating effects if their properties are suddenly changed (e.g., sublimation) due to pressure and temperature conditions to which they are accidentally exposed. If solids continue to remain in solid form, the damage will be negligible.

Any human/mechanical failure may cause large-scale spills of liquids or of compressed gases like chlorine or Liquid Petroleum Gas (LPG) which can cause BLEVE and can directly affect human lives and the environment. The release of compressed gases give rise to thermal and cryogenic stresses, which may also impact the surrounding structure or building, compounding the damage.

Initiators of Chemical Accidents

A number of factors including human errors could spark off chemical accidents with the potential to become chemical disasters. These are:

Process and Safety System Failures

i) *Technical errors:* design defects, fatigue, metal failure, corrosion etc.

ii) *Human errors:* neglecting safety instructions, deviating from specified procedures etc.

iii) *Lack of information:* absence of emergency warning procedures, nondisclosure of line of treatment etc.

iv) *Organisational errors:* poor emergency planning and coordination, poor communication with public, non-compliance with mock drills/exercises etc., which are required for ensuring a state of quick response and preparedness.

Natural Calamities

The Indian subcontinent is highly prone to natural disasters, which can also trigger chemical disasters. Damage to phosphoric acid sludge containment during the Orissa super cyclone in 1999 and the release of acrylonitrile at Kandla Port, during an earthquake in 2001, are some of the recent examples. Vulnerability to chemical disasters is further compounded by likely terrorist and warfare activities, which include sabotage and attack on HAZCHEM installations and transportation vehicles.

Impact of Chemical Disasters

In addition to loss of life, the major consequences of chemical disasters include impact on livestock, flora/fauna, the environment (air, soil, water) and losses to industry Chemical accidents may be categorised as a major accident or a disaster depending upon the number of casualties, injuries, damage to the property or environment. A major accident is defined in the Manufacture, Storage and Import of Hazardous Chemicals (MSIHC) Rules, 1989, issued under the Environment (Protection) Act, 1986, whereas 'disaster' is defined in the DM Act, 2005.

Chemical Disasters in India

India is amongst the very few countries, which have enshrined the right to live in a clean and wholesome environment as a fundamental right. The Factories Act was enacted in 1948, for ensuring safety, health and welfare at the workplace. Recognising the need to mainstream environmental concerns in all developmental activities, a separate ministry—the MoEF—was created in 1980, and was declared as the nodal ministry for the management of chemical (industrial) disasters. CDM received greater emphasis the world over only after the Bhopal disaster in 1984.

Regulatory Framework and Codes of Practises

The regulatory framework on chemical safety can be traced to the Factories Act, 1948 and chemical class-specific regulations like the Explosives Act, 1884; the Insecticide Act, 1968; and The Petroleum Act, 1934. Later, an umbrella Act, the Environment (Protection) Act, 1986, was enacted, which also deals with chemical management and safety. A number of regulations covering safety in transportation, insurance, liability and compensations were enacted thereafter. The Government of India has further reinforced the legal framework on chemical safety and management of chemical accidents by enacting new rules and by way of amendments to them.

Institutional Framework and Compliance

Institutional framework

The regulations referred to in para 2.1 above provide for institutional framework for enforcement and monitoring of chemical safety and emergency management. It involves various central/state ministries/ departments viz. MHA, MoEF, MoLE, MoA, MoP & NG, MoC & F, MoSRT & H, Ministry of Commerce and Industry (MoC & I), Department of Economic Affairs (DEA), Ministry of Finance (MoF), and others.

The MoLE, MoEF and MoSRT & H are responsible for enacting regulations. The MoLE through its state entities; the Inspectorate of Factories/Directorate of Industrial Safety and Health (DISH); the Central Pollution Control Board (CPCB) and the MoEF with its state entities, State Pollution Control Boards (SPCBs) and Pollution Control Committees (PCCs) of UTs monitors compliance of the various regulations. The MoLE is assisted in this regard by the DGFASLI and central/regional labour institutes. The MoSRT & H through the Department of Road, Transport and Highways is to ensure the development and maintenance of national highways.

On the other hand, the state governments through their respective state transport departments, transport commissioners/regional transport officers and Public Works Department (PWD) are responsible for the management of the roads and highways in the states.

With respect to petroleum products and explosives, the MoC & F through Department of Chemicals and Petrochemicals and Department of Fertilizers, MoP & NG, and Ministry of Heavy Industries and Public Enterprises (MoHI & PE) through the Petroleum and Explosives Safety Organization (PESO) monitor compliance of the regulations.

The MoH & FW through various hospitals responds to medical emergencies during chemical accidents. For prompt and effective medical response with requisite capacity building in emergency medical services, institutional linkages and statutory backups need to be urgently formalised.

Organisations/agencies like the DAE and Centre for Fire, Explosive and Environment Safety (CFEES) are responsible for preparing Off-Site emergency plans in the DAE and MoD respectively. The CFEES is an authority under the MSIHC Rules for enforcement of directions and procedures in respect of laboratories, industrial establishments and isolated storages dealing with HAZCHEMs in the MoD. Similarly, the DAE is responsible for nuclear installations.

Research institutes like the Indian Institute of Chemical Technology (IICT), Hyderabad; Industrial Toxicology Research Centre (ITRC), Lucknow; National Environmental Engineering Research Institute (NEERI), Nagpur; National Chemical Laboratory (NCL), Pune and National Institute of Occupational Health (NIOH), Ahmedabad, are working in the field of occupational hazard, safety and in aspects related to CDM. Defence Research Development Organisation (DRDO) is working on the field detection kits, personal protection equipment and measures for prophylaxis and therapy.

Limited facilities for the collection of environmental toxicants, released during a chemical disaster also exist in the Council of Scientific and Industrial Research (CSIR), the DRDO, and Indian Council of Medical Research (ICMR) laboratories, as well as in the CPCB, SPCBs, PCC, PESO and recognised laboratories in the private sector.

Autonomous bodies, professional institutes, Private Voluntary Organizations (PVOs) and NGOs play an important role in training and community awareness and also can contribute significantly in response, rehabilitation and reconstruction efforts.

Compliance

Of the 602 districts in India, 263 districts have MAH units. Of them, 170 have clusters of more than five MAH units (hazardous/industrial pockets). As on date there are 1666 MAH units in India. In addition to these, there are a large number of storages of hazardous substances; big warehouses including local factories/storage sites, some of them presently existing in residential areas. On-Site emergency plans are in place for 1628 units. Off-Site emergency plans for 166 districts have been prepared. Twenty-six of them are based on hazard analysis studies undertaken at the initiative of the MoEF. Presently, a mock drill of the On-Site plan by occupiers of MAH units every six months is a statutory requirement. However, only a few mock drills of prepared Off-Site plans have been conducted.

The MoEF has set up a Central Crisis Group (CCG) and a coordination committee at the national level. Further, out of the 28 states and seven UTs, 20 states and three UTs have set up State Crisis Groups (SCG). Nineteen states with districts having MAH units, have set up District Crisis Groups (DCGs), while 17 of the states have also set up Local Crisis Groups (LCGs). Depending on the gravity of an accident, appropriate crisis groups at local, district, state and central levels are activated.

The MoEF has set up a Crisis Control Room (CCR) as part of the CAS, for the rapid exchange of information and for coordination of activities during an emergency. The MoEF is preparing a web-based accident information system for use of all stakeholders concerned, which will have better monitoring and management of chemical disasters. A 'red book' containing duties to be performed by authorities and agencies during an emergency is published periodically and circulated. It contains names, addresses and telephone numbers of key functionaries of state governments, chief inspectorate of factories, SPCBs, PCC, experts/ institutions, etc.

A brochure entitled, 'DOs and DON'Ts during a Chemical Accident', to educate and enable the community for self protection has been published. Industries have also undertaken awareness programmes for communities residing in the vicinity of industrial units.

Other Technical Activities/Initiatives

Initiatives in installations

Major accident hazard control system

In addition to the efforts to strengthen the legal framework by amending the Factories Act, the MoLE through the DGFASLI and state factory inspectorates implemented a project called 'Establishment and Initial Operations of Major Accident Hazard Control System in India'. During the project period, the MAH units were identified and infrastructural facilities were augmented in the Chief Inspectorate of Factories (CIFs), Central Labour Institute (CLI), Mumbai, labour institutes of various states, and Regional Labour Institutes (RLIs), Kanpur, Kolkata and Chennai. Under the Major Accident Control System it is mentioned that the Major Accident Hazard Control Advisory Divisions (MAHCAD) of these institutes provide consultancy services to industries, conduct training programmes and workshops, training the officials of CIFs of various states and conduct joint safety inspections of MAH units with them to enhance safety levels of various installations.

Hazard analysis studies of industrial pockets

A sub-scheme entitled, 'Industrial Pocket-wise Hazard Analysis' has been in operation at the MoEF since the Eighth Five Year Plan. Hazard analysis studies for identifying the accident potential of industrial areas/pockets, their possible consequence and prevention strategies including rapid safety audit of MAH units have been initiated for 107 districts covering 900 MAH units. Out of these, studies of 85 districts have been completed.

GIS-based emergency management system

A pilot study entitled, 'GIS based Emergency Planning and Response System for Chemical Accidents in MAH Installations in Major Industrial Clusters' in four identified industrial states namely— Gujarat, Maharashtra, Tamil Nadu and Andhra Pradesh has been completed. The system would help existing response agencies in planning for and responding to major chemical emergencies to contain damage to a minimum. Training programmes involving members of crisis groups have been conducted. This project has been extended to the National Capital Territory (NCT) of Delhi, Rajasthan, Uttar Pradesh, Haryana, Karnataka, Kerala, West Bengal, Assam, Madhya Pradesh and Punjab.

Environment Risk Reporting and Information Systems (ERRIS)

Another unique initiative is the ERRIS prepared by the Indian Chamber of Commerce (ICC), Kolkata for the chemical units in Haldia and Durgapur in West Bengal. The industry risk management system, ERRIS, was developed under a project funded by the European Union with the technical collaboration of The Netherlands and Italy.

Emergency Response Centres (ERCs) and poison control centres

Five ERCs have been established in Manali (Tamil Nadu), Bhopal (Madhya Pradesh), Mahad (Maharastra), Vishakhapatnam (Andhra Pradesh) and Hyderabad (Andhra Pradesh), which serve as a link between the DCG and the industry during an emergency. ERCs deal with chemical emergencies in a given area and disseminate technical information relating to the chemicals involved. Presently, the ERCs do not cater to emergencies arising during the transportation of HAZCHEMs.

The first National Poison Information Centre was set up in the Department of Pharmacology in 1995, at the All India Institute of Medical Sciences, New Delhi. The main objectives of Poison Control Centres include toxico-surveillance (active survey of the prevailing and potential toxicity risks) and environmental health monitoring. It aims to help detect heavy metal contamination, occupational exposure, food, water, air, and soil contamination.

Capacity development

Financial assistance has been provided for capacity development to the National Fire Service College (NFSC), Nagpur; National Civil Defence College (NCDC), Nagpur; offices of the CIFs/DISH of states including Maharashtra, Tamil Nadu, Andhra Pradesh, Gujarat, Rajasthan and NCT Delhi.

Some other national and regional institutions (viz. National Safety Council [NSC], Disaster Management Institute [DMI]) have also been working in the areas of accident prevention, emergency preparedness and hazardous risk management. The Confederation of Indian Industry (CII), Federation of Indian Chambers of Commerce and Industry (FICCI) and the ICC are other notable leading umbrella networks of organisations of business and industry working in these fields.

Control room concept

The following five Control Rooms have been set up at the initiative of the industries in the state of Gujarat:

i) Emergency Control Room in Vadodara (registered as a Central Control Room).

ii) Atul Emergency Control Centre in Atul Ltd., Valsad.

iii) Vapi Emergency Control Centre in Vapi Industrial Association, Vapi.

iv) Disaster Prevention and Management Centre, in the Gujarat Industrial Development Corporation (GIDC) fire station, Ankleshwar.

v) Disaster Management Centre, Bharuch in the IPCL Guest House, Dahej Off-Site Emergency Control Room.

National Networking of Emergency Operation Centres (EOCs)

The national network of EOCs with links to state EOCs and other state secretariats and the district EOCs at the district collectorate form the main emergency communication network in the country for DM. The National Informatics Centre Network (NICNET) and the Police Network (POLNET) are other important satellite-based networks for emergency communications.

Responsible Care (RC)

The concept of RC is a global voluntary initiative of the chemical industry, covering all activities including research, process and product development, manufacturing and sales. It aims at an ethical and behavioural change, going away from a regulatory driven approach to a proactive approach.

RC is now licensed by 52 national industry associations worldwide. The Indian Chemical Manufacturers' Association (ICMA) now called Indian Chemical Council launched the RC initiative in 1992 and at present, 92 chemical industries have become signatories to the RC initiative in India.

Mutual Aid Response Group (MARG)

MARG, a voluntary initiative on developing 'mutual aid arrangement' for effective emergency response on a voluntary basis among neighbouring units in an industrial pocket, has emerged during the last decade. This initiative of the association of industries in an industrial pocket, is a forum to mutually help each other by sharing resources to tackle emergencies.

It has been successful in Maharashtra, where 15 MARGs are presently working. This industry initiative is promoted by the DISH, which is the regulatory agency in Maharashtra under the Factories Act. It is also found that some industrial units have entered into formal mutual aid agreements. There is a need for the expansion of MARG initiatives in other states.

Initiatives in storages

Inventory of isolated storages

An inventory of 'Isolated Storages' with chemicals and their quantities in the country was undertaken. The study identified 347 isolated storages, of which the maximum were in the states of Gujarat (41), Uttar Pradesh (38), Tamil Nadu (32), Andhra Pradesh (31), Karnataka (25), West Bengal (24), Maharastra (23), Orissa (22), Rajasthan (22), Madhya Pradesh and Punjab (17), and Delhi (14).

Initiatives in the road transport sectors

Vulnerability and risk assessment of transportation of HAZCHEM

Risk assessment and vulnerability studies have been completed in 16 stretches of national highways in four states with a high density of hazardous material transportation. Based on the identified risks, mitigation measures including preparation of DM Plans are carried out.

Hazardous material (HAZMAT) emergency response van

The NSC identified and analysed the successful experience of developing and operating HAZMAT Emergency Response Vans by leading MAH units in the Patalganga-Rasayani Industrial Area, Dist. Raigad, in Maharashtra, and published a case study on it. The approach for responding to road transport emergencies represented by this case study is considered practical and cost effective in the Indian situation and needs to be replicated at the national level.

Parallel International Efforts

International Labour Organization (ILO)

The ILO convention No. C 174, adopted on 22 June 1993, dealing with the prevention of major industrial accidents involving hazardous substances and the limitation of the consequences of such accidents, is directly relevant for CDM in India.

Awareness and preparedness for emergencies at the local level (APELL) project

APELL is a tool developed by the United Nations Environment Programme, Division of Technology, Industry and Economics office (UNEP DTIE) in 1988 to minimise the occurrence of harmful effects of technological accidents and emergencies.

The five-year (1992–97) APELL Project was implemented in India by the NSC in selected six high-risk areas in different regions across India.

The APELL project was timely and eminently suited to address the issues identified under the Major Accident Hazard Control (MAHC) project as the groundwork carried out provided a foundation for building the structure of community awareness and emergency preparedness. A systematic methodology for testing emergency plans was also developed.

The outputs achieved include:

i) Coordinating groups like the APELL setup in all the six high-risk industrial areas.
ii) Positive experience in community involvement.
iii) A systematic methodology developed for testing emergency plans.
iv) Strengthened technical capabilities at the national and local levels.
v) Further issues identified.

Above all, the APELL approach was institutionalised through the notification of the Chemical Accidents (Emergency Planning, Preparedness and Response) (CA[EPPR]) Rules.

United Nations (UN) International Strategy for Disaster Reduction (ISDR)

The UN ISDR effort is promoting chemical disaster risk reduction by educating and involving the community and civil authorities.

Recent Major International Developments

The UNEP Trans-APELL Programme

The UNEP APELL Programme is being strengthened as a key vehicle for UNEP work, at the local level in preventing and preparing for natural and other disasters, such as industrial disasters. The Trans-APELL Pilot Project is designed to channelise the proven APELL approach to dangerous goods transport emergency planning in a local community by using the Trans-APELL Handbook published by UNEP in 2000. Following the Trans-APELL Workshop organised by the NSC with the participation from all the stakeholders, two initiatives have been undertaken on a pilot basis:

i) To include the HAZMAT Response Training Module in the Curriculum of the Traffic Police Apex Institute and train their trainers.

ii) To conduct awareness programmes for communities living near identified accident prone spots along a major highway. The statutory obligations resting on the road transport operators and the improvement measures taken on the ground for achieving compliance have made the situation particularly favourable to initiate this programme.

To promote the APELL process further, the UNEP is revising, adapting and elaborating new tools and methods to repackage it as a multi-hazard programme for disaster reduction that enables local communities to identify, assess, prevent and prepare for the impact of any type of disaster. A decision to this effect was taken in the UNEP General Council meeting held recently in February 2006 at Dubai.

Strategic Approach to International Chemicals Management (SAICM)

In February 2006, over 190 countries including India acceded to the SAICM—a voluntary agreement to ensure the safe use of chemicals by 2020. India has decided to contribute to the newly created Quick Start Programme (QSP) trust fund. This initiative of UNEP consists of an overarching policy strategy and a global plan of action. There are 192 activities that have been identified for a global plan of action.

Recent National Developments

Enactment of The DM Act, 2005

The DM Act, 2005 provides for the requisite institutional mechanism for drawing up and monitoring the implementation of the DM Plans ensuring measures by various wings of government for prevention and mitigation effects of disasters and for undertaking a holistic coordinated and prompt response to any disaster situation. The Act seeks to institutionalise the mechanisms at the national, state and district levels to plan, prepare and ensure a swift response to both natural calamities and man-made disasters/ accidents. The Act, inter alia mandates:

i) The formation of a national apex body, the NDMA, with the Prime Minister of India as the ex-officio chairperson.

ii) The state governments to establish SDMAs, and also create DDMAs.

Powers and functions of the NDMA

The NDMA constituted under Section 3 of the DM Act, 2005, has the responsibility of laying down the policies, plans and guidelines for effective DM. As mandated, the NDMA may:

i) lay down policies on disaster management;

ii) approve the National Plan;

iii) approve plans prepared by the ministries or departments of the Government of India in accordance with the National Plan;

iv) lay down guidelines to be followed by the State Authorities in drawing up the State Plan;

v) lay down guidelines to be followed by the different ministries or departments of the Government of India for the purpose of integrating the measures for prevention of disaster or the mitigation of its effects in their development plans and projects;

vi) coordinate the enforcement and implementation of the policy and plan for DM;

vii) recommend provision of funds for the purpose of mitigation;

viii) provide such support to other countries affected by major disasters as may be determined by the Central Government;

ix) take such other measures for the prevention of disaster, or the mitigation, or preparedness and capacity building for dealing with the threatening disaster situation or disaster as it may consider necessary;

x) lay down broad policies and guidelines for the functioning of the National Institute of Disaster Management (NIDM).

The NDMA will be assisted by its executive committee, the National Executive Committee (NEC). The NEC is responsible for implementing the policies and plans of the NDMA. The NEC shall act as the coordinating and monitoring body for DM for the implementation of the National Plan. The NDMA is, inter alia, responsible for coordinating and ensuring the implementation of the government's policies and plans for disaster reduction/ mitigation and ensuring adequate preparedness at all levels; coordinating response to a disaster when it strikes and post-disaster relief, rehabilitation and reconstruction.

The NDMA shall maintain, build and strengthen the existing machinery, structure and mechanism. The nodal ministry will continue to be responsible for CDM, and based on the Guidelines issued by the NDMA, will prepare the detailed Action Plan for CDM. Similarly, all central ministries/departments and state governments and UTs shall prepare comprehensive DM Plans that will address all phases of the DM cycle in a coordinated manner as specified in these guidelines.

Management of Chemical Accidents

Regulations

The effectiveness of the present regulations can be gauged from fairly successful operational records/ performance of industries. However, the following are the specific gaps identified in the regulations:

i) Based on the Factories Act, 1948 (amended in 1987), the states have notified their own Factories Rules, which need to be dovetailed with the subjects of accident prevention, preparedness and mitigation.

ii) Absence of national regulations on occupational safety and health and medical emergency management.

iii) Harmonisation of classification and definitions in existing regulations including petroleum and petroleum products.

iv) Absence of regulations on storage and transportation of cryogenics.

v) Lack of legislation on risk assessment requirements and classification, labelling and packaging for industrial chemicals.

vi) Need to identify technical competent authorities and standardisation of reporting mechanisms for the status of implementation of various chemical disaster-related activities.

vii) Non-availability of statutes for grant of compensation to chemical accident victims.

viii) Harmonisation and incorporation of international laws in chemical management.

Codes of Practises, Procedures and Standards

A number of codes of practises, procedures and standards governing safety in the handling of chemicals are available. However, these are not exhaustive, do not cover all HAZCHEM and processes and are also not prescribed by the statutes.

The specific gaps in these Codes of Practises, Procedures and Standards are as follows:

i) Lack of national-level risk assessment criteria and acceptable risks for chemical plants viz., failure rate and probability of accidents, etc.

ii) Procedure for conduct of safety audit and safety report preparation.

Statutory Inspection, Safety Audit and Testing of Emergency Plans

Inspection system in factory inspectorates

There are a large number of industrial units that require inspection and the manpower to do so is limited. Inspection formats and guidelines on follow-up action also require updating.

Safety audit

A safety audit is a tool for identifying and rectifying gaps in institutional safety management systems and is currently mandated to be carried out every two years by law. This requirement is often unmet. Problems arise due to inspection by two or more different departments for the same location, for example, the Controller of Explosives, Director of Factories, Pollution Control Board and Fire Service Department. The requirement of a single inspection system has not been established.

Commissioning and decommissioning plans

There is currently no system in place to report accidents that occur during commissioning and de- commissioning of plants. It is observed that a number of accidents take place during these processes.

On-site emergency plan

The testing of On-Site emergency plans every six months is a statutory requirement. A large number of units conduct mock drills shop-floor wise or cover only a few components, while the requirement is for the installation as a whole.

Off-site emergency plans

i) A yearly mock drill of district Off-Site emergency plans is essential and mandated. Very few full-scale drills of district Off-Site emergency plans are being conducted in the country, and even those are not conducted as per the norms.

ii) Preparation of SOPs for rescue teams and other QRTs regarding the wearing of full protective gear before entering the hazardous zone and cordoning off the disaster site are required.

Medical emergency plans

District Off-Site emergency plan should include a separate section on management of medical emergencies, which should also be tested yearly during mock drills.

Technical and Technological Information

Information on chemicals

The disclosure of information via Material Safety Data Sheets (MSDS) by occupiers to workers on chemical hazards is a statutory requirement. The information in MSDS is generally complex and exhaustive, therefore, supervisory staff and workers find it difficult to comprehend the information available in them.

Technical information

i) Hazard and risk assessment information to first responders, harmonised risk assessment and management principles and case studies of accidents/major accidents/disasters in MAH units are not available.

ii) Case studies of major accidents including emergency response experience and yearly statistics of major chemical accidents are not compiled and published at the national level.

iii) There is lack of clear accessible information on potential chemical hazards and their management for ready use by local authorities. In addition, the officers responsible for issuing No Objection Certificates (NOCs) for establishing a storage facility often lack sufficient scientific knowledge and need to undergo appropriate training.

Technology

Some MAH units handling HAZCHEMs are not based on best available technologies. Many of the small and medium units continue to use obsolete and unsafe technologies.

PREPAREDNESS

Education, Training and Capacity Development

Education

DM has been introduced as a subject at the school level for classes VIII, IX and X by the Ministry of Human Resource Development. Different modules on DM are required to be developed and placed appropriately at different levels in the education system at the national and state levels. In addition, there is a need to include disaster-related technical education for professionals and medical officers in their respective institutions. Besides chemical sciences and technologies, the basic knowledge of toxicology needs to be imparted at all levels.

Training of emergency services and district authorities

i) The existing training institutes in India require up-gradation and strengthening besides adequate funds to be provided by the centre and state governments. Dedicated institutes for training on CDM have not been identified/established. Institutes for imparting training to first responders, authorities and others involved in emergency planning, preparedness and response need to be identified/established.

ii) Specific training modules need to be prepared for CDM with specialised packages for different stakeholders in a time-bound manner. These modules are required to be tested and implemented at different levels of CDM.

iii) The paramedical staff lack knowledge on DM and need to be trained with appropriate knowledge of effects of chemicals and clinical modalities for management of their toxicities.

iv) Self-inspection by the industries and corporate responsibility for safety are not practised; these measures need to be established through the training of trainers.

Capacity development

Capacity in terms of adequate skilled man power, material logistics and infrastructural facilities are grossly inadequate at various levels required in the management of chemical disasters.

i) Infrastructural

a) Adequate infrastructural facilities in installations, monitoring institutions and authorities concerned and their requirements need to be addressed.

b) There is a need to assess individually and collectively the augmentation of infrastructure and financial resources required in institutions associated with CDM.

c) Based on the concentration of MAH units, the requirement and location of ERCs and poison centres need to be identified.

d) The integration of infrastructural facilities with those of existing institutions after providing the necessary resources/expertise for process hazards and chemical disasters is required.

ii) Skilled manpower

a) Capacity in terms of skilled and trained manpower is required to be built up at the identified institutes/research departments/training centres.

b) Functional integration of various aspects of disasters in the curriculum, and linkage of this knowledge in the initial recruitment and further promotions of the employees.

c) The role of NGOs and the community is required to be defined. Resident Welfare Associations and NGOs needs to be integrated with this training network so as to develop a group of volunteers.

d) Sensitisation of functionaries at all levels about the need, measures for quick assessment and action to be taken during chemical disasters.

iii) Material logistics

a) The adoption of suitable technologies for CDM need an established mechanism to test, verify and check the technology in a rapid and time-bound manner. Once approved, the same is to be adopted at the grass-root level.

b) Inventory of Personal Protective Equipment (PPE), chemical emergency management kits, relief and response material like ambulances, evacuation vans, fire-fighting equipment including HAZMAT vehicles and other safety-related items need to be identified, tested and established.

Awareness Generation

i) The public at large is the most important stakeholder in DM. The creation of public awareness by MAH installations and the district administration/DDMA and local authorities regarding possible accidents is a statutory requirement. Even though community awareness is a priority area, it has not been adequately addressed.

ii) Public awareness about HAZCHEM, their effects, dos and don'ts during an accident and remedial measures, is grossly inadequate.

iii) Proper guidelines and a code of ethics and conduct is not available for the print and electronic media for handling sensitive issues arising out of chemical disasters. This is necessary for a disciplined, structured and panic-free approach in order to communicate any disastrous event and its immediate consequences to the public.

iv) In awareness generation, NGOs can play an effective role. There is an urgent need for identifying NGOs with experience to successfully help in handling chemical emergencies and strengthening their capacities and capabilities to support effective response during an emergency.

Institutions, Networking and Communication

Institutional framework for providing technical support services at various levels is a key requirement for sustaining proper development and implementation of an effective DM system. These have not been fully identified.

Institutions

i) National-level institutions and other academic institutions such as the Indian Institutes of Technology (IITs); the OISD; Atomic Energy Regulation Board (AERB); IICT; ITRC; NIOH; CLI; CLRI; NEERI; NFSC; NCDC; NSC; DMI; NIDM; Indian Chemical Association (ICA); and other professional bodies; industrial and corporate institutions/associations need to be further involved in CDM. The present status and strengths of these institutes need to be assessed and if required, to be strengthened to include disaster-related activities in their training and knowledge development thereof.

ii) Fire services, which are traditionally the first responders, as an institution lacks modern equipment and advance training for strategic response.

iii) Revamping of the Civil Defence and Home Guards is essential for these institutions to play an effective role in DM.

Networking and communication

Effective communication and networking between various stakeholders is currently inadequate at all levels for a successfully orchestrated response to chemical disasters.

i) Human and functional networking is needed at the following levels for coordinated planning, preparedness and response. The communication network shall include:

   a) Control rooms at all levels (district, state and centre).

   b) Industries (with district/state authorities, and state/national institutions).

   c) Emergency functional units identified in On-Site and Off-Site plans and other responders including designated authorities.

   d) Institutes/analytical laboratories/ research departments identified by the nodal ministry; other associated ministries and the NDMA at the national level along with the others that will be identified by the states need to have an effective communication network to quickly assess toxicants/chemotoxins at the incident site and for continuing effective R&D programmes.

   e) Road transport and other modes of transportation need to have an established dedicated communication system with all stakeholders and a mechanism for continuous monitoring of the transport vehicle carrying HAZCHEM all along its route.

   f) It is required to make available the exhaustive list of HAZCHEMs, their side-effects and related dos and don'ts on the internet.

ii) Coordination between different stakeholders:

   a) An effective network based on the roles of different stakeholders in a pre-rehearsed manner is required. The roles and responsibilities of different stakeholders including the first responders as identified in the various plans need to be further adequately defined and available as ready department-specific guides for better coordination during chemical disasters.

   b) Voluntary initiatives of industrial clusters for effective networking and mutual help viz. MARG, need to be encouraged at the national level. District administration/DDMAs, state authorities/ SDMAs, response agencies and the other enforcement agencies need to network with such voluntary initiatives.

Medical Preparedness and Response

Effective medical preparedness and response for a chemical emergency is a priority area. There is a need to address medical preparedness comprehensively at all levels with specific stress on chemical disaster-related aspects. The salient gaps identified are:

i) Medical preparedness is the weakest link in the emergency response system and at hospitals.

ii) It is essential to develop mechanisms for creating awareness, making available trained medical first responders, decontamination facilities, risk and resource inventory, trauma care, plans for evacuation, mechanisms to maintain uniform casualty profiles, proper chemical casualty treatment kits, mobile teams/ hospitals, hospital DM Plans and preparing and responding to public health and environmental effects.

iii) Non-availability of specific antidotes for chemicals.

iv) Inadequacy of infrastructure for trained medical and paramedical staff.

v) The SOPs for emergency medical response at incident site are not laid down. There is an absence of a separate medical emergency plan in the district Off-Site plan. There is also a lack of documentation of uniform SOPs to be followed during chemical emergencies.

vi) Gross inadequacies in terms of trained manpower and capacity in poison information centres and regional laboratories that are close to disaster-prone areas with detection facilities for HAZCHEM.

vii) Absence of mechanism for medical surveillance.

viii) There are inadequate studies on long-term effects of HAZCHEM and their medical management.

ix) Mechanisms for medical rehabilitation need addressal.

R&D Activities

Following are some of the areas where R&D activities are required to be initiated, intensified and pursued:

i) Customisation and validation of software for risk assessment and consequence modelling under Indian conditions.

ii) Critical analysis of available technology for acquisition.

iii) Development of need-based technologies for detection, protection, monitoring of common toxicants and their effective management.

iv) Development of safer and cost effective alternatives and adoption of safer, affordable and sustainable technologies and processes.

v) Epidemiological studies on high volume HAZCHEMs handled by industry.

vi) To develop and introduce new biomarkers and indicators for chemical toxicants.

vii) Collaborate, update and adopt developing new approaches to detect, evaluate and decontaminate chemical toxicants.

Response, Relief and Rehabilitation

SOPs for all the response functions to be performed by all the functionaries of CDM according to the gravity of the chemical accident need to be developed and integrated into the existing structure and function of crisis management at all levels.

Detailed minimum standards for food, water, shelter, sanitation do not exist at present. There is also the absence of SOPs for providing evacuation, shelter, food, water and relief.

Immediate relief under the Public Liability Insurance Act, 1991 needs to be revisited.

During rehabilitation, there is a need to comprehensively address all the requirements of victims including medical care for long-term effects of HAZCHEM.

Management of Transport Accidents

The major gaps include:

i) Air, maritime and rail transportation of HAZCHEM needs up-gradation in terms of loading, unloading, containerisation; their contingency plans also need to be revisited and revised to tackle any unexpected chemical emergency.

ii) Specific roles and responsibilities of consignor, consignee, transporters, drivers and authority are required to be addressed.

iii) Transport routes for HAZCHEM from the storage site to the delivery point with SOPs to be followed for transportation are essential to be defined. The safe stoppage points with the safe parking areas and an appropriate time of transportation need to be indicated in the route plans.

iv) The system of communication and training of persons involved in HAZCHEM transportation are grossly inadequate.

v) Highways are prone to numerous chemical emergencies due to bulk transportation of HAZCHEM but still no appropriate highway DM Plan exists. It needs to be comprehensively addressed.

vi) It is essential to address the modification/ harmonisation of legislations to reduce the probability of occurrence of chemical transport emergencies.

vii) The available study material on the specific highways stretches with heavy traffic density of HAZCHEM carriers needs to be replicated on other national/state highways.

viii) A national and state-wise directory of chemical/technical experts needs to be compiled and published for ready reference of traffic police and other service providers.

ix) Emergency response guidance for first responders and highway DM Plans are not available.

x) Fire services lack required technological sophistication and number of HAZMAT vehicles for quick emergency response.

xi) Transporters of chemicals including drivers lack the requisite training to discharge their roles satisfactorily during a HAZCHEM incident.

xii) Traffic police lack requisite training, basic knowledge of relevant statues, use of support tools such as TREMCARD, and their role in emergency response.

xiii) In line with the existing system of fire brigade and police, a network of communication and a four-digit number-based connectivity is essential for ambulance services and hospitals for quick medical response on highways.

xiv) Standardisation in design of vehicles and handling capacity needs to be addressed. Stress on R&D activities to address the designing of trucks and other vehicles carrying hazardous substances from the safety point-of-view is required.

xv) Recording and monitoring facilities of transport vehicles carrying HAZCHEMs on the identified routes need to be provided.

xvi) A statutory authority for inspecting the facilities on these vehicles and their monitoring and reporting mechanism is required.

xvii) In case of disasters, post-disaster cleanup needs to be dealt with.

xviii) Periodical training at regular intervals for drivers and attendants needs to be made mandatory. The syllabus for basic training and refresher courses needs to be designed and updated regularly.

xix) Rules pertaining to the issues of safety of import and export of chemicals needs to be updated according to changing global scenarios.

Implementation of Existing Regulations and Procedures

Any plan, policy, regulation or guidelines is only as good as its implementation. Lack of compliance and weak enforcement including coordination of CDM has been identified as follows:

Lack of Emphasis on CDM Functions at Various Levels

In order for DM to be effective, focused attention at various levels, namely, designated focal points in the nodal ministries viz. MoEF and MoLE at the central and state levels and designation of an emergency coordinator at the district level are essential. The lack of assigned responsibility, systems for update and clarity in functions currently plague the system.

Deficiencies in On-Site and Off-Site Emergency Plans

The Off-Site plan of a district/pocket is based on the On-Site emergency plans of MAH units in the industrial pocket. The following are some critical deficiencies observed in the On-Site emergency plans:

i) Lack of standardisation of risk assessment methodology.

ii) Non-use of standard terminology.

iii) Non-uniformity in the structure of the plan.

iv) Lack of separate documentation of the Off-Site consequences of an On-Site emergency.

v) Currently On/Off-Site emergency plans are prepared based on the maximum loss scenario. Limits for maximum credible and probabilistic loss scenario have not been evolved at the national level.

vi) Lack of graded response plans.

vii) Lack of medical response plans.

Keeping in view the responsibilities entrusted to the factory inspectorate with respect to chemical industries and management of chemical accidents, and the reliance of the district collector on the factory inspectorate during emergencies, proper infrastructure facilities at the inspectorate are inadequate. The enforcement of the CA(EPPR) Rules is not uniform among different states. The following are the inadequacies in the present system:

a) Non-availability of appointed dedicated staff in the control room.

b) Regular checking of the procedures and systems detailed in the red book.

c) Establishment of information networking with states and districts.

d) Database availability in the control room and updating.

e) The infrastructure facilities and management structure for the control room/ CAS.

f) A system for flow of information in the nodal ministry and from the accident site in the states has not been detailed and documented.

Liability and Compensation

Mechanisms to deal with social and economic impact of chemicals on human health, society and the environment, including liability, compensation and redress need to be streamlined and strengthened.

References

Bhushan, K.; G. Katyal. (2002). *Nuclear, Biological, and Chemical Warfare*. India: APH Publishing.

Cordette, Jessica, MPH. (2003). *Chemical Weapons of Mass Destruction*. Retrieved Nov. 29, 2004.

Eckerman, Ingrid (2001). *Chemical Industry and Public Health—Bhopal as an example*. Essay for MPH.

Shrishti (2002). *Toxic present—toxic future. A report on Human and Environmental Chemical Contamination around the Bhopal disaster site*. Delhi: The Other Media.

Weir D (1987). *The Bhopal Syndrome: Pesticides, Environment and Health*. San Francisco: Sierra Club Books.

5

Managing Terrorism Hazards

Terrorism is the systematic use of terror, often violent, especially as a means of coercion. In the international community, however, terrorism has no legally binding, criminal law definition. Common definitions of terrorism refer only to those violent acts which are intended to create fear (terror), are perpetrated for a religious, political or, ideological goal; and deliberately target or disregard the safety of non-combatants (civilians). Some definitions now include acts of unlawful violence and war. The use of similar tactics by criminal organizations for protection rackets or to enforce a code of silence is usually not labeled terrorism though these same actions may be labeled terrorism when done by a politically motivated group. Perhaps, it is less oppressive in itself than through the effects of the precautions taken to protect its likely victims.

The word "terrorism" is politically and emotionally charged, and this greatly compounds the difficulty of providing a precise definition. Studies have found over 100 definitions of "terrorism". The concept of terrorism may itself be controversial as it is often used by state authorities (and individuals with access to state support) to delegitimize political or other opponents, and potentially legitimize the state's own use of armed force against opponents.

Terrorism has been practiced by a broad array of political organizations for furthering their objectives. It has been practiced by both right-wing and left-wing political parties, nationalistic groups, religious groups, revolutionaries, and ruling governments. An abiding characteristic is the indiscriminate use of violence against noncombatants for the purpose of gaining publicity for a group, cause, or individual. The symbolism of terrorism can leverage human fear to help achieve these goals.

The definition of terrorism has proved controversial. Various legal systems and government agencies use different definitions of terrorism in their national legislation. Moreover, the international community has been slow to formulate a universally agreed, legally binding definition of this crime. These difficulties arise from the fact that the term "terrorism" is politically and emotionally charged. In this regard, Angus Martyn, briefing the Australian Parliament, stated that "The international community has never succeeded in developing an accepted comprehensive definition of terrorism. During the 1970s and 1980s, the United Nations attempts to define the term foundered mainly due to differences of opinion between various members about the use of violence in the context of conflicts over national liberation and self-determination."

These divergences have made it impossible for the United Nations to conclude a Comprehensive Convention on International Terrorism that incorporates a single, all-encompassing, legally binding, criminal law definition terrorism. Nonetheless, the international community has adopted a series of sectoral conventions that define and criminalize various types of terrorist activities. Moreover, since 1994, the United Nations General Assembly has repeatedly condemned terrorist acts using the following political description of terrorism: "Criminal acts intended or calculated to provoke a state of terror in the general public, a group of persons or particular persons for political purposes are in any circumstance unjustifiable, whatever the considerations of a political, philosophical, ideological, racial, ethnic, religious or any other nature that may be invoked to justify them."

Pejorative Use

The terms "terrorism" and "terrorist" (someone who engages in terrorism) carry strong negative connotations. These terms are often used as political labels, to condemn violence or the threat of violence by certain actors as immoral, indiscriminate, unjustified or to condemn an entire segment of a population. Those labeled "terrorists" by their opponents rarely identify themselves as such, and typically use other terms or terms specific to their situation, such as separatist, freedom fighter, liberator, revolutionary, vigilante, militant, paramilitary, guerrilla, rebel, patriot, or any similar-meaning word in other languages and cultures. Jihadi, mujaheddin, and fedayeen are similar Arabic words which have entered the English lexicon. It is common for both parties in a conflict to describe each other as terrorists.

On the question of whether particular terrorist acts, such as killing civilians, can be justified as the lesser evil in a particular circumstance, philosophers have expressed different views: while, according to David Rodin, utilitarian philosophers can (in theory) conceive of cases in which the evil of terrorism is outweighed by the good which could not be achieved in a less morally costly way, in practice the "harmful effects of undermining the convention of non-combatant immunity is thought to outweigh the goods that may be achieved by particular acts of terrorism". Among the non-utilitarian philosophers, Michael Walzer argued that terrorism can be morally justified in only one specific case: when "a nation or community faces the extreme threat of complete destruction and the only way it can preserve itself is by intentionally targeting non-combatants, then it is morally entitled to do so".

In his book Inside Terrorism Bruce Hoffman offered an explanation of why the term terrorism becomes distorted:

> On one point, at least, everyone agrees: terrorism is a pejorative term. It is a word with intrinsically negative connotations that is generally applied to one's enemies and opponents, or to those with whom one disagrees and would otherwise prefer to ignore. 'What is called terrorism,' Brian Jenkins has written, 'thus seems to depend on one's point of view. Use of the term implies a moral judgment; and if one party can successfully attach the label terrorist to its opponent, then it has indirectly persuaded others to adopt its moral viewpoint.' Hence the decision to call someone or label some organization terrorist becomes almost unavoidably subjective, depending largely on whether one sympathizes with or opposes the person/group/cause concerned. If one identifies with the victim of the violence, for example, then the act is terrorism. If, however, one identifies with the perpetrator, the violent act is regarded in a more sympathetic, if not positive (or, at the worst, an ambivalent) light; and it is not terrorism.

The pejorative connotations of the word can be summed up in the aphorism, "One man's terrorist is another man's freedom fighter". This is exemplified when a group using irregular military methods is an ally of a state against a mutual enemy, but later falls out with the state and starts to use those methods against its former ally. During World War II, the Malayan People's Anti-Japanese Army was allied with the British, but during the Malayan

Emergency, members of its successor (the Malayan Races Liberation Army), were branded "terrorists" by the British. More recently, Ronald Reagan and others in the American administration frequently called the Afghan Mujahideen "freedom fighters" during their war against the Soviet Union, yet twenty years later, when a new generation of Afghan men are fighting against what they perceive to be a regime installed by foreign powers, their attacks are labelled "terrorism" by George W. Bush.

Groups accused of terrorism understandably prefer terms reflecting legitimate military or ideological action. Leading terrorism researcher Professor Martin Rudner, director of the Canadian Centre of Intelligence and Security Studies at Ottawa's Carleton University, defines "terrorist acts" as attacks against civilians for political or other ideological goals, and said:

There is the famous statement: 'One man's terrorist is another man's freedom fighter.' But that is grossly misleading. It assesses the validity of the cause when terrorism is an act. One can have a perfectly beautiful cause and yet if one commits terrorist acts, it is terrorism regardless.

Some groups, when involved in a "liberation" struggle, have been called "terrorists" by the Western governments or media. Later, these same persons, as leaders of the liberated nations, are called "statesmen" by similar organizations. Two examples of this phenomenon are the Nobel Peace Prize laureates Menachem Begin and Nelson Mandela. WikiLeaks whistleblower Julian Assange has been called a "terrorist" by Sarah Palin and Joe Biden.

Sometimes states which are close allies, for reasons of history, culture and politics, can disagree over whether or not members of a certain organization are terrorists. For instance, for many years, some branches of the United States government refused to label members of the Irish Republican Army (IRA) as terrorists while the IRA was using methods against one of the United States' closest allies (the United Kingdom) which the UK branded as terrorism. This was highlighted by the Quinn v. Robinson case. For these and other reasons, media outlets wishing to preserve a reputation for impartiality try to be careful in their use of the term.

Types of Terrorism

In early 1975, the Law Enforcement Assistant Administration in the United States formed the National Advisory Committee on Criminal Justice Standards and Goals. One of the five volumes that the committee wrote was entitled Disorders and Terrorism, produced by the Task Force on Disorders and Terrorism under the direction of H.H.A. Cooper, Director of the Task Force staff. The Task Force classified terrorism into six categories.

1. *Civil disorder* – A form of collective violence interfering with the peace, security, and normal functioning of the community.
2. *Political terrorism* – Violent criminal behaviour designed primarily to generate fear in the community, or substantial segment of it, for political purposes.
3. *Non-Political terrorism* – Terrorism that is not aimed at political purposes but which exhibits "conscious design to create and maintain a high degree of fear for coercive purposes, but the end is individual or collective gain rather than the achievement of a political objective."
4. *Quasi-terrorism* – The activities incidental to the commission of crimes of violence that are similar in form and method to genuine terrorism but which nevertheless lack its essential ingredient. It is not the main purpose of the quasi-terrorists to induce terror in the immediate victim as in the case of genuine terrorism, but the quasi-terrorist uses the modalities and techniques of the genuine terrorist and produces similar consequences and reaction. For example, the fleeing felon who takes hostages is a quasi-terrorist, whose methods are similar to those of the genuine terrorist but whose purposes are quite different.
5. *Limited political terrorism* – Genuine political terrorism is characterized by a revolutionary approach; limited political terrorism refers to "acts of terrorism which are committed for ideological or political motives but which are not part of a concerted campaign to capture control of the state.
6. *Official or state terrorism* –referring to nations whose rule is based upon fear and oppression that reach similar to terrorism or such proportions. It may also be referred to as Structural Terrorism defined broadly as terrorist acts carried out by governments in pursuit of political objectives, often as part of their foreign policy.

Motivation of Terrorists

Attacks on 'collaborators' are used to intimidate people from cooperating with the state in order to undermine state control. This strategy was used in the USA in its War of Independence and in Ireland, in Kenya, in Algeria and in Cyprus during their independence struggles.

Attacks on high profile symbolic targets are used to incite counter-terrorism by the state to polarise the population. This strategy was used by Al Qaeda in its attacks on the USA in September 2001. These attacks are also used to draw international attention to struggles which are otherwise unreported such as the Palestinian airplane hijackings in 1970 and the South Moluccan hostage crises in the Netherlands in 1975.

Abrahm suggests that terrorist organizations do not select terrorism for its political effectiveness. Individual terrorists tend to be motivated more by a desire for social solidarity with other members of their organization than by political platforms or strategic objectives, which are often murky and undefined.

Perpetrators

The perpetrators of acts of terrorism can be individuals, groups, or states. According to some definitions, clandestine or semi-clandestine state actors may also carry out terrorist acts outside the framework of a state of war. However, the most common image of terrorism is that it is carried out by small and secretive cells, highly motivated to serve a particular cause and many of the most deadly operations in recent times, such as the September 11 attacks, the London underground bombing, and the 2002 Bali bombing were planned and carried out by a close clique, composed of close friends, family members and other strong social networks. These groups benefited from the free flow of information and efficient telecommunications to succeed where others had failed.

Over the years, many people have attempted to come up with a terrorist profile to attempt to explain these individuals' actions through their psychology and social circumstances. Others, like Roderick Hindery, have sought to discern profiles in the propaganda tactics used by terrorists. Some security organizations designate these groups as violent non-state actors. A 2007 study by economist Alan B. Krueger found that terrorists were less likely to come from an impoverished background (28% vs. 33%) and more likely to have at least a high-school education (47% vs. 38%). Another analysis found only 16% of terrorists came from impoverished families, vs. 30% of male Palestinians, and over 60% had gone beyond high school, vs. 15% of the populace.

To avoid detection, a terrorist will look, dress, and behave normally until executing the assigned mission. Some claim that attempts to profile terrorists based on personality, physical, or sociological traits are not useful. The physical and behavioral description of the terrorist could describe almost any normal person. However, the majority of terrorist attacks are carried out by military age men, aged 16–40.

Tactics

Terrorism is a form of asymmetric warfare, and is more common when direct conventional warfare will not be effective because forces vary greatly in power.

The context in which terrorist tactics are used is often a large-scale, unresolved political conflict. The type of conflict varies widely; historical examples include:

- Secession of a territory to form a new sovereign state or become part of a different state
- Dominance of territory or resources by various ethnic groups
- Imposition of a particular form of government
- Economic deprivation of a population
- Opposition to a domestic government or occupying army
- Religious fanaticism

Terrorist attacks are often targeted to maximize fear and publicity, usually using explosives or poison. There is concern about terrorist attacks employing weapons of mass destruction. Terrorist organizations usually methodically plan attacks in advance, and may train participants, plant undercover agents, and raise money from supporters or through organized crime. Communications occur through modern telecommunications, or through old-fashioned methods such as couriers.

Chemical Terrorism

In November 2004 a United Nations (UN) panel described terrorism as 'an act intended to cause death or serious bodily harm to civilians or non-combatants with the purpose of intimidating a population, or compelling a government or an international organization to do or abstain from doing any act'. A terrorist attack involving chemical agents differs from other terrorist attacks as it presents specific health effects to a larger population in the shortest possible period, hence creating great panic in the community.

The major targets of terrorists include important persons, densely populated and crowded locations, market places, religious congregations, public functions, convention centres, sports events, food and entertainment facilities, utility services like electricity, gas, or water supplies, important places like government institutions including key economic, military, scientific or other sensitive installations, etc. The likely purpose of terrorist attacks is to create panic, kill, injure, incapacitate or destroy life, and cause damage to critical infrastructure, and the environment.

Terrorists, the world over, are not only getting more and more aggressive in their activities but also adopting newer modalities, techniques, and technologies in their modes of operation. Access to advanced science and technology, cyber technology, state-of-the-art communication systems, sophisticated military grade weaponry, global financial channels, both open and confidential, have given an undue impetus to the capabilities of terrorist groups. Use of terrorism as a state policy by some countries and the emergence of fundamentalism and suicide bombers has further compounded the threat of terrorism. This threat has shown a gradual but steady rise globally over the recent past. In the present global threat scenario posed by Al Qaida and other fundamental groups, India is equally prone to terrorist activities. The management of chemical weapons and other related intelligence issues are in the domain of the Ministry of Home Affairs (MHA), Cabinet Secretariat and intelligence agencies. However, since the preparedness for management of Chemical (Terrorism) Disasters (CTD) is common for all three bodies, the details given here are also pertinent to all of them.

There is a global intellectual consensus that acts of terror shall not be accepted under any circumstances. Preparing the nation to address the threat of chemical terrorism is a formidable challenge because anticipating such attacks and dealing with the devastating consequences of the chemical agents involved are difficult and complex propositions.

There are a large number of toxic chemicals that have been used either in warfare or for terrorist activities. Although instances of what might be styled as chemical weapons date back to antiquity, much of the lore of chemical weapons as viewed today has its origin in World War I. Development of chemical weapons in World War I was predominantly the adaptation of a chemical 'fill' to standard munitions. The chemicals used were commercial chemicals with well-known properties or their variants or derivatives. Chlorine gas was used for the first time during World War I in pressurised cylinders, the effectiveness of which depended upon the wind direction. Shortly thereafter, a projectile containing phosgene was used to cause more severe damage and this method became the principal means of delivery. Phosgene is more lethal than chlorine gas and its effects are delayed. Cyanide was introduced sometime in the middle of the world war. Mustard shells were employed in July 1917, and simultaneously Diphenyl Chloroarsine was tried as a mask breaker. During the World War, it was estimated that at one stage 30 per cent of all artillery shells from both sides contained some kind of poison gas. After World War I, research on new chemical warfare agents called nerve agents began, which were many times more potent and lethal than chemical agents used in World War I. Significant among them were Di-isopropylphosphoro Fluoridate, Tabun, Sarin, Soman, and VX. 'Agent Orange' and 'Super Orange' were the nicknames given to a defoliant used extensively between 1961 and 1971. Agent Orange, a 50-50 mix of two herbicide chemicals, known conventionally as 2,4-Dichlorophenoxy Acetic Acid (2,4-D) and 2,4,5-Trichlorophenoxy acetic acid (2,4,5-T), was by far, the most frequently employed of the so-called 'rainbow herbicides'. The earliest health concerns regarding Agent Orange arose when it was found contaminated with 2,3,7,8-Tetrachlorodibenzo-p-dioxin (TCDD), or Dioxin. Degradation of Agent Orange released dioxins, which caused severe damage to the health of those exposed to it during the Vietnam War. The 1980s witnessed the use of mustard gas as a chemical warfare agent. The end of the Cold War has ushered in political and economic turbulence, along with the rise of fundamentalism and state-sponsored terrorism.

The terrorist organisation—'Aum Shinrikyo' in Japan used a single-front company to purchase 180 tonnes of phosphorous tri-chloride, along with other toxic industrial chemicals. They produced sarin gas from these chemicals and released it in two separate attacks in 1994 and 1995. There were five coordinated attacks in the second incident in which 12 persons were killed and nearly 5,000 persons were affected, causing many of them temporary vision problems. All these amply illustrate the potential of Chemical Warfare Agents (CWA) to wreak long-term destruction upon humans and their environment. However the damage causing capacity of CWA has increased manifold in present times.

The numerous industrial accidents involving Hazardous Chemicals (HAZCHEM), which have occurred in the recent past, provide important learning lessons. The foremost of these are the Flixborough explosion of Cyclohexane, the Beek disaster consequent to the release of propylene under pressure, the Seveso disaster, involving Dioxin or TCDD, the Mississagua accident due to collision of railway wagons containing chlorine and propane, the Houston accident involving an anhydrous ammonia tanker truck, the Sommerville, Massachusetts spill of phosphorous trichloride, the Mexico explosion in 1983 involving liquefied petroleum gas, and the worst of all—the Bhopal Gas Tragedy.

Chlorine gas is still being used in conjunction with conventional vehicle-borne explosive devices. Initially, attacks were poorly executed, probably because much of the chemical agent was rendered non-toxic by the heat of the accompanying explosives. Subsequently, with techniques becoming more refined, attacks resulted in hundreds of injuries, but did not prove to be viable means of inflicting massive loss of life. Their primary impact was widespread panic, with a large number of civilians suffering non-life threatening, but nonetheless highly traumatic injuries. These attacks demonstrate that human society is quite vulnerable to chemical threats.

India's unique geo-climatic conditions make it vulnerable to natural disasters. However, sociopolitical conditions in the Indian Subcontinent have made this region particularly vulnerable to man-made disasters including chemical terrorism. Chemical terrorism relates to acts of terrorism using chemical agents. Terrorists sponsored by states, and non-state actors with substantial financial resources and technical expertise, may acquire explosives, incendiaries, and chemical agents similar to those used by military services. Toxic industrial chemicals or materials, together with their hazardous waste, as well as Chemical Warfare (CW) agents are included in the quadrate of Chemical, Biological, Radiological and Nuclear (CBRN) agents due to their widespread accessibility, availability of dual technology, lesser complexity of production, ease of use, and potential toxicity.

Types of Chemical Agents

Toxic chemicals which can be used in terrorism may be generally classified in the following broad categories based on their toxicity and usage.

i) CW agents.

ii) Dual use chemicals.

iii) Toxic Industrial Chemicals/Materials.
iv) HAZCHEM and their waste by-products.
v) Agricultural chemicals.
vi) Other poisonous substances.
vii) Natural gas and petroleum products.

Chemical Warfare Agents

CW agents include toxic chemicals, their precursors, ammunition, and equipment for the dispersal of chemical agents. These agents exist in liquid, gas, or solid form. They can be classified based on their chemical nature, like organo-phosphorus, organo-sulphur, organo-fluorine, arsenicals, and others; and persistency or dose-dependent lethal and incapacitating properties. Above all, the most widely used classification is based on their physiological effects. The categories include nerve agents, blistering agents, blood agents, lung injurants, psychic incapacitants, riot control agents, and toxins. The toxicity data, mechanism of action, and toxic effects including signs. The effectiveness of CW agents depends on many factors. The important ones include:

i) The efficiency of the delivery system, such as munitions and low-flying aircraft.
ii) Modes of dispersal or dissemination, like spray tanks.
iii) Vulnerability of the potential target.
iv) Meteorological conditions, like wind velocity and direction, humidity, temperature, etc.

Dual Use Chemicals

Dual use chemicals are those that can be used for military warfare though they have important industrial applications as well. These industrial chemicals may act as potential precursors of CW agents and are identified in Schedule 2 and 3 of the Chemical Weapons Convention (CWC) list of chemicals. The important ones are phosgene, cyanogen chloride, hydrogen cyanide, and chloropicrin. Production and use of these chemicals is regulated by industrial verifications.

Important Toxic Industrial Chemicals/ Materials

TIC/TIM are manufactured, stored, transported and used throughout the country and are easily accessible by terrorists, and also vulnerable to them.

Facilities handling them in large amounts, like Major Accident Hazard (MAH) units, storages, and during transportation of HAZCHEM or Hazardous Materials (HAZMAT) through ports, railroads, and highways in large, unprotected quantities, are prone to sabotage by terrorists which can lead to toxic spillages/ releases. Some of the important TICs that can be exploited by terrorists include chlorine gas used in water treatment facilities, phosgene gas used in the urethane foam industry, and anhydrous ammonia used in agriculture, refrigeration, and chemical installations. The important physical effects are generally caused by fire, explosion, and leakage of skin toxicants. Chemically, the agents may affect the lungs, eyes, skin, and blood. Many of them may act as carcinogens.

Hazardous Chemical Wastes

The toxic properties of hazardous waste generated by industries not only critically damages the environment but is also under the constant threat of being exploited by terrorists. Hazardous waste can be explosive, inflammable or prone to spontaneous combustion, corrosive, and susceptible to the unpredictable deadly combinations of non-compatible wastes and off-specification properties, etc. They can cause devastation if used selectively and intelligently after due diligence and study of the specifications. Hazardous wastes are also poisonous and can be utilised to contaminate the

drinking water supply of a township or a locality with dire consequences. Thus, terrorists may turn to hazardous waste as a resource for toxicants, or for the synthesis of explosives, e.g., chromium, cyanide etc., are highly poisonous in nature, while lead nickel, iron, and other metals in dissolvable form can result in toxic effects. Waste containing chromium, arsenic, cyanide, acids, alkalis, or unstable compounds can trigger violent reactions.

Agricultural Chemicals

Agrochemicals include chemicals such as pesticides, herbicides, and fungicides used in agriculture to destroy insects, fungi, bacteria, pests, and weeds, and to regulate plant growth. Pesticides are chemicals which are used to kill harmful animals or plants. They are used especially in agriculture and around areas where humans live. Some pesticides are harmful to humans, either from direct contact or as residue on food, or are harmful to the environment because of their high toxicity, such as DDT. Pesticides include fungicides, herbicides, insecticides, and rodenticides. Herbicides are used for the control of weeds. Insecticides are used for the control of insects. The Bhopal Gas Tragedy underlined the dangers arising out of the storage of pesticides or their intermediates. Similar risks are inherent in the manufacture, formulation, and transport of pesticides and their raw materials, formularies, and intermediates. Fertilisers can be organic, or inorganic. Following the Oklahoma city bombing using ammonium nitrate in 1995, the threat of fertiliser being used as a weapon has manifested itself in a menacing manner.

Natural Gas and Petroleum Products

There are many examples of heavy metal poisoning which have caused heavy casualties.

i) The methyl mercury poisoning catastrophe in Iraq during the early 1970s in which an estimated 10,000 people died and 100,000 were severely and permanently brain damaged.

ii) The Minamata methyl mercury poisoning (Japan) affecting 2,955 people, which was first reported officially in 1956, caused by dumping of toxic waste by two factories, contaminating the fish in the waters around the area, which were consumed by the local population.

iii) Arsenic poisoning of milk consumed by infants in Okayama causing 130 fatalities and affecting over 12,000 people.

iv) The prevalent cases of chronic arsenic poisoning in West Bengal, Taiwan, and Bangladesh underline the inherent potential of heavy metals for terrorist activities.

v) Further, the high incidence of lung cancer reported in 1960 from the factory of Nippon-Denki at Kiryama on the Islands of Hokkaido, in which 30 deaths occurred due to inhalation of dust containing highly oxidised chromium (VI).

Lead is also one of the major environmental poisons and its wide usage in a number of daily use products and medical accessories expose the population to associated risks. Other metals include cadmium which has a disruptive effect on the reproductive and endocrine systems, and cyanide which is well known for its lethal potential. The water solubility and acute toxicity potential of heavy metals like arsenic, mercury, cyanide, or related compounds make them a potential choice to poison food and water.Natural gas and petroleum products can be used as agents for creating havoc and casualties. LNG being transported by tankers can be used as a cryogenic agent for causing large fires, thereby creating mass panic reaction and fatalities. CNG cascades can have a devastating effect if a detonator is placed inside them. Terrorists may also target petroleum and petroleum product pipelines operated for transmission and the distribution network.

Acquisition and Delivery of Chemical Agents

Usually ordinary chemical agents are not used for chemical terrorism activities because of the large quantities required to produce significant effects, which complicate logistics. Several other factors that limit the use of chemical agents by terrorists include controlled access to precursor chemicals, difficulty and danger in producing the agents, problems with their dispersion without military munitions, and security issues linked to chemical agents.

Many terrorist groups are well organised, technically sound, have well-connected global networks, and have easy accessibility to methodologies for preparing various 'homemade' agents for chemical terrorism. Among CBRN agents, terrorist organisations prefer to use chemical weapons as an ideal mode of attack as they are cheap, relatively accessible, and easy to transport. A wide range of potentially deadly chemical agents are available, including various insecticides, industrial chemicals, and potent toxins such as ricin, which are relatively easy to produce or acquire. A skilled chemist can readily synthesise most of these chemical agents if the precursors are available. These organisations have purportedly developed manuals that cover inter alia, techniques of assassination including details for the production of poisonous gases, pesticides, fungicides, mustards, arsine, phosgene, and other poisons like ricin, etc. Though somewhat unlikely, it may also be possible to steal deadly agents from civilian research facilities or military stockpiles. A state sponsor of terrorism—most of whom have active programmes for Weapons of Mass Destruction (WMD)—would be willing to provide terrorists with chemical weapons or materials, if it could establish 'plausible deniability' while using a surrogate group to inflict a devastating blow on an enemy.

The lethality of some types of highly toxic chemical agents depends crucially on their delivery system, which predominantly affects the resultant exposure. The common mode of dispersal of chemical agents for terrorism may include:

i) Dissemination of aerosolised or gaseous vapour in confined or open spaces.
ii) Premeditated mass poisoning of water supply at water reservoirs and bottling plants.
iii) Contamination of personal items and belongings, like handkerchiefs, blankets, etc.
iv) Contamination of packaged food products and pharmaceutical products.
v) The hijacking, sabotage and/or use of any conveyance have effectively been utilised in attacks on the World Trade Center, Mumbai local trains, Glasgow, and recent such attacks in Iraq.

Many factors influence the effectiveness of a delivery system. For instance, open-air release of an agent may be crucially affected by meteorological conditions, while the release of an agent even in a confined space is influenced by the individual dose and air circulation patterns.

Effects of Chemical Agents

Terrorists use chemicals simultaneously with explosives and other dangerous materials for spreading panic and terror. Poisonous chemical agents have deleterious effects on people, animals, plants, and the environment. The tragic sequel of terrorist attacks involving chemicals also varies in its magnitude and impact.

Health Effects

Chemicals agents cause a variety of harmful effects with different degrees of severity. Most of them are capable of causing serious chemical burns, heat burns, injuries, poisoning, disabilities, and chronic health conditions, causing high morbidity and mortality. Contamination of ambient air is the most significant pathway by which the toxic chemical attacks the target organ i.e., eye, lung, skin, etc., in major chemical disasters. Intake by inhalation or absorption through skin and mucous membranes constitute the main routes of entry. In the case of contaminated water or food, the targets will be the digestive and assimilative systems. When the source of drinking water is contaminated, delayed effects will manifest themselves. The variation in magnitude and impact on human life in terms of severity of injuries depends mainly on the type and amount of the chemical agent used, the potential of the implicated chemical to interact with diverse anatomical structures and physiological functions, the mode of dispersal or delivery, climatic conditions, the route of entry and absorption, the individual's susceptibility, the degree and duration of exposure, and the state of preparedness to counter immediate effects. The long-term effects like carcinogenicity and mutagenicity must also be kept in mind for medical follow up of disaster victims.

Psycho-Social Trauma and Community Behaviour

Although people are often tragically killed and wounded by terrorists in their attacks, terrorism by its nature is designed to have far-reaching psychological effects beyond the immediate victims or objects of their violence. It is meant to instil a sense of fear and thereby intimidate or otherwise affect the behaviour of the terrorists' target. Since fear is deliberately created and exploited during such attacks, it can undeniably be regarded as a form of psychological warfare affecting the behaviour of a much wider target population. Cyber based exchange of information which can be used to cause a CTD presents a tough challenge to democratic societies and liberal values. Terrorism adversely affects normal daily life by threatening personal safety, thereby tearing the social fabric by destroying its business and cultural life and the mutual trust upon which society is based. Common responses to the fear generated by the uncertainty of where and when the next terrorist attack will occur may result in refusal of people to go to religious places, shopping malls, sporting events, theatres, cinema halls, concerts, or to travel. It is often difficult to differentiate psychological harm caused by chemical terrorism from other illnesses. Previous events across the globe demonstrate that a large number of patients with psychological distress will impact emergency response and potentially overwhelm the health care system. Strategies must be developed to diminish fear and hopefully decrease subsequent mass psychological distress that is likely to occur following a mass incidence of chemical exposure.

Research and documentation is lacking in India on these aspects, specifically for CTD. International experience and research has evidence that the affected population and survivors experience panic reactions as an immediate response. Individuals' concern for their own safety and for their near and dear ones, leads to extreme emotional reactions of breaking down, shouting, or running around looking for safety. The individual behavioural response pattern in itself can lead to active physical danger, e.g., jumping out of windows from high rise buildings; but more importantly the behavioural response pattern of groups and crowds becomes critical in terrorism related disasters. A stampede or other such phenomena resulting from the collective behaviour response pattern add to and further compound death and injuries. In the Indian experience of terrorism-related disasters, there have been media reports and indirect evidence, but specific evidence from research is not yet available.Scientific literature suggests the possibility of Post Traumatic Stress Disorder (PTSD) and 'survivor guilt syndrome' besides other depressive disorders. In India, although there have been a few studies on the psychological fallout of terrorism, which have reported moderate rates of psychiatric symptoms and syndromes like PTSD, there is very little systematic research on the psychological aspects including behavioural response patterns.

Effects on Environment

Chemical terrorism disasters may result in the discharge of toxic chemicals into any one of the compartments of environment, viz., soil, water bodies, and atmosphere. The impact on the environment as a consequence of chemical terrorism activity varies in severity. Re-suspension of chemicals occurs by wind and water mediated erosion and human activities. In the aquatic environment, chemicals present in living and non-living compartments keep recycling at a faster pace and the aquatic biota plays an important role in their phase distribution. Transfer of chemicals from the atmosphere to terrestrial and aquatic ecosystems involve deposition, interception, and retention, however, the particle size and nature of the chemical, the nature of the vegetation, ground surface aspects, prevailing weather conditions, the state of growth of ground cover, and the physico-chemical nature of the water bodies play an important role.

The pervasion of the environmental compartments by toxic chemicals results in perceptible and insidious effects on human health as a long-range target in the course of bio-magnification through the food chain of living organisms. Plants absorb chemicals from the environment through foliage and roots. Once in the plant, the chemicals are translocated and stored. Since plants are primary producers, accumulation of chemicals in them have considerable consequences on consumers in the food web.

Surveillance Mechanism

Besides the MHA, which is the designated nodal agency for developing and coordinating the intelligence and surveillance mechanism, the important line ministries mainly involved in coordinating the response and relief in the aftermath of terrorist attacks include MoD, Ministry of Health and Family Welfare (MoH&FW), Ministry of Agriculture (MoA), and Ministry of Environment and Forests (MoEF). MHA also draws technical help from the Chief of Integrated Defence Staff (CIDS), Armed Forces, Defence Research and Development Organisation (DRDO), Armed Forces Medical Services (AFMS), paramilitary forces and state machinery.

Mechanisms are in place to oversee the command and control function at the national level through various Crisis Management Groups (CMGs), which coordinate the response of the government sectors, and monitor the situation in terrorist events. Other agencies at the national level concerned with chemical terrorism include Ministry of External Affairs (MEA), Ministry of Information and Broadcasting, Department of Drinking Water Supply, Department of Animal Husbandry and Dairying (DAH&D); and technical agencies like Directorate General Health Services (DGHS), AFMS, Indian Council of Medical Research (ICMR), and Drug Controller General of India.

MHA interacts with states and technical institutes at periodic intervals to share intelligence inputs. The other backup technical structure includes the various technical laboratories of AFMS, DRDO, Council for Scientific and Industrial Research (CSIR), Department of Science and Technology (DST), and ICMR, as also certain autonomous and semi-autonomous laboratories.

Similar machinery exists at the state level, backed up by various ministries and departments. The main organisations and functionaries concerned at the state level for effective management of chemical terrorism are the Department(s) of Health Services, Public Health Engineering, Transport Services, Agriculture, Animal Husbandry and Dairying, etc. The states also have regional offices of various central ministries to liaise with the central government.

At the district level, the district collector, with the help of various departments and committees, is responsible for planning, preparing, and management of CTD. As applicable, the collector, deputy commissioner, district magistrate, commissioner of police, and superintendent of police have been designated to be a part of the command and control functions.

Legislative and Regulatory Framework

At the national level, India has created a comprehensive infrastructure of legislative and executive measures to synergise and coordinate actions against terrorist groups. The repealed Prevention of Terrorism Act, 2002, contained provisions to deal with terrorist activities including WMD. These provisions have largely been retained in the Unlawful Activities (Prevention) Amendment Act, 2004, which covers a wide spectrum of activities including WMD. The provisions incorporated in the Act include the definition of 'unlawful association', punishment for possession of substances capable of producing WMD, etc. Relevant provisions under the Civil Procedure Code and Criminal Procedure Code can be invoked to detain and question persons involved in criminal acts, which include terrorism in their ambit. Other provisions under the existing mechanism can be invoked for establishing law and order, for cordoning off the incident area, and for traffic and crowd management. There are a number of regulations in place for manufacture, storage, transportation, insurance, liability and compensation, and environmental issues related to potentially dangerous chemicals.

Ministry of Defence

The armed forces have a network of hospitals all over the country, which can support clinical case management. Further, the armed forces have the capacity to evacuate casualties by ambulance, ship, and aircraft. However, it is necessary to develop a fleet of ambulances fitted with Nuclear, Biological, and Chemical (NBC) filters. MoD is the nodal ministry for coordinating war-related matters. The AFMS has mobile field hospitals, which can be moved to the affected areas for administering treatment at the incident site itself. The medical and paramedical staff are well trained to handle patients resulting from any disaster. Training is imparted at the time of induction, and refresher courses are conducted regularly.

Role of the armed forces

i) The armed forces by their inherent organisational infrastructure, training, leadership, communication, etc., are ideally suited to be first responders in any national level calamity or disaster.

ii) Response to a chemical terrorist attack would be different from a response to any other disaster due to the specialised facilities required to be created, including protection, detection, and decontamination facilities.

iii) Since this type of disaster would be more towards the management of providing immediate specialised medical assistance, the nodal agency to coordinate and provide assistance as first responders and would be orchestrated by the Director General, Armed Forces Medical Services (DG AFMS). This would be in the form of earmarking command-wise response, relating to assigned areas of responsibilities. Basically, the following may be included:

a) Upgrade necessary infrastructure and develop capacity by equipping the responders with Personal Protective Equipment (PPE), detection, and decontamination facilities to respond adequately and effectively.

b) Training of earmarked medical personnel in the management of casualties during a chemical attack, as these would be different in nature from war casualties or casualties occurring in any other disaster.

c) Creating specialised ambulances for CBRN casualty evacuation.

d) Decontamination facilities, specialised treatment wards, and adequate specialised laboratory support is necessary for the management of CTD.

e) Earmarking of command-wise first responders from all medical resources of the army, navy, and the air force.

f) Adequate mechanisms and provisions are required to be created for providing specialised support to manage chemical casualties.

g) Creation of adequate stockpiles of necessary antidotes, decontamination agents, and essential drugs along with their turnover policy, under various commands.

h) Conduct periodic exercises to ensure efficacy of CTD response plans.

i) Upgradation of the existing infrastructure and provisions is a continuous process based upon the National Guidelines.

j) Regular interaction with nodal ministries (MHA and MoH&FW) directly or through the National Executive Committee (NEC).

The National Crisis Management Committee (NCMC), under the chairmanship of the cabinet secretary, is mandated to coordinate and monitor response to crisis situations. The NDMA provides advocacy on policy, and shall issue guidelines on the subject for the purpose of prevention, mitigation, and preparedness for strengthening response.

Initiatives at the State Level

Many states have taken the initiative of making Standard Operating Procedures (SOPs) to handle chemical incidents. National policy provides extended support to the state governments in the management of such incidents. At present, state crisis groups exist along with Emergency Operations Centres (EOCs) and Emergency Response Centres (ERCs) for the management of such disasters. However, there is no particular institutional mechanism in most of the states for tackling CTD. Various states are now in the process of setting up state/district authorities. Some of these authorities have taken initiatives to prepare 'all hazard' DM plans, which also include man-made disasters, and preparedness measures to manage CTD based on the guidelines issued by NDMA or the State Disaster Management Authority (SDMA).

Other Technical Initiatives

India has a number of technical institutes under various organisations/departments dealing with the management of different aspects of disasters involving chemicals and toxicants. The various technical capacities available are as follows:

i) MoD established the Inter-Services Coordination Committee to monitor the CW programme, wherein the DRDO is also a participant. Research is carried out by DRDO to design and fabricate protective clothing and equipment for troops in the battlefield in case of a chemical weapons attack. The Defence Research and Development Establishment (DRDE) at Gwalior is the primary establishment for studies in toxicology and biochemical pharmacology. Research on the effects of chemical agents and heavy metal toxins is also carried out here. There are ongoing R&D activities in the areas of upgrading the design and manufacture of protective clothing and equipment, detection equipment, decontamination systems, and medical protection equipment like face masks, canisters, casualty evacuation bags, etc. DRDO is also developing reconnaissance vehicles and mobile laboratories for evaluating the situation during an attack or suspected attack.

ii) Research institutes like the Indian Institute of Chemical Technology (IICT), Hyderabad; Industrial Toxicology Research Centre (ITRC), Lucknow; National Environmental Engineering Research Institute (NEERI), Nagpur; National Chemical Laboratory (NCL), Pune; and

National Institute of Occupational Safety and Health (NIOSH), Ahmedabad, are working in the field of occupational hazard, safety, and other aspects related to the management of CTD.

iii) Limited facilities, for the collection of environmental toxicants released during a chemical disaster, also exist in the laboratories of CSIR, DRDO, and ICMR, as well as in the Central Pollution Control Boards (CPCBs), State Pollution Control Boards (SPCBs), Pollution Control Committee (PCC), Petroleum and Explosive Safety Organisation (PESO), and some recognised laboratories in the private sector.

iv) Fire and emergency services for the management of CTD are not yet fully developed. A few HAZMAT vehicles are available with the fire and emergency services in some states.

v) The first National Poisons Information Centre (NPIC) was set up in 1995 in the Department of Pharmacology, All India Institute of Medical Sciences (AIIMS), New Delhi. NPIC works in the areas of:

   a) Detection of heavy metal contamination, occupational exposure, food, water, air, and soil contamination.

   b) Environmental health monitoring.

   c) Toxico-surveillance (active survey of prevailing and potential toxicity risks).

vi) In addition to the National Poisons Information Centre functioning at the AIIMS, there are other poison information centres functioning at (a) NIOSH, Ahmedabad; (b) Department of Toxicology, Amrita Institute of Medical Sciences and Research, Cochin; and (c) Toxiclogy and IMCU Unit, Government General Hospital, Chennai.

vii) State-level forensic laboratories have limited capabilities for detection of chemical substances.

viii) Five ERCs have been established in Manali (Tamil Nadu), Bhopal (Madhya Pradesh), Mahad (Maharastra), Vishakhapatnam (Andhra Pradesh), and Hyderabad (Andhra Pradesh), which deal with chemical emergencies in a given area and disseminate technical information relating to the chemicals involved. The MoEF has recently approved the proposal to establish three more Emergency Response Centres (ERCs) at Vijaywada, Kurrool and Kakinada in Andhra Pradesh.

ix) The Petroleum and Natural Gas Regulatory Board (PNGRB) has taken the initiative of forming sub-committees which provide necessary guidelines for safety and other standards used by various segments covered under oil and gas mid-stream and down-stream sectors. The PNGRB has also framed the Emergency Response and Disaster Management Plan (ERDMP) which also highlights the means of averting such disasters.

International Conventions and Global Initiatives

There is an increasing reliance on restrictive regimes and the use of punitive action to confront terrorism which is a threat to international peace and security. A number of global initiatives have been taken for non-proliferation, counter-proliferation, and consequence management of CTD, which have contributed in mitigating the overall risks.

Chemical Weapons Convention

India signed the CWC on 14 January 1993, as a pioneer signatory, and deposited the instrument of ratification on 3 September 1996. Consequently, India enacted the CWC Act, 2000, that gave effect to the convention on the prohibition of the development, production, stockpiling, and use of chemical weapons, and on their destruction, to provide for matters connected thereof. Each country was to enact legislation and constitute an authority for this purpose. Accordingly, the National Authority of Chemical Weapons Convention [NA(CWC)] was constituted under the provision of the Indian CWC Act, 2000, for the implementation of the CWC.

According to the CWC, 'all toxic chemicals and their precursors are chemical weapons, as long as the type and quantities are intended for use prohibited under the convention'. It includes the chemical action on life processes causing death, temporary incapacitation, or permanent harm to human beings or animals. CWC has classified toxic chemicals as Schedule 1: A—toxic chemicals and B—precursors; Schedule 2: A—toxic chemicals and B—precursors, and Schedule 3: A—toxic chemicals and B—precursors.

As of now, 182 countries are state parties to the CWC, among which India is one of the original signatories. Six other countries have signed the CWC but not ratified it, and there are seven non-signatory nations. The major ones among the latter are Egypt, Iraq, Lebanon, Syria, and North Korea. The former category includes Congo, Israel, and Myanmar.

The CWC stipulates certain responsibilities and requirements of the signatory countries. Some of the important responsibilities are as follows:

i) Each state party to this convention undertakes, never under any circumstances:

   a) To develop, produce, otherwise acquire, stockpile, or retain chemical weapons, or transfer, directly or indirectly, chemical weapons to anyone.

   b) To use chemical weapons.

   c) To engage in any military preparations to use chemical weapons.

   d) To assist, encourage, or induce, in any way, anyone to engage in any activity prohibited to a state party under this convention.

ii) Each state party undertakes to destroy chemical weapons it owns or possesses, or that are located in any place under its jurisdiction or control, in accordance with the provisions of this convention.

iii) Each state party undertakes to destroy chemical weapons it abandoned on the territory of another state party, in accordance with the provisions of this convention.

v) Each state party undertakes to destroy any chemical weapons production facilities it owns or possesses, or that are located in any place under its jurisdiction or control, in accordance with the provisions of this convention.

v) Each state party undertakes not to use riot control agents as a method of warfare.

vi) To fulfil the criterion identified under this convention, the following initiatives for its implementation were taken:

   i) For purposes of equitable geographical representation in the decision-making organs of the convention, regional groups are recognised.

   ii) Implementation of this convention is expected to facilitate a global trade in chemical products and encourage international cooperation between state parties in the peaceful application of chemistry.

   iii) The CWC calls for declarations from signatory parties on their stockpiles, detailing types and quantities and also chemical weapon production facilities, both past and present. This includes inspection of storage and production facilities related to destruction of chemical weapons and production facilities.

However, the CWC stipulates that destruction must be ecologically and environmentally friendly, and open-pit burning, deep sea dumping and other non-environmentally friendly methods must be avoided.

iv) CWC makes it clear that any toxic chemical can be produced as long as the type and quantity are useful for non-prohibited purposes. A state party can even produce and stockpile a very toxic agent, like VX, to a maximum extent of one tonne, provided the material is used for protective, medical, or research purposes. While medical and research purposes are clear, protective purposes need adequate explanation. This means these chemicals can be used for testing defensive equipment that is for CW detection, or protection from it, or for training personnel.

v) Consequence management preparedness activities carried out bilaterally or through multilateral entities, like the Euro-Atlantic Disaster Response Coordination Centre, have contributed in mitigating the risk of chemical terrorism. Such an initiative is also required for Asian countries.

vi) There are many precursor chemicals that are required for chemical weapon production. While the negotiations were on, it was realised that these precursors, and even some of the toxic chemicals like hydrogen cyanide or phosgene, have legitimate industrial use, and curtailing their production would impede technological developments. It is therefore, clear that while the verification and inspection of chemical weapons and production facilities is expected to cease in a 10-year period, the non-diversion and non-use of industrial chemicals for chemical weapons will continue forever. It was to address these issues that the Organisation for Prohibition of Chemical Weapons (OPCW) was established at The Hague in The Netherlands, which oversees the implementation of CWC.

OPCW and its Role in Implementation of CWC

OPCW is an international agency that empowers the state parties to understand and manage the real and proven threats of chemical terrorism. It has been well understood that in-spite of speedy implementation of the CWC, there is always the possibility of a state party becoming a victim of chemical weapon attack, or being subjected to their use, or making use of riot control agents as a method of warfare, which is also prohibited. The issue of terrorism involving the use of WMD is a concern for the world community. To compound the issue, a state party can be threatened by the action and activities of another state party related to CW use. In such instances not only can the state party that is subjected to a CW attack get assistance from OPCW, but an investigation can also be ordered, which is called 'Alleged Use Inspection'.

Initiatives Taken by the UN Security Council

Addressing the General Assembly in 2001, the UN Secretary General said, 'While the world was unable to prevent the 11 September attacks, there is much we can do to help prevent future terrorist acts carried out with WMD. The greatest danger arises from a non-state group—or even an individual—acquiring and using a nuclear, biological, or chemical weapon. Such a weapon could be delivered without the need for any missile or other sophisticated delivery system'. The UN has since dealt with the threat posed by terrorism and WMD and has made certain useful recommendations. Further steps need to be taken in the UN framework since this is not a problem specific to a particular country or region. Given the global implications, it will not be sufficient to address the problem behind the closed doors of select clubs. The UN has identified the probability of using chemical agents as terrorist weapons, and to prevent such disasters, has passed the following resolutions:

i) *Resolution 1540 (2004) of the UN Security Council (UNSC)* This Resolution affirms that proliferation of nuclear, chemical, and biological weapons as well as their means of delivery, constitute a threat to international peace and security. It also calls for all states to refrain from providing any form of support to non-state actors that attempt to develop, acquire, manufacture, possess, transport, transfer, or use nuclear, chemical, or biological weapons and their means of delivery.

ii) United Nations Security Council Resolution 1373

The 9/11 World Trade Center attack by Al Qaida led to the UNSC Resolution 1373 making it obligatory on the part of all states to undertake legal, administrative, and other measures to deal with WMD. The UNSC at its 4385th meeting, on 28 September 2001, adopted Resolution 1373. Operational paragraph 3 (a) also calls upon all states to find ways of intensifying and accelerating the exchange of operational information, especially regarding actions or movements of terrorist persons or networks, forged or falsified travel documents, trafficking in arms, explosives or sensitive materials, use of communication technologies by terrorist groups, and the threat posed by the possession of WMD by terrorist groups.

Container Security Initiative

Containerised shipping is a critical component of international trade. As terrorist organisations have increasingly turned to destroying economic infrastructure to make an impact on nations, the vulnerability of international shipping has come under scrutiny. The Container Security Initiative (CSI) was launched in 2002 by the US Bureau of Customs and Border Protection (CBP), an agency of the Department of Homeland Security. Its purpose was to increase security for container cargo shipped to the US. As the CBP puts it, the intent is to 'extend [the] zone of security outward so that American borders are the last line of defense, not the first'. Under the CSI programme, teams of CBP officials deployed to work with host nation counterparts target and screen all containers that pose a potential threat with regard to terrorism, WMD, their delivery systems, related technologies, and advanced conventional weapons.

Initiative by Europe and Eurasia

i) Registration, Evaluation, Authorisation and Restriction of Chemicals (REACH), is a new European community regulation on chemicals and their safe use. The aim of REACH is to improve the protection of human health and the environment through better and earlier identification of the intrinsic properties of chemical substances. The new law came into force on 1 June 2007. The REACH Regulation gives greater responsibility to industry to manage risks from chemicals and to provide safety information on the substances. The benefits of the REACH system will gradually become evident as more and more substances are brought within the purview of REACH.

ii) Operation Active Endeavour (OAE): The North Atlantic Treaty Organisation (NATO) plays a key role in combating terrorism at the regional level in Europe. The OAE is part of NATO's multifaceted response to the terrorist threat—a naval operation aimed at combating terrorism by monitoring maritime traffic in the Mediterranean Sea. It is designed to prevent the movement of terrorists, or WMD, as well as to enhance the security of shipping in general. It began on 4 October 2001, as one of the eight NATO responses to 11 September 2001 attacks. The operation aims to demonstrate NATO's solidarity and resolve in the fight against terrorism and to help detect and deter terrorist activities in the Mediterranean Sea. So far, over 100,000 merchant ships have been hailed and 148 vessels boarded. Recently the OAE has developed good relations with similar operations in the Arabian and Black Seas.

ASEAN's Concerns about Weapons of Mass Destruction

The Association of Southeast Asian Nations, commonly referred to as ASEAN, is a geopolitical and economic organisation of 10 countries located in Southeast Asia. The ASEAN Regional Forum (ARF) is the principal forum for security dialogue in Asia. It draws together 23 countries, which have a bearing on the security of the Asia-Pacific region. They have been deliberating on the growing dangers posed by the proliferation of WMD and their means of delivery, and reaffirmed their commitment to make further joint efforts to tackle the problem.

The Basel Convention on the Control of Transboundary Movement of Hazardous Wastes and their Disposal

India is a party to the Basel Convention on the Control of Transboundary Movements of Hazardous Wastes and their Disposal. The basic objectives of the Basel Convention are the control and reduction of transboundary movement of hazardous and other wastes, subject to the convention; prevention and minimisation of their generation, environmentally sound management of such wastes, and for active promotion of the transfer and use of cleaner technologies. As a party to the convention, India is obliged to regulate and minimise the import of hazardous waste or other wastes for disposal or recycling, and also to prevent export of waste to parties, which have prohibited the import of such wastes. As a party to this convention, India is also required to minimise generation of hazardous waste in the country, taking into account social, technological, and economic aspects. Further, hazardous waste generated in the country is also required to be managed in an environmentally sound manner. India, as a party, can prevent the import of hazardous waste or other waste if it has reason to believe that the waste in question will not be managed in an environmentally sound manner. The sound management of hazardous waste would also reduce its probable usage in chemical terrorism activities.

Preparedness for Chemical Terrorism Disasters

Like many other developed and developing countries of the world, India too, is vulnerable to all kinds of terrorist activities. An analysis of existing institutional mechanisms for CTD revealed various gaps. Guidelines for preparedness have been developed based on the gaps identified in the existing mechanism with incorporation of well-tested global best practices and technological advances in the field. One of the major requirements for the management of CTD is the development of reliable detection technologies coupled with a continuous surveillance system. Such surveillance systems will be integrated with inputs from national and international intelligence agencies. A management framework based upon advanced technologies for the management of CTD by harmonisation of various activities is required to enhance the capacities at district, state, and national levels. Infrastructure must be developed or upgraded to prevent, mitigate and manage illness and injury caused by chemical agents used in terrorist activities. The national approach to chemical terrorism will not be a stand-alone plan but will be incorporated into the 'all hazard' mitigation strategy for combating all types of man-made disasters. The strategy can be made effective by adoption of a three-step approach, namely, identifying the potential risks and assessing their impact, building the necessary capabilities to respond effectively, and continually evaluating and testing preparedness, which includes identifying lessons from mock-exercises and real-life events.

Counter-Terrorism Strategies

The key aim of the counter-terrorism strategy will be the adoption of appropriate measures, which will mitigate the overall risk of CTD, based on vulnerability and threat assessment. Necessary counter-terrorism strategies will be aimed to minimise the various socio-economic factors that lead to terrorism. This will be followed by reduction of the perceived terrorist threat by using the following measures:

i) Crucial surveillance data and intercepted information gathered by intelligence agencies will be shared with authorised stakeholders on a need-to-know basis.

ii) Surveillance technologies will be updated to keep up with global best practices.

iii) Adequate steps will be taken to enhance and update surveillance capabilities. The help and support of telecommunication companies and internet service providers will also be taken for this purpose.

iv) Regular monitoring and continuous follow up of terrorist activities and changing trends will be done by gathering intelligence inputs.

v) The ability to identify and understand the various factors enhancing possible terrorist threats will be improved.

vi) Various deterring and disrupting measures will be adopted to limit the factors that lead to emergence of terrorism.

vii) International cooperation with overseas partners will strengthen intelligence inputs to help prevention and mitigation of various factors that lead to terrorist activities.

viii) Border security will be strengthened, and identity management improved.

ix) Enhanced protection of installations, storages, and pipelines carrying HAZCHEM by working in conjunction with the corporate sector.

x) Steps will be taken to reduce the risk and impact of attacks during transportation of toxic chemicals and materials by adopting advanced security and technological measures.

xi) Appropriate financial strategies will be adopted to scuttle the flow of funds through illegal means from unauthorised sources to various terrorist and other undesirable organisations. This will be achieved by:

    a) Developing secure networks of intelligence and law-enforcement agencies.

    b) Seeking cooperation from national and international financial and banking agencies, and other financial regulatory bodies.

Risk and Vulnerability Assessment

Risk and vulnerability assessment must precede emergency management plans for mitigation of CTD. It requires inputs from several agencies and a coordination mechanism which will be supported by documented information and continuing research in the relevant areas of chemical safety and security.

A comprehensive risk management approach will focus on the intent and capabilities of potential terrorists, the vulnerability of various possible targets, and the possible consequences of such attacks.

The criterion of risk and vulnerability assessment includes development of indicators which are as follows:

i) Factors to define vulnerable locations and thereby development of risk-zonation maps for possible chemical attacks based upon intelligence inputs or surveillance reports.

ii) Define priority activities that require strengthening to prevent or mitigate the effects of terrorist activities.

iii) Mechanism to define field variables followed by their testing.

iv) Mechanism for identification of major plausible hazards and indicators that show the progression of the severity of CTD at different time intervals.

v) Modes to promptly identify various vulnerable groups and their prioritisation.

vi) Identify and establish resource inventories and existing counter-terrorism measures to limit the impact of CTD.

vii) Carry out risk assessment studies based on global incidents to determine the risk potential in the Indian context.

Information and inputs derived from the above indicators will help in the proper assessment of risks. Such information will also be integrated with the existing risk management framework.

Surveillance and Environmental Monitoring

The information collected from surveillance and continuous environmental monitoring ultimately helps in risk-zonation at the micro level. The important priority areas are:

i) Preparation of a secure database of all the chemicals which have potential for use in different chemical terrorism activities or as a potential target for terrorist attacks. Such information should be made available to various stakeholders who are involved in the management of CTD.

ii) Assessment of the impact of all plausible worst-case scenarios.

iii) Establishment of a mechanism to synergise technical cooperation and coordination between the intelligence gathering agencies, technical institutes, and other emergency functionaries.

iv) The zoning of vulnerable sites susceptible to chemical attacks is required urgently. Exit pathways must also be identified. The above shall be done after considering the effects of identified toxic chemicals/ chemical agents. The vulnerability assessment mapping will be based on the following factors:

   a) GIS-based modelling—taking into account the topography of the area and the prevailing climatic conditions.

   b) The vulnerable population (children, women, elderly people, disabled, patients, etc.), medical care facilities, schools, important government buildings, financial institutions, and public utilities that need extra care during such attacks.

   c) The number and quality of shelters available, the access routes for people out of the incident site, as well as awareness in the community about various chemical risks and necessary response measures.

   d) Existing negative factors like presence of densely populated and industrial clusters, absence of evacuation routes, inadequate health care facilities, lack of communication facilities, and measures to mitigate them.

   e) Reservoirs, water bodies, ecologically important sites, food storages, wildlife sanctuaries, and cattle sheds, etc., that would intensify the vulnerability of the area.

   f) The level of resilience and capacity to respond in the local population.

   g) Vulnerability of important routes used for HAZCHEM transportation.

   h) Variables like proximity of urban areas, and the effect of an attack on important installations.

The surveillance module will also include a model for CTD based chemical mock-exercises and their periodical testing at the ground level. Mock-exercises will be designed specifically for high risk sites and areas based on the vulnerability and surveillance module threat assessment.

Chemical Security and Early Warning System (EWS)

A large number of dual-use chemicals can be targeted for CTD activity. The toxic industrial chemical infrastructure is spread all over India and hence it presents a special challenge. The security of such chemicals at the installation level, during transport, and at isolated storages and pipelines is necessary for effective prevention of their misuse. Specialised areas of concern such as management of TICs/TIMs, hazardous waste, and strategies for mitigation of indirect risks requires effective planning at all levels and needs to be addressed carefully. The effect of attacks can be optimally mitigated with an efficient EWS. Mechanism for chemical security and EWS will be developed based on the following:

i) Development of indicators for the possible mode of delivery and the effects of chemical agents for terrorist activities. Such indicators will be used to develop an effective EWS. Conducting mock-drills to validate the above indicators of EWS using scenarios of intentional chemical attacks is also necessary.

ii) Understanding the terrorist's motivation and capabilities regarding use of TIC/TIMs for chemical attacks or as targets.

iii) Develop innovative approaches to deny terrorist access to TIC facilities, associated chemicals, or other capabilities they would require to carry out chemical attacks.

iv) Tailor the deterrence strategies at national and state levels to counter terrorists and those who might help or facilitate a chemical attack.

v) There is a need to detect and disrupt the flow of toxic industrial chemicals, funds, and other resources and inputs required by terrorists and likely anti-national elements to carry out a chemical attack.

vi) Institute measures to strengthen response, should an attack be imminent, and in the event of a chemical release, take measures to alleviate the consequences by creation of an infrastructure equipped with the latest forensic and investigative techniques and qualified manpower.

vii) Networking of intelligence services for countering chemical terrorism is recommended at all levels, especially in and around installations, storages, and vulnerable transportation routes of chemicals for close information sharing, and for updating the law enforcement agencies about the various threats and changed emerging trends. The level of intelligence-sharing with other stakeholders will be decided by law-enforcement agencies.

viii) Create awareness, and vigilance about the need for chemical security provisions, amongst all those who produce, hold, and utilise chemical agents, and educate government functionaries, and the community by:

a) Sharing of data regarding chemicals and adoption of infallible and concise chemical security provisions.

b) Communication to increase dialogue and consultations.

ix) Periodical review of risk-vulnerability studies, and environmental and surveillance mechanisms, analysis of the security aspects of different emergency plans to continuously upgrade the existing indicators of threat perception, where intelligence agencies and other stakeholders participate.

x) Creation and regular updating of resource inventory of key contacts from industries, regulatory bodies, intelligence agencies, and other stakeholders.

There is no doubt that under initiatives and instructions from MoEF and MHA, the chemical industry has taken initiatives to enhance security and safeguard its infrastructure. The regulatory system, however, needs to be put in place, in line with the Guidelines on Chemical (Industrial) Disasters, already issued by NDMA.

Prevention of Illegal Trafficking of Hazardous Waste

The illegal trafficking of hazardous waste and its potential usage in CTD is an important aspect that requires immediate attention. Adequate attention is required to be given to issues pertaining to hazardous waste generation, storage, and disposal from origin to destination. This category includes a wide variety of chemicals, with hazardous by-products of unknown nature, which are produced during the degradation process, and may serve as an important target or source of chemical terrorism activities. The mechanism for prevention of illegal trafficking of hazardous waste includes the following:

i) A systematic approach will be adapted in chemical terrorism risk mitigation to evolve a fail-safe approach against terrorists seeking to acquire and make improvised chemical devices using hazardous waste.

ii) Security provisions employing public and private partnership will be put in place to optimise collective and individual risk-reduction efforts.

iii) These provisions will be extended to all modes of transportation, i.e., air, water, and land.

iv) Illegal dumping sites will be identified and removed to prevent terrorists access to hazardous waste.

v) National, state and district level planning needs to ensure the implementation of the following recommendations:

   a) A monitoring system will be developed to keep surveillance on industries involved in transfer of chemicals and hazardous waste including cyanide, toluene, sulphur waste, and used oil, etc.

   b) Identifying and listing industries using chemicals like ammonia (anhydrous), chlorine, epi-chlorohydrin, hydrogen chloride (hydrochloric acid), hydrogen fluoride (hydrofluoric acid), sulphur dioxide (anhydrous), sulphur trioxide, tri-nitro toluene, potassium chlorate, ammonium nitrate and aluminium powder, mercury fulminate and peroxide which could be used in conjunction with Improvised Explosive Devices (IEDs), etc.

   c) Drawing up an inventory of all hazardous waste and materials from waste generators and Treatment, Storage, and Disposal Facilities (TSDF) operators will be carried out and included in the secure web-based system for online tracking of its movement and disposal by Central and State Pollution Control Boards, Indian Port and Customs Authority, Directorate General of Foreign Trade, manufacturers, and transporters. All data from the recycler facilities will be maintained and tracking of waste should be an ongoing exercise.

   d) The inventory data will be linked with Value Added Tax (VAT) data maintained by all generators, transporters, and TSDF operators.

   e) Establishment or adoption of a classification system for hazardous waste. This would help in standardising the definitions regarding name, nature, storage, handling, and disposal of hazardous waste.

   f) Strict implementation of import and export of hazardous waste and materials as per existing rules.

g) CPCB will develop mechanisms for identification of states and districts which are more prone to hazardous waste exports, imports, production, and recycling, as also the modes of transportation.

h) Establish citizen watch programmes with the help of local communities to monitor and report any illegal or suspicious transfer or dumping of hazardous waste. SPCBs, based upon the directions issued by CPCB, can then keep a watch on the activities of recyclers in the 'Red List' to prevent illegal sales or dumping.

i) The database should necessarily include the quantity and quality of hazardous waste generators, and lists of those adopting environmentally sound technologies for waste reduction and recycling and those which are neglecting this vital aspect.

j) Invigorate 'Right-to-Information' and enlighten the community in order to promote public awareness and information programmes on hazardous waste.

k) CPCB, in coordination with SPCBs will develop a resource inventory including network of professionals working in the area of hazardous waste.

l) Reinforce national capacities to detect and halt any illegal attempt to introduce hazardous waste into the country, state or district.

m) Promote regional agreements and strengthen international cooperation in the management of trans-boundary movement of hazardous waste based upon the Basel Convention.

n) Spread awareness to prevent the illegal trafficking of crucial electrical components like timer machines, switches, detonators, remote and time-delay switches, and electrical, mechanical, and impact detonators, which may serve as important components for IEDs by terrorists.

o) Upgradation of chemical laboratories and PICs for analysis of hazardous waste samples collected by the customs department.

Planning for Mitigation of Indirect Risks Associated with CTD

CTD pose a number of indirect risks thereby enhancing the overall vulnerability status. It also needs to be dealt in state and district DM plans to develop effective mitigation measures. Indirect risks can be classified as those risks that affect a location or an enterprise whose infrastructure may be exploited during the planning or execution of a chemical terrorist attack. The important measures to mitigate these indirect risks are as follows:

i) Transporters who unwittingly provide chemical transport services may face liability for transporting chemicals to 'actors' whose background they should have checked more thoroughly. Thus, necessary provisions should be laid down for verifying the true identity of the buyers.
ii) Financial intermediaries and banks that provide funds to front companies moving or transporting HAZCHEM, dual-use chemicals, and chemical weapons to terrorist organisations can suffer substantial loss of reputation and face liability for the same. It is imperative to develop SOPs that can maintain a strict vigilance on these issues, and develop newer models to counter these indirect risks by private sector risk managers and security professionals. The contours of enterprise liability related to the facilitation of acts of terrorism need to be defined in the plans.
iii) A mechanism will be developed to integrate the internet service providers in the intelligence and surveillance systems since they can help detect plans in cyberspace that involve nefarious designs to sabotage chemical facilities and pass such information on to law enforcement agencies for appropriate action.

Prevention of Disaster and Terrorist Activities for Petroleum, Petroleum Products, Pipelines, Storages and Process Plants

A pipeline integrity assessment system will be brought out by PNGRB which will help in the prevention of disasters. Other measures like regular patrolling, Supervisory Control and Data Acquisition (SCADA), periodic inspection, etc., will be carried out for the prevention of disasters. Similar provisions will be incorporated in the respective regulations if needed.

Preparedness

Preparedness for CTD involves planning, infrastructure, and knowledge management for both capability and capacity development, and commensurate human resources to cope with chemical emergencies. Preparedness includes a range of time-sensitive special emergency tasks carried out by all emergency response units, responder organisations and their networks, health care providers, network of laboratories, voluntary organisations in the private sector, international organisations and other stakeholders based upon the need and threat assessment of the area. It requires increased chemical terrorism awareness among all stakeholders about chemical agents, and likely injuries they can inflict. EWS based on risk and vulnerability assessment will be developed. Protection, detection, decontamination, quick evacuation, and prompt emergency response are the crucial components of medical preparedness and emergency medical response at the incident site, during evacuation of casualties, and treatment at hospitals. SOPs will be evolved containing definite standards of individual and collective protection, detection, decontamination facilities, and essential medical countermeasures as a part of preparedness plans. The various areas are discussed in detail in the following paragraphs.

Preparedness for Emergency Response at the Incident Site

Rapid and efficient response to a chemical terrorist incident is essential to save lives and prevent further casualties. The initial stages of response in such attacks are also equally dangerous to the first responders themselves.

Responders rushing to the scene of the chemical attack who are not well-informed, well-versed, and prepared (protected) or properly equipped will most likely become part of the problem and not the solution. The impulse to hurriedly rush into an event may be fatal for these responders. The emergency response at the incident site requires coordination between numerous agencies. It begins with the initiation of the following activities:

i) Define and create infrastructure and SOPs for emergency responders including, detection of chemical agents, search and rescue teams, fire and emergency services, MFR network, PPE, secure communication network, and early medical response.

ii) Response teams will work at the incident site and at residential locations from where the communities are to be evacuated.

iii) MFRs/QRMTs will provide BLS and resuscitation at the incident site and also support the rescue workers. They will be trained for triage, field decontamination, emergency administration of antidotes, and psycho-social first aid.

iv) Other teams of the different emergency functionaries will play an active role based upon their area of specialisation.

v) All the rescue teams will work with full integration and coordination under the overall supervision of the incident commander.

Some of the specific key issues of preparedness for emergency response to CTD at the incident site are described below.

Protection

The availability of appropriate PPE is important for protecting and inculcating confidence amongst the rescue workers dealing with management of CTD. The major recommendations are as follows:

i) Development of capabilities for individual respiratory and body protection to prevent exposure to chemical agents. The essential characteristics of air tightness and non-permeability to gases will be maintained. Respiratory protection will be achieved by using either Self-Contained Breathing Apparatus (SCBA) or face masks fitted with NBC filters. The NBC respirator, NBC canister, protective clothing, impermeable protective clothing, gloves, over-boots etc.

ii) Based on risk assessment, collective protection (physical protection for a group of individuals with the aim of reducing the discomfort of wearing gas masks and clothing) may need to be established. Temporary inflatable shelters maintained at positive pressure with separate entry and exit doors located at perpendicular positions will be catered for. The shelters will be fitted with NBC filters for detoxification of contaminated air.

iii) Depending upon the risk and threat perception, adequate number of protective gear will be stocked at the district level and other important locations for all first responders including NDRF, SDRF, police, fire and emergency services, MFRs, and other personnel connected with management of CTD. The protocols for quick wearing, leak testing, and removal of protective gear will also be laid down. They will be checked from time to time for proper functionality.

It is necessary for the responders to understand the limitations of the different protective gear and their probable usage under different circumstances to protect themselves prior to saving the lives of others.

Detection

Early detection of the type and quantity of chemical agent(s) used in CTD is vital for proper management of the victims. The knowledge of the exact nature of the chemical used in the event will facilitate proper antidote administration and effective treatment for early recovery. The characterisation of chemical compounds depends upon the reliability and accuracy of the detection technologies used. The major points for addressal are mentioned below.

i) EWS will have an inbuilt mechanism to monitor different regions and if the concentration of any chemical agent goes above the threshold level which may be harmful, a response will be activated. Any undue alarm or suspicion will be obviated by due verification.

ii) A mechanism will be established for monitoring the progress of the chemical event, to provide real-time data of the changing dynamics of the chemical agent. Indigenous industries will be encouraged to develop such instruments in collaboration with research institutes which are able to operate under extreme climatic differences as observed at various vulnerable locations in the country.

iii) SOPs regarding the usage of different detection techniques will be laid down as per their priority.

iv) Fire and emergency services will be equipped with HAZMAT vans for speedy detection of the nature of chemicals used in an attack. District authorities will have at least one HAZMAT response van depending upon the vulnerability status of the area. The firefighting teams will also be properly trained to use the various detectors. Rapid field detection kits for detection and characterisation of chemical agents and advanced online monitoring technologies will be developed.

v) Surveillance for detection of illness and injuries resulting from chemical terrorism shall be integrated into the existing surveillance programme, while developing new mechanisms for detecting, evaluating, and reporting suspicious events that might represent terrorist acts. As part of this effort, central, state, and district health authorities will form partnerships with front line medical personnel in hospital emergency departments, hospital care facilities, PICs, laboratory networks, and other institutions to enhance detection and reporting of unexplained injuries and illnesses as part of the routine surveillance mechanism for chemical terrorism.

vi) Detection teams shall not enter the defined 'risk areas' contaminated with toxic chemicals without special protective equipment.

vii) Detection technology shall be upgraded from time to time to ensure accuracy of the identification of chemical agents by minimising false positive signals.

viii) A multi-level chemical laboratory network for chemical terrorism will be created for an early characterisation of chemicals so as to identify short-term and long-term effects.

ix) Detection and surveillance will include the provision of mapping vulnerable areas so that evacuation routes can be defined.

x) A mobile chemical laboratory fitted with a chemical analyser will be made available for highly vulnerable areas.

Detection and characterisation of the chemical agent is the first step in initiating the response activity. Therefore, it is imperative to develop adequate detection technologies with skilled and trained staff in every district.

Decontamination

Decontamination is a process that removes or neutralises chemical agents physically and also prevents their absorption through the skin. An ideal decontamination agent will rapidly and completely remove all chemical toxic agents either by cleaning, disinfection, or sterilisation.

The complete decontamination process at the incident site includes:

i) Mobile decontamination facilities established at the incident site but outside the risk area. The models of temporary mobile decontamination facilities will be developed, tested, and made available at the district level.

ii) The first step is the physical removal by brushing off, washing, or adsorption of the chemicals by using adsorbent materials like Fuller's Earth, Dutch Powder, and other substances like ion exchange and resin-based decontamination materials.

iii) The next step is the use of chemical methods like soap and water including detergents, etc., based upon the principles of oxidation, and acid or base hydrolysis. Mustard (HD) and the persistent nerve agent VX contain sulphur molecules that are readily subject to oxidation reactions. VX and the other nerve agents contain phosphorus groups that can be hydrolysed. Therefore, most chemical decontaminants are designed to oxidise HD and VX and to hydrolyse nerve agents. All the necessary equipment, decontamination agents, and methodologies will be available to the emergency responders. Necessary decontamination procedures including wound and skin decontamination and gas phase decontamination will be laid down. SOPs will include detailed decontamination processes for specific CW agents.

iv) It is imperative to use different chemical agents that are able to destroy these toxic chemicals specifically in case of CW agents. For example, hypochlorite removes VX in 15 minutes at pH 10 while it may take a longer time to remove mustard agents. On the other hand, vesicants may penetrate at a very fast rate prior to the reactive detoxification process. Thus, necessary SOPs will be laid down for usage of different decontamination processes and training will also be imparted through mock-drills.

v) New updated technologies for decontamination will be adopted after testing and validating the procedures.

vi) Necessary mechanisms will be developed under the guidance of a specific level of medical authority, to prevent the spread of contaminated water due to the runoff reaction.

vii) Self-decontamination procedures to be followed by the community exposed to the chemicals include:

   a) Self-removal of clothing will be done, and if necessary by cutting or tearing off the clothes to avoid spreading the chemical agent on the body. While rendering help to others, it is recommended that contaminated areas should not be touched to prevent any possible secondary or cross-contamination. In this case also, the clothes should be cut or torn off if necessary.

   b) Wash the affected portions with lots of water and soap. Remove contact lenses if any, and irrigate the eyes to contain or prevent any likely irritation.

   c) Dispose soiled and contaminated clothes in a plastic bag while wearing rubber gloves if possible to avoid contact with the same. Seal the above bag and put it in another bag for handing over to the authorities for proper disposal. Fresh uncontaminated clothes from a closed suitcase or cupboard should be worn.

Preparedness for emergency medical response

Medical preparedness will be based upon upgradation of the regular practice of medicine to enable it for emergency medical response in the event of a CTD. Emergency medical response commences with prompt establishment of medical posts as a part of ICS within the golden hour. Treatment begins by providing BLS at the incident site itself, which reduces morbidity and mortality. Mechanism for enhancing the coping capacity of health care providers for an effective medical response is necessary. The preparedness for emergency medical response will focus on:

i) SOPs for establishing an ICP post including the provision of emergency medical care and dedicated mobile teams trained to work in the chemical scenario.

ii) Specific provisions will be ensured for providing emergency medical care during evacuation of the victims from the contaminated environment. Mechanism for coordination between the various health care institutions and other agencies like the police, fire and emergency services, NGOs and other humanitarian agencies shall be established.

iii) Problem solving procedures based on the past experience of similar disasters and lessons learnt during mock-exercises will be incorporated.

iv) Injuries, illness, and public health problems including psycho-social trauma will be addressed by integration of medicine and public health in the overall comprehensive medical management plans.

v) Indicators suitable for assessing the progression of disasters will be developed. Continuous real time and accurate information will be provided to public health authorities and the public through a dedicated PA system or locally available means.

vi) Protection and detection equipment will be available with various mobile teams and various rescue services which are essentially required for the initial assessment and management of CTD.

vii) Risk and resource inventory of protection and detection equipment, decontamination and decorporation agents, and chemical casualty treatment kits will be prepared at all levels of the medical management planning process.

viii) Immediate clean-up actions using various neutralisation techniques will be initiated to reduce the concentration of chemical agents at the incident site in the case of a CTD involving TICs/TIMs and hazardous waste as potential targets.

ix) QRMTs/MFRs will have first aid medical kits containing important antidotes like pyridostigmine tablets, injection obidoxime, atropine sulphate, dimercaprol, sodium thiosulphate, and other essential components including syringes, needles, and Gudel airways etc., which are specific for CW agents.

x) Reserves of medical bricks containing CBRN related emergency medicines, antidotes, and BLS equipment will be developed and maintained by periodic rotation of stocks. Necessary provisions will be developed for pooling in extra requirements and backup medical services.

xi) Medicos and paramedics will be trained in the medical management of the acute health risks associated with CW agents, usage of different antidotes, providing BLS and psycho-social first aid to reduce panic reaction and acute stress, etc.

xii) Training of specialised MFRs for CTD on the aspects of first aid and resuscitation measures, triage, decontamination and decorporation agents, and treatment modalities will be provided.

xiii) Chemical casualty treatment profiles will be standardised.

xiv) SOPs to collect biological samples of casualties and various environmental samples will be laid down.

References

Croddy, Eric. (2001). *Chemical and Biological Warfare*, Copernicus.

Chaliand, Gerard. (2007). *The History of Terrorism: From Antiquity to al Qaeda.* Berkeley: University of California Press.

Hoffman, Bruce. *(1988). Inside Terrorism.* New York: Columbia University Press.

Smart, Jeffery K., M.A. (1997). *History of Biological and Chemical Warfare.* Retrieved Nov. 24, 2004.

Sublette, Carey. (2007). "Types of nuclear weapons". *FAQ*. The Nuclear Weapon Archive. Retrieved 2010-02-13.

6

Warfare: Threat Assessment and Management

Man-made catastrophes are a little easier to explain because we can identify the cause. Wars are the classic example of man-made disasters. If we want to compare what we have done to ourselves with what nature has done to us in recent centuries, we are going to find that we have been much more destructive to ourselves. In the 20th century the conservative estimate is that, with the two world wars, the ethnic and political purges of Stalin, Hitler and Pol Pot, the Chinese revolution and other conflicts in nations too numerous to mention, people killed 130 million of their fellow human beings.

Consider, for instance, more recent civil strife that usually doesn't get much of the world's attention. One million were killed in the Congo, 1 million in Rwanda and 2 million in southern Sudan (not including the recent conflict in the Darfur region). Any one of these far outstrips the Indian Ocean tsunami that took some 280,000 lives.

Definition of War

War is an organized, armed, and, often, a prolonged conflict that is carried on between states, nations, or other parties typified by extreme aggression, social disruption, and usually high mortality. War should be understood as an actual, intentional and widespread armed conflict between political communities, and therefore is defined as a form of political violence. The set of techniques used by a group to carry out war is known as warfare. An absence of war (and other violence) is usually called peace.

In 2003, Nobel Laureate Richard E. Smalley identified war as the sixth (of ten) biggest problem facing the society of mankind for the next fifty years. In the 1832 treatise On War, Prussian military general and theoretician Carl von Clausewitz defined war as follows: "War is thus an act of force to compel our enemy to do our will."

While some scholars see warfare as an inescapable and integral aspect of human culture, others argue that it is only inevitable under certain socio-cultural or ecological circumstances. Some scholars argue that the practice of war is not linked to any single type of political organization or society. Rather, as discussed by John Keegan in his History of Warfare, war is a universal phenomenon whose form and scope is defined by the society that wages it. Another argument suggests that since there are human societies in which warfare does not exist, humans may not be naturally disposed for warfare, which emerges under particular circumstances. The ever changing technologies and potentials of war extend along a historical continuum. At the one end lies the endemic warfare of the Paleolithic with its stones and clubs, and the naturally limited loss of life associated with the use of such weapons. Found at the other end of this continuum is nuclear warfare, along with the recently developed possible outcome of its use, namely the potential risk of the complete extinction of the human species.

History of Warfare

Before the dawn of civilization, war likely consisted of small-scale raiding. One half of the people found in a Nubian cemetery dating to as early as 12,000 years ago had died of violence. Since the rise of the state some 5,000 years ago, military activity has occurred over much of the globe. The advent of gunpowder and the acceleration of technological advances led to modern warfare. According to Conway W. Henderson, "One source claims 14,500 wars have taken place between 3500 BC and the late 20th century, costing 3.5 billion lives, leaving only 300 years of peace."

In War Before Civilization, Lawrence H. Keeley, a professor at the University of Illinois, says that approximately 90–95% of known societies throughout history engaged in at least occasional warfare, and many fought constantly.

Keeley explained several styles of primitive combat such as, small raids, large raids, and massacres. All of these forms of warfare were perpetrated by primitive societies. The use of the massacre by pre-state societies can be exhibited by the Dogrib tribes of the subarctic in North America. The Dogrib tribe eventually destroyed the Yellowknife tribe by killing 4 men, 13 women, and 17 children which accounted for 20 percent of the population. This was a devastating blow from which the Yellowknife tribe never recovered. Keeley further explains how small raids are not organized due to the lack of leadership and any formal training. This causes raids to be short and quick with relatively low numerical casualties but may significantly damage a percentage of a population. The deficit of resources also can account for a lack of fortifications and defensive structures in primitive prestate societies. The protection provided by a defensive could not justify the valuable resources used and labor implemented to build it.

William Rubinstein wrote that "Pre-literate societies, even those organised in a relatively advanced way, were renowned for their studied cruelty ... 'archaeology yields evidence of prehistoric massacres more severe than any recounted in ethnography [ie, after the coming of the Europeans]'. At Crow Creek, South Dakota, as noted, archaeologists found a mass grave of 'more than 500 men, women, and children who had been slaughtered, scalped, and mutilated during an attack on their village a century and a half before Columbus's arrival".

In Western Europe, since the late 18th century, more than 150 conflicts and about 600 battles have taken place

The Human Security Report 2005 documented a significant decline in the number and severity of armed conflicts since the end of the Cold War in the early 1990s. However, the evidence examined in the 2008 edition of the Center for International Development and Conflict Management's "Peace and Conflict" study indicated that the overall decline in conflicts had stalled.

Recent rapid increases in the technologies of war, and therefore in its destructiveness, have caused widespread public concern, and have in all probability forestalled, and may hopefully altogether prevent the outbreak of a nuclear World War III. At the end of each of the last two World Wars, concerted and popular efforts were made to come to a greater understanding of the underlying dynamics of war and to thereby hopefully reduce or even eliminate it all together. These efforts materialized in the forms of the League of Nations, and its successor, the United Nations.

Shortly after World War II, as a token of support for this concept, most nations joined the United Nations. During this same post-war period, with the aim of further delegitimizing war as an acceptable and logical extension of foreign policy, most national governments also renamed their Ministries or Departments of War as their Ministries or Departments of Defense, for example, the former US Department of War was renamed as the US Department of Defense.

In 1947, in view of the rapidly increasingly destructive consequences of modern warfare, and with a particular concern for the consequences and costs of the newly developed atom bomb, Albert Einstein famously stated, "I know not with what weapons World War III will be fought, but World War IV will be fought with sticks and stones." Fortunately, the anticipated costs of a possible third world war are currently no longer deemed as acceptable by most, thus little motivation currently seems to exist on an international level for such a war.

Still since the close of World War II, limited non-nuclear conflicts continue, and surprisingly enough, some outspoken celebrities and politicians have even advocated for the proclamation of another world war. Mao Zedong urged the socialist camp not to fear nuclear war with the United States since, even if "half of mankind died, the other half would remain while imperialism would be razed to the ground and the whole world would become socialist."

Types of Warfare

War, to become known as one, must entail some degree of confrontation using weapons and other military technology and equipment by armed forces employing military tactics and operational art within the broad military strategy subject to military logistics. War Studies by military theorists throughout military history have sought to identify the philosophy of war, and to reduce it to a military science.

In general, modern military science considers several factors before a National defence policy is created to allow a war to commence: the environment in the area(s) of combat operations, the posture national forces will adopt on the commencement of a war, and the type of warfare troops will be engaged in.

Conventional warfare is an attempt to reduce an opponent's military capability through open battle. It is a declared war between existing states in which nuclear, biological, or chemical weapons are not used or only see limited deployment in support of conventional military goals and maneuvers.

The opposite of conventional warfare, unconventional warfare, is an attempt to achieve military victory through acquiescence, capitulation, or clandestine support for one side of an existing conflict.

Nuclear warfare is warfare in which nuclear weapons are the primary, or a major, method of coercing the capitulation of the other side, as opposed to a supporting tactical or strategic role in a conventional conflict.

Civil war is a war where the forces in conflict belong to the same nation or political entity and are vying for control of or independence from that nation or political entity.

Asymmetric warfare is a conflict between two populations of drastically different levels of military capability or size. Asymmetric conflicts often result in guerrilla tactics being used to overcome the sometimes vast gaps in technology and force size.

Intentional air pollution in combat is one of a collection of techniques collectively called chemical warfare. Poison gas as a chemical weapon was principally used during World War I, and resulted in an estimated 91,198 deaths and 1,205,655 injuries. Various treaties have sought to ban its further use. Non-lethal chemical weapons, such as tear gas and pepper spray, are widely used, sometimes with deadly effect.

Warfare Environment

The environment in which a war is fought has a significant impact on the type of combat which takes place, and can include within its area different types of terrain. This, in turn, means that soldiers have to be trained to fight in a specific types of environments and terrains that generally reflects troops' mobility and limitations.

The behaviour of troops in warfare varies considerably, both individually and as units or armies. In some circumstances, troops may engage in genocide, war rape and ethnic cleansing. Commonly, however, the conduct of troops may be limited to posturing and sham attacks, leading to highly rule-bound and often largely symbolic combat in which casualties are much reduced from that which would be expected if soldiers were genuinely violent towards the enemy. Situations of deliberate dampening of hostilities occurred in World War I by some accounts, e.g., a volley of gunfire being exchanged after a misplaced mortar hit the British line, after which a German soldier shouted an apology to British forces, effectively stopping a hostile exchange of gunfire. Other examples of non-aggression, also from World War I, are detailed in "Good-Bye to All That." These include spontaneous ceasefires to rebuild defences and retrieve casualties, alongside behaviour such as refusing to shoot at enemy during ablutions and the taking of great risks (described as 1 in 20) to retrieve enemy wounded from the battlefield. The most notable spontaneous ceasefire of World War I was the Christmas truce.

The psychological separation between combatants, and the destructive power of modern weaponry, may act to override this effect and facilitate participation by combatants in the mass slaughter of combatants or civilians, such as in the bombing of Dresden in World War II. The unusual circumstances of warfare can incite apparently normal individuals to commit atrocities.

Effects of War

Nations customarily measure the 'costs of war' in dollars, lost production, or the number of soldiers killed or wounded. Rarely do military establishments attempt to measure the costs of war in terms of individual human suffering. Psychiatric breakdown remains one of the most costly items of war when expressed in human terms.

On soldiers

Soldiers subject to combat in war often suffer psychological and physical casualties, including depression, Post Traumatic Stress Disorder, disease, injury, and death.

During World War II, research conducted by US Army Brigadier General S.L.A. Marshall found that, on average, only 15% to 20% of American riflemen in WWII combat fired at the enemy. In Civil War Collector's Encyclopedia, F.A. Lord notes that of the 27,574 discarded muskets found on the Gettysburg battlefield, nearly 90% were loaded, with 12,000 loaded more than once and 6,000 loaded 3 to 10 times. These studies suggest that most soldiers resist firing their weapons in combat, that – as some theorists argue – human beings have an inherent resistance to killing their fellow human beings. Swank and Marchand's WWII study found that after sixty days of continuous combat, 98% of all surviving soldiers will become psychiatric casualties. Psychiatric casualties manifest themselves in fatigue cases, confusional states, conversion hysteria, anxiety, obsessional and compulsive states, and character disorders.

Additionally, it has been estimated that anywhere from 18% to 54% of Vietnam war veterans suffered from Post Traumatic Stress Disorder.

Based on 1860 census figures, 8% of all white American males aged 13 to 43 died in the American Civil War, including about 6% in the North and approximately 18% in the South. The war remains the deadliest conflict in American history, resulting in the deaths of 620,000 soldiers. United States military casualties of war since 1775 have totaled over two million. Of the 60 million European soldiers who were mobilized in World War I, 8 million were killed, 7 million were permanently disabled, and 15 million were seriously injured.

During Napoleon's retreat from Moscow, more French soldiers died of typhus than were killed by the Russians. Felix Markham thinks that 450,000 crossed the Neman on 25 June 1812, of whom less than 40,000 recrossed in anything like a recognizable military formation. More soldiers were killed from 1500–1914 by typhus than from all military action during that time combined. In addition, if it were not for the modern medical advances there would be thousands of more dead from disease and infection. For instance, during the Seven Years' War, the Royal Navy reported that it conscripted 184,899 sailors, of whom 133,708 died of disease or were 'missing'.

On Civilians

Many wars have been accompanied by significant depopulations, along with destruction of infrastructure and resources (which may lead to famine, disease, and death in the civilian population). Civilians in war zones may also be subject to war atrocities such as genocide, while survivors may suffer the psychological aftereffects of witnessing the destruction of war. During the Thirty Years' War in Europe, for example, the population of the German states was reduced by about 30%. The Swedish armies alone may have destroyed up to 2,000 castles, 18,000 villages and 1,500 towns in Germany, one-third of all German towns.

Estimates for the total casualties of World War II vary, but most suggest that some 60 million people died in the war, comprising around 20 million soldiers and 40 million civilians. The Soviet Union lost around 27 million people during the war, about half of all World War II casualties. Since a high proportion of those killed were young men, the postwar Soviet population was 45 to 50 million fewer than post–1939 projections would have led one to expect. The largest number of civilian deaths in a single city was 1.2 million citizens dead during the 872-day Siege of Leningrad.

On the Economy

Once a war has ended, losing nations are sometimes required to pay war reparations to the victorious nations. In certain cases, land is ceded to the victorious nations. For example, the territory of Alsace-Lorraine has been traded between France and Germany on three different occasions.

Typically speaking, war becomes very intertwined with the economy and many wars are partially or entirely based on economic reasons such as the American Civil War. In some cases war has stimulated a country's economy (World War II is often credited with bringing America out of the Great Depression) but in many cases, such as the wars of Louis XIV, the Franco-Prussian War, and World War I, warfare serves only to damage the economy of the countries involved. For example, Russia's involvement in World War I took such a toll on the Russian economy that it almost collapsed and greatly contributed to the start of the Russian Revolution of 1917.

Factors Ending a War

The political and economic circumstances, in the peace that follows war, usually depend on the facts on the ground. Where evenly matched adversaries decide that the conflict has resulted in a stalemate, they may cease hostilities to avoid further loss of life and property. They may decide to restore the antebellum territorial boundaries, redraw boundaries at the line of military control, or negotiate to keep or exchange captured territory. Negotiations between parties involved at the end of a war often result in a treaty, such as the Treaty of Versailles of 1919, which ended the First World War.

A warring party that surrenders or capitulates may have little negotiating power, with the victorious side either imposing a settlement or dictating most of the terms of any treaty. A common result is that conquered territory is brought under the dominion of the stronger military power. An unconditional surrender is made in the face of overwhelming military force as an attempt to prevent further harm to life and property. For example, the Empire of Japan gave an unconditional surrender to the Allies of World War

II after the atomic bombings of Hiroshima and Nagasaki, the preceding massive strategic bombardment of Japan and declaration of war and the immediate invasion of Manchuria by the Soviet Union. A settlement or surrender may also be obtained through deception or bluffing.

Many other wars, however, have ended in complete destruction of the opposing territory, such as the Battle of Carthage of the Third Punic War between the Phoenician city of Carthage and Ancient Rome in 149 BC. In 146 BC the Romans burned the city, enslaved its citizens, and razed the buildings.

Some wars or aggressive actions end when the military objective of the victorious side has been achieved. Others do not, especially in cases where the state structures do not exist, or have collapsed prior to the victory of the conqueror. In such cases, disorganised guerilla warfare may continue for a considerable period. In cases of complete surrender conquered territories may be brought under the permanent dominion of the victorious side. A raid for the purposes of looting may be completed with the successful capture of goods. In other cases an aggressor may decide to end hostilities to avoid continued losses and cease hostilities without obtaining the original objective, such as happened in the Iran–Iraq War.

Somc hostilities, such as insurgency or civil war, may persist for long periods of time with only a low level of military activity. In some cases there is no negotiation of any official treaty, but fighting may trail off and eventually stop after the political demands of the belligerent groups have been reconciled, a political settlement has been negotiated, the combatants are gradually killed or decide the conflict is futile, or the belligerents cease active military engagement but still threaten each other. An example is the Chinese Civil War which essentially ceased by 1950 but the People's Republic of China fought diplomatically to isolate Taiwan, but it still threatens Republic of China (commonly known as Taiwan) with an invasion. For this reason, some historians consider the war not ended but continuing.

War Ethics

The seeming contradiction between warfare and morality has led to serious moral questions, which have been the subject of debate for thousands of years. The debate, generally speaking, has two main viewpoints: Pacifists, who believe that war is inherently immoral and therefore is never justified regardless of circumstances, and those who believe that war is sometimes necessary and can be moral.

There are two different aspects to ethics in war, according to the most prominent and influential thought on justice and war: The Just War Theory. First is Jus ad bellum (literally translated as "right to war"), which dictates which unfriendly acts and circumstances justify a proper authority in declaring war on another nation. There are six main criteria for the declaration of a just war: first, any just war must be declared by a lawful authority; second, it must be a just and righteous cause, with sufficient gravity to merit large-scale violence; third, the just belligerent must have rightful intentions – namely, that they seek to advance good and curtail evil; fourth, a just belligerent must have a reasonable chance of success; fifth, the war must be a last resort; and sixth, the ends being sought must be proportional to means being used.

Once a just war has been declared, the second standard, or aspect, is put into effect. Jus in bello, which literally translates to "right in war", are the ethical rules of conduct when conducting war. The two main principles in jus in bello are proportionality and discrimination. Proportionality regards how much force is necessary and morally appropriate to the ends being sought and the injustice suffered. The principle of Discrimination determines who are the legitimate targets in a war, and specifically makes a separation between combatants, who it is permissible to kill, and non-combatants, who it is not. Failure to follow these rules can result in the loss of legitimacy for the just war belligerent, and so thereby forfeit the moral right and justice of their cause.

The Just War standard is as old as Western Civilization itself, and still has significant impact on thinking about the morality of wars and violence today. Just War Theory was foundational in the creation of the United Nations and in International Law's regulations on legitimate war.

These two positions generally cover the broad philosophical and ethical bents mainstream society. However, there are several theories on and about War which are in the minority in culture, but which, because of the influence they have had in recent history, demand mention here. These strains of thought on human society and war can be broken up into two main camps: Marxist and Fascist, both of which view war as purely practical.

Marxism, and other such historicist ideals, hold that history advances through a set of dialectics (as stated by Heinrich Moritz Chalybäus: thesis, antithesis, synthesis). Marx, and his followers, in particular held that history advances through violence. Marxism-Leninism, in fact, held the belief that outright incitement to violence and war was necessary to topple Capitalism and free the proletariat. In these theories, the question of ethics has no place, as the value of the war is entirely dependent on whether it advances the revolution or synthesis.

Fascism, and the ideals it encompasses, such as Pragmatism, Racism, and Social Darwinism, hold that violence is good. Pragmatism holds that war and violence can be good if it serves the ends of the people, without regard for universal morality. Racism holds that violence is good so that a master race can be established, or to purge an inferior race from the earth, or both. Social Darwinism thinks that violence is sometimes necessary to weed the unfit from society so that civilization can flourish. These are broad archetypes for the general position that the ends justify the means.

Nuclear Warfare

Nuclear warfare (sometimes atomic warfare or thermonuclear warfare), is a military conflict or political strategy in which nuclear weaponry is used to inflict damage on an opponent. Compared to conventional warfare, nuclear warfare can be vastly more destructive in range and extent of damage, and in a much shorter time scale. A major nuclear exchange could have severe long-term effects, primarily from radiation release, but also from the production of high levels of atmospheric pollution leading to a "nuclear winter" that could last for decades, centuries, or even millennia after the initial attack. A large nuclear war is considered to bear existential risk for civilization on Earth.

Only two nuclear weapons have been used in the course of warfare, both by the United States near the end of World War II. On August 6, 1945, a uranium gun-type device (code name "Little Boy") was detonated over the Japanese city of Hiroshima. Three days later, on August 9, a plutonium implosion-type device (code name "Fat Man") was detonated over Nagasaki, Japan. These two bombings resulted in the deaths of approximately 200,000 Japanese people (mostly civilians) from acute injuries sustained in the detonations.

After World War II, nuclear weapons were also developed by the Soviet Union (1940s), the United Kingdom and France (1950s), and the People's Republic of China (1960s), which contributed to the state of conflict and extreme tension that became known as the Cold War. In the 1970s, India, and in the 1990s, Pakistan, two countries that were openly hostile toward each other, developed nuclear weapons. Israel (1960s) and North Korea (2000s) are also thought to have developed stocks of nuclear weapons, and made the political decision to refrain from openly acknowledging them to the present time. South Africa also manufactured several complete nuclear weapons in the 1980s, but subsequently became the first country to voluntarily destroy their domestically made weapons stocks and abandon further production (1990s).

Nuclear weapons have been detonated on over two thousand occasions for testing purposes and demonstrations.

After the collapse of the Soviet Union in 1991 and the resultant end of the Cold War, the threat of a major nuclear war between the two nuclear superpowers was generally thought to have declined. Since then, concern over nuclear weapons has shifted to the prevention of localized nuclear conflicts resulting from nuclear proliferation, and the threat of nuclear terrorism.

Types of Nuclear Warfare

The possibility of using nuclear weapons in war is usually divided into two subgroups, each with different effects and potentially fought with different types of nuclear armaments.

The first, a limited nuclear war (sometimes attack or exchange), refers to a small-scale use of nuclear weapons by two (or more) belligerents. A "limited nuclear war" could include targeting military facilities - either as an attempt to pre-emptively cripple the enemy's ability to attack as a defensive measure, or as a prelude to an invasion by conventional forces, as an offensive measure. This term could apply to any small-scale use of nuclear weapons that may involve military or civilian targets (or both).

The second, a full-scale nuclear war, could consist of large numbers of nuclear weapons used in an attack aimed at an entire country, including military, economic, and civilian targets. Such an attack would almost certainly destroy the entire economic, social, and military infrastructure of the target nation, and would probably have a devastating effect on Earth's biosphere.

Some Cold War strategists such as Henry Kissinger argue that a limited nuclear war could be possible between two heavily armed superpowers (such as the United States and the Soviet Union). Some predict, however, that a limited war could potentially "escalate" into a full-scale nuclear war. Others have called limited nuclear war "global nuclear holocaust in slow motion" - arguing that once such a war took place, others would be sure to follow over a period of decades, effectively rendering the planet uninhabitable in the same way that a "full-scale nuclear war" between superpowers would, only taking a much longer (and arguably more agonizing) path to the same result.

Even the most optimistic predictions of the effects of a major nuclear exchange foresee the death of many millions of victims within a very short period of time. More pessimistic predictions argue that a full-scale nuclear war could potentially bring about the extinction of the human race, or at least its near extinction, with only a relatively small number of survivors (mainly in remote areas) and a reduced quality of life and life expectancy for centuries afterward. Such a horrific catastrophe would almost certainly cause permanent damage to most complex life on the planet, its ecosystems, and the global climate - particularly if predictions about the production of a nuclear winter are accurate.

A study presented at the annual meeting of the American Geophysical Union in December 2006 asserted that even a small-scale regional nuclear war could produce as many direct fatalities as all of World War II and disrupt the global climate for a decade or more. In a regional nuclear conflict scenario in which two opposing nations in the subtropics each used 50 Hiroshima-sized nuclear weapons (ca. 15 kiloton each) on major population centers, the researchers predicted fatalities ranging from 2.6 million to 16.7 million per country. Also, they estimated that as much as five million tons of soot could be released, producing a cooling of several degrees over large areas of North America and Eurasia (including most of the grain-growing regions). The cooling would last for years and could be "catastrophic", according to the researchers.

Either a limited or full-scale nuclear exchange could occur during an accidental nuclear war, in which the use of nuclear weapons is triggered unintentionally. Postulated triggers for this scenario have included malfunctioning early warning devices and/or targeting computers, deliberate malfeasance by rogue military commanders, consequences of an accidental straying of warplanes into enemy airspace, reactions to unannounced missile tests during tense diplomatic periods, reactions to military exercises, mistranslated or misscommunicated messages, and others. A number of these scenarios actually occurred during the Cold War, though none resulted in the use of nuclear weapons. Many such scenarios have been depicted in popular culture, such as in the 1962 novel Fail-Safe (released as a film in 1964), and the film Dr. Strangelove or: How I Learned to Stop Worrying and Love the Bomb, also released in 1964.

Atomic Bombings of Hiroshima and Nagasaki

During the final stages of World War II in 1945, the United States conducted two atomic bombings against the Japanese cities of Hiroshima and Nagasaki, the first on August 6, 1945, and the second on August 9, 1945. These two events are the only use of nuclear weapons in war to date.

For six months before the atomic bombings, the United States intensely fire-bombed 67 Japanese cities. Together with the United Kingdom and the Republic of China, the United States called for the unconditional surrender of Japan in the Potsdam Declaration issued July 26, 1945. The Japanese government ignored this ultimatum. By executive order of President Harry S. Truman, the U.S. employed the uranium-type nuclear weapon code named "Little Boy" on the city of Hiroshima on Monday, August 6, 1945, followed three days later by the detonation of the plutonium-type weapon code named "Fat Man" over the city of Nagasaki on August 9.

Within the first two to four months after the bombings, acute effects killed 90,000–166,000 people in Hiroshima and 60,000–80,000 in Nagasaki, with roughly half of the deaths in each city occurring in the first 24 hours. The Hiroshima prefectural health department estimates that - of the people who died on the day of the detonation - 60% died from flash or flame burns, 30% from falling or flying debris, and 10% from other causes. During the following months, large numbers died from the chronic effects of burns, radiation sickness, and other injuries, compounded by illnesses. In a U.S. estimate of the total immediate and short-term causes of death, 15–20% died from radiation sickness, 20–30% from flash burns, and 50–60% from other injuries, compounded by illnesses. In both cities, most of the dead were civilians.

Six days after the detonation over Nagasaki, on August 15, 1945, Japan announced its surrender to the Allied Powers, signing the Instrument of Surrender on September 2, 1945, officially ending the Pacific War and, therefore, World War II, as Germany had already signed its Instrument of

Surrender on May 7, 1945, ending the war in Europe. The two atomic bombings led, in part, to post-war Japan's adopting of the Three Non-Nuclear Principles, which forbade the nation from developing nuclear armaments. The role of the bombings in the surrender of Japan, the ethical justification of the US for using them, as well as their strategic importance, is still hotly debated.

Immediately After the Japan Bombings

Immediately after the atomic bombings of Japan, the status of atomic weapons in international and military relations was unclear. Presumably, the United States hoped atomic weapons could offset the Soviet Union's larger conventional ground forces in Eastern Europe, and possibly be used to pressure Soviet leader Joseph Stalin into making concessions. Under Stalin, the Soviet Union pursued its own atomic capabilities through a combination of scientific research and espionage directed against the American program. The Soviets believed that the Americans, with their limited nuclear arsenal, were unlikely to engage in any new world wars, while the Americans were not confident they could prevent a Soviet takeover of Europe, despite their atomic advantage.

Within the United States the authority to produce and develop nuclear weapons was removed from military control and put instead under the civilian control of the United States Atomic Energy Commission. This decision reflected an understanding that nuclear weapons had unique risks and benefits that were separate from other military technology known at the time.

For several years after World War II, the US developed and maintained a strategic force based on the Convair B-36 bomber that would be able to attack any potential enemy from bomber bases in the US. It deployed atomic bombs around the world for potential use in conflicts. Over a period of a few years, many in the US defense community became increasingly convinced of the invincibility of the United States to a nuclear attack. Indeed, it became generally believed that the threat of nuclear war would deter any strike against the United States.

Many proposals were suggested to put all US nuclear weapons under international control (by the newly formed United Nations, for example) as an effort to deter both their usage and an arms race. However, no terms could be arrived at that would be agreed upon by both the US and the USSR.

US and USSR Nuclear Stockpiles

On August 29, 1949 the USSR tested its first nuclear weapon at Semipalatinsk in Kazakhstan. Scientists in the United States from the Manhattan Project had warned that, in time, the Soviet Union would certainly develop nuclear capabilities of its own. Nevertheless, the effect upon military thinking and planning in the US was dramatic, primarily because American military strategists had not anticipated the Soviets would "catch up" so soon. However, at this time, they had not discovered that the Russians had conducted significant nuclear espionage of the project from spies at Los Alamos, the most significant of which was done by the theoretical physicist Klaus Fuchs. The first Soviet bomb was more or less a deliberate copy of the Fat Man plutonium device.

With the monopoly over nuclear technology broken, worldwide nuclear proliferation accelerated. The United Kingdom tested its first independent atomic bomb in 1952, followed by France in 1960 and then the People's Republic of China in 1964. While much smaller than the arsenals of the US and the USSR, Western Europe's nuclear reserves were nevertheless a significant factor in strategic planning during the Cold War. A top-secret White Paper, compiled by the Royal Air Force and produced for the British Government in 1959, estimated that British atomic bombers were capable of destroying key cities and military targets in the Soviet Union, with an estimated 16 million deaths in the USSR (half of whom were estimated to be killed on impact and the rest fatally injured) before bomber aircraft from the US Strategic Air Command reached their targets.

The 1950s

Though the USSR had nuclear weapon capabilities in the beginning of the Cold War, the US still had an advantage in terms of bombers and weapons. In any exchange of hostilities, the US would have been capable of bombing the USSR, while the USSR would have more difficulty carrying out the reverse mission.

The widespread introduction of jet-powered interceptor aircraft upset this imbalance somewhat by reducing the effectiveness of the US bomber fleet. In 1949 Curtis LeMay was placed in command of the Strategic Air Command and instituted a program to update the bomber fleet to one that was all-jet. During the early 1950s the B-47 and B-52 were introduced, providing the ability to bomb the USSR more easily. Before the development of a capable strategic missile force in the Soviet Union, much of the war-fighting doctrine held by western nations revolved around using a large number of smaller nuclear weapons used in a tactical role. It is debatable whether such use could be considered "limited" however, because it was believed that the US would use their own strategic weapons (mainly bombers at the time) should the USSR deploy any kind of nuclear weapon against civilian targets. Douglas MacArthur, an American general, was fired by President Harry Truman, partially because he persistently requested permission to use his own discretion in deciding whether to use atomic weapons on the People's Republic of China in 1951 during the Korean War. Mao Zedong, China's communist leader, gave the impression that he would welcome a nuclear war with the capitalists because it would annihilate their imperialist system.

Several scares about the increasing ability of the USSR's strategic bomber forces surfaced during the 1950s. The defensive response by the US was to deploy a fairly strong "layered defense" consisting of interceptor aircraft and anti-aircraft missiles, like the Nike, and guns, like the Skysweeper, near larger cities. However, this was a small response compared to the construction of a huge fleet of nuclear bombers. The principal nuclear strategy was to massively penetrate the USSR. Because such a large area could not be defended against this overwhelming attack in any credible way, the USSR would lose any exchange.

This logic became ingrained in US nuclear doctrine and persisted for much of the duration of the Cold War. As long as the strategic US nuclear forces could overwhelm their USSR counterparts, a Soviet preemptive strike could be averted. Moreover, the USSR could not afford to build any reasonable counterforce, as the economic output of the United States was far larger than that of the Soviets, and they would be unable to achieve "nuclear parity".

Soviet nuclear doctrine, however, did not match US nuclear doctrine. Soviet planning expected a large-scale nuclear exchange, followed by a "conventional war" which itself would involve heavy use of tactical nuclear weapons. Unfortunately, US doctrine rather assumed that Soviet doctrine was similar, with the mutual in Mutually Assured Destruction necessarily requiring that the other side see things in much the same way, rather than believing - as the Soviets did - that they could fight a large-scale, "combined nuclear and conventional" war.

A revolution in nuclear strategic thought occurred with the introduction of the intercontinental ballistic missile (ICBM), which the USSR first successfully tested in August 1957. In order to deliver a warhead to a target, a missile was much faster and more cost-effective than a bomber, and enjoyed a higher survivability due to the enormous difficulty of interception of the ICBMs (due to their high altitude and extreme speed). The USSR could now afford to achieve nuclear parity with the US in terms of raw numbers, although for a time, they appeared to have chosen not to.

Photos of Soviet missile sites set off a wave of panic in the US military, something the launch of Sputnik would do for the American public a few months later. Politicians, notably then-US Senator John F. Kennedy suggested that a "missile gap" existed between the Soviets and the US. The US military gave missile development programs the highest national priority, and several spy aircraft and reconnaissance satellites were designed and deployed to observe Soviet progress.

Early ICBMs and bombers were relatively inaccurate, which led to the concept of countervalue strikes — attacks directly on the enemy population, which would theoretically lead to a collapse of the enemy's will to fight. During the Cold War the USSR invested in extensive protected civilian infrastructure, such as large "nuclear-proof" bunkers and non-perishable food stores. In the US, by comparison, smaller scale civil defense programs were instituted starting in the 1950s, where schools and other public buildings had basements stocked with non-perishable food supplies, canned water, first aid, and dosimeter and Geiger counter radiation-measuring devices. Many of the locations were given "Fallout Shelter" designation signs. Also, CONELRAD Radio information systems were adopted, whereby the commercial radio sector would broadcast on two AM frequencies in the event of a Civil Defense (CD) emergency. These two frequencies-640 and 1240 marked with small CD triangles on the tuning dial can still be seen on 1950s-vintage radios on online auction sites and museums. Also, the occasional backyard fallout shelter was built by private individuals.

1960s

An extensive, complicated, and worrisome situation developed in 1962, in what is called the Cuban Missile Crisis. The Soviet Union placed medium-range ballistic missiles 90 miles (140 km) from the US - a move considered by many as a direct response to American Jupiter missiles placed in Turkey.

After intense negotiations, the Soviets ended up removing the missiles from Cuba and decided to institute a massive weapons-building program of their own. In exchange, the US dismantled its launch sites in Turkey, although this was done secretly and not publicly revealed for over two decades. Khrushchev did not even reveal this part of the agreement when he came under fire by political opponents for mishandling the crisis.

By the late 1960s, the number of ICBMs and warheads was so high on both sides that it was believed that both the US and the USSR were capable of completely destroying the infrastructure and population of the other country. Thus, a balance of power system known as mutually assured destruction (or MAD) came into being. It was thought that any full-scale exchange between the powers could not produce a victorious side, and thus neither would willingly risk initiating one.

One drawback of the MAD doctrine was the possibility of a nuclear war occurring without either side intentionally striking first. Warning system\Early Warning Systems (EWS) were notoriously error-prone. For example, on 78 occasions in 1979 alone, a "missile display conference" was called to evaluate detections that were "potentially threatening to the North American continent". Some of these were trivial errors and were spotted quickly, but several went to more serious levels. On September 26, 1983, Stanislav Petrov received convincing indications of a US first strike launch against the USSR, but positively identified the warning as a false alarm. Though it is unclear what role Petrov's actions played in preventing a nuclear war during this incident, he has been honored by the United Nations for his actions.

Similar incidents happened many times in the US, due to failed computer chips, misidentifications of large flights of geese, test programs, and bureaucratic failures to notify early warning military personnel of legitimate launches of test or weather missiles. For many years, US strategic bombers were kept airborne on a daily rotating basis "around the clock", until the number and severity of accidents, the 1968 Thule Air Base B-52 crash in particular, persuaded policymakers it was not worthwhile.

1970s

By the late 1970s, citizens in the US and USSR (and indeed the entire world) had been living with the concept of MAD for about a decade, and it became deeply ingrained into the popular culture. Such an exchange would have killed many millions of individuals directly, and possibly induced a nuclear winter which could have led to the death of a large portion of humanity and - potentially - the collapse of global civilization.

On May 18, 1974, India conducted its first nuclear test in the Pokhran test range. The name of the operation was Smiling Buddha, and India termed the test as a "peaceful nuclear explosion".

According to the 1980 United Nations report General and Complete Disarmament: Comprehensive Study on Nuclear Weapons: Report of the Secretary-General, it was estimated that there were a total of about 40,000 nuclear warheads in existence at that time, with a potential combined explosive yield of approximately 13,000 megatons. By comparison, when the volcano Mount Tambora erupted in 1815 - turning 1816 into the Year Without A Summer due to the levels of ash expelled) - it exploded with a force of roughly 1,000 megatons. Many people believed that a full-scale nuclear war would result in the extinction of the human species, though not all analysts agreed on the assumptions required for these models.

The idea that any nuclear conflict would eventually escalate was a challenge for military strategists. This challenge was particularly severe for the United States and its NATO allies because it was believed (until the 1970s) that a Soviet tank invasion of Western Europe would quickly overwhelm NATO conventional forces, leading to the necessity of the West escalating to the use of tactical nuclear weapons.

This strategy had one major (and possibly critical) flaw, which was soon realised by military analysts but highly underplayed by the US military: conventional NATO forces in the European theatre of war were far outnumbered by similar Soviet and Warsaw Pact forces, and it was assumed that in case of a major Soviet attack (commonly envisioned as the "Red tanks rolling towards the North Sea" scenario) that NATO - in the face of quick conventional defeat - would soon have no other choice but to resort to tactical nuclear strikes against these forces. Most analysts agreed that once the first nuclear exchange had occurred, escalation to global nuclear war would likely become inevitable.

The 1980s

In the late 1970s and, particularly, during the early 1980s under US President Ronald Reagan, the US renewed its commitment to a more powerful military, which required a large increase in spending on US military programs. These programs, which were originally part of the defense budget of US President Jimmy Carter, included spending on conventional and nuclear weapons systems. Under Reagan, defensive systems like the Strategic Defense Initiative became emphasized as well.

Another major shift in nuclear doctrine was the development and the improvement of the submarine-launched, nuclear-armed, ballistic missile, or SLBM. It was hailed by many military theorists as a weapon that would make nuclear war less likely. SLBMs - which can move with "stealth" (greatly lessened detectibility) virtually anywhere in the world - give a nation a "second strike" capability (i.e. after absorbing a "first strike"). Before the advent of the SLBM, thinkers feared that a nation might be tempted to initiate a first strike if it felt confident that such a strike would incapacitate the nuclear arsenal of its enemy, making retaliation impossible. With the advent of SLBMs, no nation could be certain that a first strike would incapacitate its enemy's entire nuclear arsenal. To the contrary, it would have to fear a (near certain) retaliatory second strike from SLBMs. Thus a first strike was a much less of feasible (or desirable) option, and a (deliberately initiated) nuclear war was thought to be less likely to start.

However, it was soon realized that submarines could "sneak up" close to enemy coastlines and decrease the "warning time" (the time between detection of the missile launch and the impact of the missile) from as much as half an hour to possibly under three minutes. This effect was especially significant to the United States, Britain, India and China, whose capitals all lay within 100 miles (160 km) of their coasts. Moscow was much more secure from this type of threat, due to its considerable distance from the sea. This greatly increased the credibility of a "surprise first strike" by one faction and (theoretically) made it possible to knock out or disrupt the chain of command of a target nation before any counterstrike could be ordered (known as a "decapitation strike"). It strengthened the notion that a nuclear war could possibly be "won" - resulting not only in greatly increased tensions and increasing calls for fail-deadly control systems, but also in a dramatic increase in military spending. The submarines and their missile systems were very expensive, and one fully equipped nuclear-powered and nuclear-armed missile submarine could cost more than the entire GNP of a developing country). It was also calculated, however, that the greatest cost came in the development of both sea- and land-based anti-submarine defenses and in improving and strengthening the "chain of command", and as a result, military spending skyrocketed.

South Africa developed a nuclear weapon capability during the 1970s and early 1980s. It was operational for a brief period before being dismantled in the early 1990s.

On Sept. 1, 1983, Korean Air Lines Flight 007 was shot down by Soviet jet fighters. On the 26th, a Soviet early warning station under the command of Stanislav Petrov falsely detected 5 inbound intercontinental ballistic missiles from the US. Petrov correctly assessed the situation as a false alarm, and hence did not report his finding to his superiors. It is quite possible that his actions prevented "World War III", as the Soviet policy at that time was immediate nuclear response upon discovering inbound ballistic missiles.

The world came unusually close to nuclear war - although perhaps not as close as during the Cuban Missile Crisis - when the Soviet Union thought that the NATO military exercise Able Archer 83 was a ruse or "cover up" to begin a nuclear first strike. The Soviets responded by raising readiness and preparing their nuclear arsenal for immediate use. Soviet fears of an attack went away once the exercise concluded without incident.

Post–Cold War

Although the dissolution of the Soviet Union ended the Cold War and greatly reduced tensions between the United States and the Russian Federation (the Soviet Union's formal successor state), both nations remained in a "nuclear stand-off" due to the continuing presence of a very large number of deliverable nuclear warheads in both nations. Additionally, the end of the Cold War led the United States to become increasingly concerned with the development of nuclear technology by other nations outside of the former Soviet Union. In 1995, a branch of the US Strategic Command produced an outline of forward-thinking strategies in the document "Essentials of Post–Cold War Deterrence".

The former chair of the United Nations disarmament committee stated that there are more than 16,000 strategic and tactical nuclear weapons ready for deployment and another 14,000 in storage, with the U.S. having nearly 7,000 ready for use and 3,000 in storage, and Russia having about 8,500 ready for use and 11,000 in storage. In addition, China is thought to possess about 400 nuclear weapons, Britain about 200, France about 350, India about 80-100, and Pakistan 100-110. North Korea is confirmed as having nuclear weapons, though it is not known how many, with most estimates between 1 and 10. Israel is also widely believed to possess usable nuclear weapons. NATO has stationed about 480 American nuclear weapons in Belgium, the Netherlands, Italy, Germany, and Turkey, and several other nations are thought to be in pursuit of an arsenal of their own.

A key development in nuclear warfare during the decade of the 2000s and after has been the proliferation of nuclear weapons to the developing world, with India and Pakistan both publicly testing several nuclear devices, and North Korea conducting an underground nuclear test on October 9, 2006. The US Geological Survey measured a 4.2 magnitude earthquake in the area where the North Korean test is said to have occurred. A further test was announced by the North Korean government on May 25, 2009. Iran, meanwhile, has embarked on a nuclear program which - while officially for civilian purposes - has come under close scrutiny by the United Nations and many individual states.

Recent studies undertaken by the CIA cite the enduring India-Pakistan conflict as the one "flash point" most likely to escalate into a nuclear war. During the Kargil War in 1999, Pakistan came close to using its nuclear weapons in case the conventional military situation underwent further deterioration. Pakistan's foreign minister had even warned that it would "use any weapon in our arsenal", hinting at a nuclear strike against India. The statement was condemned by the international community, with Pakistan denying it later on. This conflict remains the only war (of any sort) between two declared nuclear powers. The 2001-2002 India-Pakistan standoff again stoked fears of nuclear war between the two countries. Despite these very serious and relatively recent threats, relations between India and Pakistan have been improving somewhat over the last few years. A bus line directly linking Indian- and Pakistani-administered Kashmir has recently been established. However, with the November 26, 2008 Mumbai terror attacks, India currently will not rule out war with Pakistan.

Another potential geopolitical issue which is considered particularly worrisome by military analysts is a possible conflict between the United States and the People's Republic of China over Taiwan. Although economic forces are thought to have decreased somewhat the possibility of a military conflict, there remains the worry that the increasing military buildup of China (China is rapidly increasing their naval capacity, and that any move toward Taiwan independence could potentially spin out of control).

Israel is thought to possess somewhere between one hundred and four hundred nuclear warheads. It has been asserted that the submarines which Israel received from Germany have been adapted to carry missiles with nuclear warheads, so as to give Israel a second strike capability. Israel has been involved in wars with its neighbors in the Middle East (and with other "non-state actors") on numerous prior occasions, and its small geographic size and population could mean that, in the event of future wars, the Israeli military might have very little time to react to an invasion or other major threat. Such a situation could escalate to nuclear warfare very quickly in some scenarios.

Biological Warfare

Biological warfare agents have gained attention in recent years. They have been discussed in Congress and in the medical literature, and have been the subject of frequent commentaries. The mention of 'biological warfare' often elicits a sense of deadly mystery, as summarized by a Russian journalist

'Biological Warfare' (BW) is defined as the 'employment of biological agents to producc casualties in man or animals or damage to plants.' An early BW attack took place in the Black Sea port of Kaffa in 1346. Rats and their fleas carried the disease to attacking Tatar soldiers. In spite, the Tatars catapulted the bodies of victims at the defending Genoese who contracted plague and left Kaffa. The same rats afflicting the Tatars likely brought disease to the Genoese.

Another attempted use of biological warfare occurred between 1754 and 1767 when the British infiltrated smallpox-infested blankets to unsuspecting American Indians during the French and Indian war. Smallpox decimated the Indians, but it is unclear if the contaminated blankets or endemic disease brought by the Europeans caused these epidemics. In 1932, the Japanese began a series of horrific experiments on human beings at 'Unit 731' outside Harbin, Manchuria, China. At least 11 Chinese cities were attacked with the agents of anthrax, cholera, shigellosis, salmonella, and plague, and at least 10,000 died during their gruesome experiments.

The United States started an offensive biological warfare program at Camp Detrick in Frederick, Maryland in 1943. Ten years later, the defensive program began. By 1969, the U.S. had weaponized the agents causing anthrax, botulism, tularemia, brucellosis, Venezuelan equine encephalitis, and Q fever.

These were soon destroyed after President Nixon unilaterally ended the U.S. offensive biological warfare program that year. 1972 the U.S. signed the Biological Weapons Convention stating that it would never develop, produce, stockpile, acquire, or retain BW agents or the means to deliver them.

Despite this convention, the development of BW weapons has continued. Controversial evidence suggests that 'yellow rain' (trichothecene mycotoxins) attacks in Southeast Asia caused thousands of deaths between 1974 and 1981. In 1978, Bulgarian dissident Georgi Markov was assassinated using an 'umbrella gun' that shot ricin into his thigh. At least 66 people died of inhalational anthrax when an aerosol of *Bacillus anthracis* spores was accidentally released from a BW research facility in Sverdlovsk, USSR in 1979.

By 1991, the Iraqis had weaponized anthrax, botulinum toxin, and aflatoxin. Fortunately, these were not used during Desert Shield or Desert Storm. The United Nations destroyed the final remains of the Iraqi offensive program in 1996.

Finally, in 1995, the Aum Shinrikyo cult, that released sarin nerve gas in a Japanese subway, was found to possess rudimentary biological weapons including anthrax, botulism, and Q fever.

Nature of Biological Warfare

BW agents can cause large numbers of casualties with minimal logistical requirements. Perpetrators can escape long before BW agents cause casualties, due to the incubation periods of the agents. Weapons are easy and cheap to produce and can be used to selectively target humans, animals, or plants. The costs of conventional weapons ($2000), nuclear armaments ($800), and chemical agents ($600) would far outstrip the bargain-basement price of biological weapons ($1) to produce 50% casualties per square kilometer (1969 dollars).

Agents can be easily procured from the environment, universities, biological supply houses, and clinical specimens. In fact, a white supremacist received a vial of *Yersinia pestis* shipped to his home by the American Type Culture Collection in Rockville, MD. Common fermentation techniques used for producing antibiotics, toxoid vaccines, foods, and beverages can be used to grow large quantities of biological agents. Simple aerosol generating devices mounted on planes or trucks, as used for crop-dusting, can generate

1-5 micron particles ideal for causing infectious aerosols. Aerosol particles 0.5-5 microns in diameter settle in the alveoli; larger particles are cleared by respiratory mucosa, and smaller particles float in and out of the alveoli without settling. BW agents are typically invisible in aerosol clouds and may not be detected until humans become ill. Panic would result as medical capabilities are quickly overwhelmed.

Disadvantages to using BW agents as weapons include hazards to the user, their dependence on optimal weather conditions to result in effective dispersal, and their possible inactivation by solar irradiation and other climatic conditions. BW attacks would most likely occur late at night or early in the morning when agents would be less likely to undergo inactivation by ultraviolet radiation. At these times, atmospheric temperature inversions would allow an agent cloud to travel at low altitude to cover its target.

BW Agents

Pathogens may be used against personnel, animals, or plants. Agents may kill or incapacitate victims. Incapacitating agents may be more effective in battle by both preventing a unit from carrying out its mission and overwhelming medical and evacuation assets. Agents with short incubation times would be most effective in a tactical setting, while those with longer incubation periods would appeal more to terrorists.

Biological attacks against large populations would most likely be disseminated by aerosol. A respiratory portal of entry may cause different clinical features than naturally occurring disease.

Biological attacks could be attempted by contaminating food and water supplies, although modern water purification and the dilution effects in large volumes of water would negate the effectiveness of a water-borne attack. While intact skin is an excellent barrier to most biological warfare agents, some agents, such as trichothecene mycotoxins, can penetrate the integument and cause systemic illness. Ingestion and cutaneous penetration are currently considered unimportant potential routes of exposure. More unusual methods of dispersion could include releasing agents in their natural arthropod vectors.

Person-to-person transmission of several agents could perpetuate an epidemic. Nosocomial transmission could result from blood and body fluid exposures.

In 1970, WHO predicted that a city of 500,000 people would be devastated following an aerosol release of as little as 50 kg of BW agent.

Current unclassified information reveals that, despite the 1972 Geneva Biological Weapons Convention, at least seventeen countries are known or suspected of having offensive biological weapons programs. Clearly, BW is a credible threat to military, as it was during Desert Shield/Storm. Terrorist use of BW agents could kill many people to create an unparalleled medical, political, and social crisis. Despite the fact the biological weapons have never been used against the United States, we must prepare for a new age of terrorism. Civilian health-care workers must know how to recognize a BW attack in the event of terrorist use of BW agents on civilian populations.

Burkholderia Pseudomallei

Burkholderia (formerly *Pseudomonas*) *pseudomallei* is a gram-negative bacillus isolated from soil, stagnant streams, ponds, rice paddies, and market produce in endemic areas and can cause epizootics in sheep, goats, swine, horses, and seals. Humans contract disease from contamination of abrasions with soil but may also ingest or inhale organisms. Melioidosis is endemic to southeast Asia and northern Australia, but it may occur anywhere between 20 degrees north and south latitudes. It is most widespread in Thailand where it accounts for 19% of hospitalizations and 40% of deaths from community-acquired septicemia. Mild or subclinical infections are common; 80% of Thai children are seropositive by age five years.

Melioidosis most commonly presents as an acute pulmonary infection, but it may present as an acute localized skin infection or septicemia. Chronic suppurative infections often develop with secondary abscesses in the skin, brain, lungs, myocardium, liver, spleen, bones, lymph nodes, or eyes. Melioidosis may remain latent for years. Even months of treatment with appropriate antibiotics do not necessarily eradicate the disease. Histologically, caseating granulomas as found in tuberculosis are seen.

Melioidosis has been called the 'Great Imitator' because the disease does not show any specific clinical features except perhaps the presentation of suppurative parotitis in children. Fulminant respiratory failure, multiple pustular and necrotic skin lesions, or the radiologic appearance of tuberculosis without isolating any mycobacteria suggests the diagnosis of melioidosis. Definitive diagnosis requires culturing organisms from blood or body fluids. No carrier state exists; recovery of organisms denotes active disease.

Antibiotic treatment should be based on sensitivities. Ceftazidime has been most responsible for reducing mortality. Treatment must continue at least 30 days, but 60-150 days is recommended for pulmonary disease and 6-12 months for suppurative extrapulmonary disease. Before antibiotics, 95% of patients died. The mortality rate for septicemic disease is over 50% and 20% for localized disease despite treatment. Overall, mortality is 40%. There are no available vaccines.

Severe urticaria has been reported with pulmonary melioidosis. Flushing and cyanosis may develop during septicemia. No cutaneous lesion, however, is specific or diagnostic of melioidosis, nor is any likely to be present with acute pulmonary disease. Inhalational melioidosis could lead to any of the skin manifestations mentioned below, but only after metatstatic abscesses to the skin formed, and this would likely take months. Many patients in endemic areas present with pustules or cutaneous abscesses associated with lymphangitis, cellulitis, or regional lymphadenitis. Draining sinuses from lymph nodes or even bone may be present. Abscesses may ulcerate, and rarely, ecthyma gangrenosum-like lesions may form.

B. pseudomallei would most likely be delivered as an aerosol. However, its long incubation period would make it a less effective agent than anthrax. The lack of a vaccine and its high mortality despite treatment may increase its utility as a BW agent. Acute pneumonia could be confused with plague given the similar appearance of stained organisms.

Yersinia Pestis

Because of its high mortality, *Yersinia pestis* has attracted attention for development as a possible BW agent.

This gram-negative bacillus develops an anti-phagocytic carbohydrate protein envelope (F1 capsular antigen) during growth above 33° C. A single gene encodes the Pla protease that provides both fibrinolytic and coagulase activities. At 37° C, fibrinolysis is most active; at 28° C, coagulation predominates. This enzyme helps organisms grow and remain in flea guts or spread through tissues in mammals. Other virulence factors act in concert with these such that only 2-10% of the bacteria needed to cause death in mammals at 25° C is necessary at 37° C.

At least 30 types of fleas and over 200 species of mammals in 73 genera serve as reservoirs. Flea infection is restricted to the alimentary canal where bacilli either are passed or stay in the midgut (stomach). There they multiply in a fibrinoid mass of blood on needle-like spines in the proventriculus. These spines aid the rupture of red blood cells and normally prevent the regurgitation of a blood meal. Such 'blocked' fleas cannot digest their food and ultimately die. However, this state makes them ravenously hungry. In an attempt to feed, blood sucked from a mammalian host mixes with bacilli which are regurgitated back into the host. Fleas become unblocked and plague transmission ceases at temperatures above 28° C. This may be caused by differential effects of Pla protease at different temperatures.

After a flea injects a blood meal into an unsuspecting host, neutrophils and monocytes engulf the bacilli and transport them to regional lymph nodes. While the neutrophils can destroy bacilli, the monocytes cannot. In monocytes, *Y. pestis* multiplies and develops its anti-phagocytic capsule that prevents even neutrophils from digesting it. Bacilli then multiply in lymph nodes and the blood and travel throughout the body, but especially to the spleen, liver, lungs, and meninges.

Every continent except Australia and Antarctica maintains enzootic foci of plague. Between 1979 and 1993, 16,312 worldwide cases resulted in over 1600 deaths.

Clinical Features

Most endemic plague presents with tender, erythematous lymphadenopathy, most commonly in the groin and causes bubonic plague (Greek *boubon* = groin). Buboes may point and drain spontaneously. Bubo location is primarily a function of the region of the body in which an infected flea inoculates plague bacilli.

A lesion is seen at the site of a flea bite no more than 10% of the time. Spread to the bloodstream results in septicemic plague. From the blood, the meninges may become infected. Spread to the lungs results in pneumonic plague that is rapidly fatal and transmissible. Because bacilli in pneumonic plague lesions possess an anti-phagocytic capsule, transmission by cough or sneeze can lead to death in a healthy individual within one to two days. The median infective inhaled dose is 100-500 bacilli. However, as only 1-10 bacilli can infect rodents or primates via the oral, intradermal, subcutaneous, or intravenous route. Respiratory droplets can be inhaled by those within two to five feet. The ensuing flu-like illness progresses rapidly to overwhelming pneumonia with cough and bloody sputum. If not treated within 24 hours of symptoms, pneumonic plague patients almost all die. One must have a high index of suspicion to diagnose plague in the absence of buboes. Stains and cultures of blood, bubo aspirates, sputum, cerebrospinal fluid, or even skin scrapings may be helpful in isolating the organism.

The formalin-killed plague vaccine protects against bubonic, but not inhalational plague. Attempts at more immunogenic live-attenuated vaccines result in no increase in immunogenicity and sporadic reversion of vaccine strains to virulent, wild type bacteria. Most strains of *Y. pestis* are sensitive to streptomycin, gentamicin, tetracycline, chloramphenicol, trimethoprim/sulfamethoxazole, and doxycycline. Although *in vitro* testing has demonstrated the effectiveness of quinolones, rifampin, third-generation cephalosporins, and amoxicillin, these have not been used to any great degree in human cases. The U.S. military currently requires the vaccine only for those traveling or deploying to high risk areas and for those employed in high risk occupations (entomologists or laboratory workers using *Y. pestis*).

Terminal pneumonic and septicemic plague patients, as would be seen in a BW scenario, would develop livid cyanosis and large ecchymoses on the back. Septicemia could cause petechiae, purpura, ecchymoses, and acral necrosis.

The petechiae and ecchymoses may even mimic meningococcemia. Dark cyanotic lesions, large ecchymoses, and/or the acral necrosis may have given rise to the Medieval epithet, 'the Black Death.' Rose-colored purpuric lesions gave rise to the nursery rhyme "Ring around the rosy." The "Pocket full of posies" referred to the attempted prophylactic measure of flowers carried by the healthy, especially physicians, "Ashes, ashes" referred to the impending mortality ("Ashes to ashes, dust to dust"), or alternatively "A-choo, A-choo" referred to the sneeze of pneumonic plague, and "All fall down" referred to the terminal event—death.

No chest x-ray pattern is characteristic of plague, but bilateral interstitial infiltrates are most commonly seen. Rare cases of ecthyma gangrenosum-like lesions and carbuncles due to plague have been reported.

Pharyngitis associated with cervical lymphadenopathy has been reported in contacts of bubonic plague patients. Of course the most common cutaneous manifestation of plague, the bubo, would not be present in a BW scenario unless the Japanese plan of releasing infected fleas was resurrected.

While *Yersinia pestis* would most likely be aerosolized for a BW attack, the Japanese employed a more creative approach in China during World War

II. Human fleas (*Pulex irritans*) were multiplied and then infected with *Y. pestis*. These organisms were released into several Chinese cities where small epidemics of plague ensued. Normally, animal hosts die in epizootics before humans are infected, but in these cases, humans died first and then animals began dying of plague.

Plague would most likely be transmitted as an aerosol in the event of BW. The possibility of rapid death combined with possible person-to-person transmission make plague an ominous BW threat. The United States studied *Y. pestis* as a potential offensive weapon in the 1950s. Other countries are suspected of weaponizing plague.

Trichothecene Mycotoxins

Trichothecene mycotoxins are the only potential BW toxins with cutaneous activity and manifestations. Mycotoxins are a diverse group of small molecular weight compounds produced by fungi. They can occur at toxic levels in moldy grains and other agricultural products and are mainly produced by members of five fungal genera: *Aspergillus, Penicillium, Fusarium, Alternaria,* and *Claviceps*. Eating contaminated foodstuffs and perhaps inhaling aerosolized toxins uncommonly causes natural human or animal disease.

Human intoxication is rare. An entity known as alimentary toxic aleukia, reported in Russia since the 19th century, is thought to result from ingestion of mycotoxins while eating foods prepared from moldy grain. Signs and symptoms include vomiting, diarrhea, 'skin inflammation,' leukopenia, hemorrhage, and sepsis.

More recently, and closer to home, trichothecene mycotoxins are thought to have caused fatal pulmonary hemorrhage in Cleveland area infants. In one area of Cleveland, it may have accounted for 5% of cases of sudden infant death syndrome between 1993-95. In all cases, the fungus *Stachybotrys atra* was found growing in water-saturated cellulose in the walls of poorly maintained homes.

At low doses (nanograms), severe skin irritation with erythema, edema, and necrosis is observed. Vesication often occurred with 'Yellow Rain' attacks; T-2 (one of the trichothecenes) mycotoxin is estimated to be 400 times more potent than alkylating agents (mustards) in producing skin injury.

T-2 mycotoxins can be absorbed through the skin and cause death with an LD_{50} of 2-12 mg/kg compared to that for mustards (4500 mg/kg) and lewisite (37 mg/kg). In Southeast Asia, the skin was thought to be the major site of deposition of aerosol spray or coarse mists.

Epidemiologic, intelligence, and trichothecene assay evidence suggest that trichothecene mycotoxins were used in Southeast Asia between 1974 and 1981. Nearly 400 alleged attacks reportedly resulted in approximately 10,000 deaths. In Laos, the attacks were described as 'yellow rain,' a sticky yellow liquid that fell and sounded like rain or looked like a yellow cloud of dust, powder, mist, smoke, or insect spray. The liquid dried rapidly to form a powder. Most attacks used yellow pigment, but some attacks used red, green, white, or brown smoke or vapor. More than 80% of attacks were by air to surface rockets.

Microgram exposure caused eye irritation, corneal damage, and impaired vision. At 0.1-0.2 LD_{50}, emesis and diarrhea occurred. Aerosols caused death within minutes to hours by destroying alveoli. The toxins affect rapidly proliferating tissues and are cytotoxic to most eukaryotic cells by inhibiting protein and RNA synthesis. After entering the circulation, regardless of portal of entry, they affect all rapidly proliferating tissues.

A protective mask and full-body clothing should be donned at the first sign of a 'yellow rain' attack. Afterwards, battle dress uniforms (BDUs) and contaminated areas of skin should be washed with soap and water followed by a water rinse. Washing within 4-6 hours of exposure removes 80-98% of the toxin and prevented death and dermal lesions in experimental animals. No known specific therapy exists, although high doses of systemic steroids decreases primary and secondary toxin injury.

Poxviridae

Poxviruses, the largest of all viruses, differ from other DNA viruses by replicating in the cytoplasm where they produce eosinophilic inclusion bodies. They are relatively resistant to drying and many disinfectants. The Orthopox genus includes at least nine species. Three viruses interest in a BW context: variola, monkeypox, and vaccinia.

Variola is an orthopox virus very similar to vaccinia but with different host predilections. There was no animal reservoir; this factor enabled global eradication of this disease. Variola retains its transmissibility for one year in dust and cloth. Person-to-person transmission requires close contact. Patients were most infective 4-6 days after the illness started, and respiratory spread was probably the most common route of transmission. Only 30% of susceptible contacts became infected.Monkeypox was first identified in 1958 as a pathogen of cynomolgus monkeys; in 1971 it was linked to human disease. The virus exists in an enzootic state in arboreal squirrels of tropical rain forests of western and central Africa. Person-to-person transmission by respiratory droplet occurs.

Thirty years ago, smallpox was endemic in 31 countries affecting 15 million people each year. Survivors often remained disfigured or blinded for life. A 10-year WHO program eradicated the disease as of October, 1977.

Smallpox featured an incubation period of 7-17 days and a prodrome of 2-4 days. During the prodrome, 10% of light-skinned patients develop an erythematous rash. An enanthem on the buccal and pharyngeal mucosa started on about the second day. These lesions shed virus and allowed for aerosol spread, the most important means of viral transmission. The typical lesions started on the face, spread to the forearms and hands, and finally appeared on the lower limbs and trunk within about one week. Macules progressed to papules, vesicles, pustules (sometimes umbilicated), and crusts distributed in a centrifugal pattern (in distinction to varicella) over a 1-2 week period.

More lesions were present in convex than concave areas. Crusts would detach in about 3 weeks leaving depressed, hypopigmented scars. Virus could be cultured from crusts throughout convalescence.

Several clinical varieties of smallpox were described. 'Ordinary' smallpox (variola major), present in 80% of patients, led to 3% mortality among the vaccinated but 30% among the unvaccinated.

The most virulent form, hemorrhagic smallpox, was seen in less than 3% of patients. 96% of these patients died, usually before they developed typical pox lesions.

Flat smallpox occurred in 2-5% of patients with severe systemic toxicity and slow evolution of flat, soft, focal skin lesions. 66% of the vaccinated and 95% of the unvaccinated died. Alastrim, or variola minor, was a mild illness featuring diminutive cutaneous lesions, mild systemic disease, and a case fatality rate of less than 5%.

Modified smallpox occurred as a "form fruste" among vaccinees and was usually a mild disease. Finally, 'variola sine eruption' occurred in 30-50% of vaccinated contacts of smallpox patients. Serologic studies showed increased antibody titers after exposure, but no skin lesions appeared.

Monkeypox greatly resembles variola with a pustular eruption, fever, respiratory symptoms, and death in 3-10% of cases.

The only distinguishing feature appears to be cervical and inguinal lymphadenopathy. Secondary bacterial pneumonia is associated with a 50% mortality. An outbreak in Zaire between February and August 1996 led to 71 cases with 6 deaths in 13 villages in a region of 15,000 people. Unlike smallpox, monkeypox possesses a non-human reservoir, an arboreal squirrel. In February, 1997, a search in 12 villages found 92 possible cases among 4000 people (2% attack rate). Fifteen of 84 had a smallpox vaccination scar. Communicability may be related to declining vaccinia-induced immunity. Vaccinia immunization seems to provide 85% protection against monkeypox.

Smallpox has been eradicated, but at least two sites, the Centers for Disease Control and Prevention in Atlanta and the Russian State Research Center of Virology and Biotechnology in Koltsovo, Russia still maintain viable variola. The extent of clandestine stockpiles remains a matter of debate and concern. WHO has set June 30, 1999 as the day all variola stocks are to be destroyed. If variola were ever released by an enemy or by terrorists, morbidity and mortality could be considerable. The person-to-person aerosol infectivity, high mortality, and stability make variola (and possibly monkeypox) a potential BW threat.

Other animal poxviruses could be genetically engineered to be virulent in humans. While WHO has 200-300 million doses of smallpox vaccine stored, the vaccine is gradually losing virulence, and the number of smallpox-naïve individuals continues to increase as vaccination has virtually ceased.

Hemorrhagic Fever Viruses

Hemorrhagic fever (HF) is a clinical syndrome featuring fever, myalgia, malaise, haemorrhage, and in some cases, hypotension, shock and death. The hemorrhagic fever viruses belong to four families of lipid enveloped viruses with single-stranded RNA genomes. Transmission of HF viruses varies with the specific virus. However, all of the HF viruses, with the exception of dengue, are potentially transmitted via aerosol, underscoring their possible role as BW agents.

Hemorrhagic fever viruses are transmitted by arthropod vectors or contact with infected animal reservoirs. Arenaviruses and Hantaviruses are transmitted by inhalation of aerosolized rodent excreta, while Rift Valley

Fever and Congo-Crimean hemorrhagic fever (CCHF) can be aerosolized during the butchering of infected livestock. The reservoir for filoviruses remains a mystery Person-to-person spread may occur via direct contact with infected patients or their blood and body fluids. Four viral hemorrhagic fevers (VHFs) have a high risk of nosocomial spread and are quarantinable conditions: Lassa fever, CCHF, Ebola fever, and Marburg disease. While epidemiologic studies indicate that respiratory transmission of viral hemorrhagic fevers does not occur among humans, such transmission has occurred among non-human primates. In addition, subclinical human infections due to a filovirus virulent for monkeys (Ebola-Reston) have occurred after respiratory exposure to infected animals.

In addition, infectious aerosols may be generated during endotracheal suctioning and other medical procedures. Although nosocomial transmission of HF in Africa has been interrupted by standard universal precautions without additional respiratory measures, adding respiratory protection as an infection control measure is advised by the Centers for Disease control and Prevention because information regarding exposure and transmission in humans is limited. Infections can be prevented by avoiding contact with vectors and reservoirs, practising standard hospital infection control procedures, patient isolation, disinfection, and reporting cases to public health officials.

Viral hemorrhagic fevers present as acute febrile illnesses characterized by malaise, myalgias, and prostration dominated by generalized abnormalities of vascular permeability because the target organ for viral replication is the endothelial cell. Initial signs include flushing, conjunctival injection, periorbital edema, petechiae, hypotension, and a positive tourniquet test. Early in the disease course, signs and symptoms are non-specific and make differentiation from endemic febrile illnesses very difficult. Full-blown disease develops into shock and generalized mucosal haemorrhage. Neurologic, hematopoietic, or pulmonary involvement is often present. Diffuse bleeding often occurs as a result of widespread vascular damage, hepatic dysfunction and/or disseminated intravascular coagulation (DIC). Life-threatening blood loss rarely occurs.

Some clinical features may differentiate the hemorrhagic fevers. An exanthem is common with the filoviruses, sometimes occurs in hemorrhagic fever with renal syndrome and dengue fever, is uncommon with Lassa fever, and is absent in CCHF. Capillary leak syndrome is most common in Lassa fever while haemorrhage and neurological manifestations are uncommon. Neurologic and hemorrhagic complications are common among the South American Arenaviruses. Rift Valley Fever rarely causes haemorrhage. While CCHF exhibits no edema, it results in DIC and the most severe hemorrhage among HF viruses. Filoviruses also exhibit significant DIC.

Sequelae of VHFs include hair loss, Beau's lines, deafness (Lassa, Ebola), retinitis (RVF, KFD), uveitis (RVF, Marburg), encephalitis (AHF, BHF, RVF, KFD, and OHF), pericarditis (Lassa), and renal insufficiency (HFRS).

Treatment is supportive with special attention to fluid and electrolyte balance, and treatment for shock, blood loss, renal failure, seizures, and coma. These may require intensive care interventions such as mechanical ventilation, dialysis, and neurological support.

The role of heparin therapy for DIC is controversial and should be reserved for patients with clinically significant hemorrhage and laboratory evidence of DIC. Aspirin and other medications that impair platelet function are contraindicated, as are intramuscular injections. The use of intravascular devices needs to be carefully considered in the context of potential benefit versus the risk of hemorrhage. Surgical interventions should be offered if indicated.

Specific antiviral therapy is limited. Clinical studies support the use of intravenous ribavirin for the treatment of Lassa fever, Argentine and Bolivian hemorrhagic fevers, hemorrhagic fever with renal syndrome due to Hantaan virus, and CCHF. Intravenous and oral ribavirin are available through human use protocol only but are reasonable options for any infection due to an Arenavirus or Bunyavirus.

Immunotherapy with convalescent plasma has been beneficial in the treatment of Argentine and Bolivian hemorrhagic fevers. Passive immunization does not work, however, for Lassa fever or CCHF.

A live attenuated yellow fever vaccine is the only licensed immunization for the viral hemorrhagic fevers available in the United States. A live, attenuated vaccine against Argentine Hemorrhagic Fever (Junin virus) has proven safe and effective in endemic areas. It also protects monkeys against aerosol exposure to Bolivian Hemorrhagic Fever (Machupo). Other investigational vaccines include a formalin-inactivated vaccine and a live attenuated vaccine for Rift Valley fever and a vaccinia-vectored vaccine against HFRS due to Hantaan virus. Hemorrhagic fevers may produce a variety of cutaneous manifestations. Most of these are due to vascular instability and bleeding. Flushing, petechiae, purpura, ecchymoses, and edema may occur in the discussed diseases except for Rift Valley Fever. No skin manifestations are typically associated with this disease.

Lassa Fever patients have a high incidence of facial edema, probably due to extensive capillary leak Skin eruptions are uncommon. The South American arenaviruses more commonly cause petechiae, purpura, ecchymoses, and palatal hyperemia.

Cutaneous manifestations of HFRS appear on about day three of illness. A petechial rash manifests on the neck, anterior and posterior axillary folds, upper arms, and thorax. A morbilliform eruption may also occur. Flushing may be seen about the head, neck, and upper torso. This may be most apparent in a malar distribution as a 'sunburn flush' accompanied by facial edema. Dermatographism is often present. Hemorrhages are often seen on mucosal surfaces and may be severe in the conjunctivae. Of the other Bunyaviruses, Rift Valley Fever typically causes no skin lesions while CCHF patients generally develop the worst hemorrhagic manifestations

The Filovirus diseases frequently exhibit an exanthem, particularly noted in lighter-skinned patients. Filovirus disease presents with a deep reddening of the soft palate that spreads to the hard palate.

The most reliable diagnostic sign is a pin-head-sized papular, erythematous eruption appearing at days 5-7 on the buttocks, trunk, and lateral arms. After 24 hours, the eruption develops into large, well-demarcated, coalescent macules and papules. In some cases, the rash appears hemorrhagic. In severe cases, a dark, livid erythema develops on the face, trunk, and extremities that disappears in several days. Cyanosis sometimes accompanies the erythema. After the 16th day, palms, soles, dorsal feet, and extremities desquamate for a few days to two weeks. The exanthem is often accompanied by scrotal dermatitis or labial erythema.

Like Marburg disease, Ebola fever starts abruptly with fever, myalgias, headache, and other influenza-like symptoms. Early findings include conjunctival injection and adenopathy. Around day 5, a morbilliform eruption followed by petechiae, ecchymoses, and even hemorrhage is seen. Most commonly, the rash is nonpruritic, maculopapular, and centripetal with variable erythema that desquamates by day 7. Patients have expressionless, ghost-like facies. Psychosis, delirium, seizures, and coma are often noted. With progressive disease, hemorrhage exudes from mucous membranes, venipuncture sites, and body orifices. Death occurs between six and 16 days after hemorrhage begins. Mortality rate in pregnancy is 100%. Death is due to a combination of hemorrhage, capillary leak, shock due to vasodilatation and hemodynamic deregulation, and end organ failure.

Dengue typically features a morbilliform eruption sparing the palms and soles. Infection due to one of the four serotypes grants lifelong immunity to that serotype only, and predisposes to dengue hemorrhagic fever or dengue shock syndrome following reinfection due to a heterologous strain.

Hemorrhagic fever viruses cause high morbidity and, in some cases, high mortality. Some may replicate well enough in cell culture to permit weaponization.

Filoviruses could be maliciously adapted as BW agents because they are highly infectious, lethal, and can be stabilized for aerosol dissemination. The Russians experimented with filoviruses as potential BW agents, but apparently discontinued development in the mid-1990s for financial reasons. They successfully enhanced the viability of aerosolized filoviruses. Marburg virus can be stabilized in 10% glycerin so that viral inactivation occurs at a rate of 1.5%/minute instead of 11.5%/minute. This rate of inactivation is in the range of that for influenza virus (1.9%/minute) which spreads naturally by aerosol. Filoviruses, however, are considered too dangerous to use because of the lack of protective vaccines and therapeutic measures to protect the users. The Russians evaluated CCHF as a BW agent, but did not weaponize it. The susceptibility of Bunyaviruses to heat, drying, and ultraviolet light make them poor candidates as BW agents. Hantaviruses replicate poorly in cell culture and are not considered to be significant BW threats. The Flaviviridae are unlikely to be used as BW agents. Dengue is not infectious by aerosol, and troops are routinely immunized for yellow fever.

Complications of BW Prevention

Vaccinia

The Orthopox virus vaccinia is distinct from cowpox, has little virulence for immunocompetent humans, and has recently been used as a vector for experimental vaccines. Vaccinia would not be used as a BW agent, but it could cause disease when used to prevent smallpox. The origin of vaccinia is obscure; it may have developed from an extinct animal poxvirus, such as horsepox, or may represent a cowpox mutant, which developed during multiple human passages during the early vaccine era. Smallpox vaccine was prepared by inoculating shaved abdomens of calves, sheep, or water buffalo. Infectious exudative lymph was harvested from inoculation sites and bottled with phenol and brilliant green as bacteriostatic agents. Human cell culture-derived vaccinia is being developed at USAMRIID.

Vaccine is administered percutaneously with a bifurcated needle. This process became known as 'scarification' because of the resulting permanent scar. Infectious virus replicated in the lesion. It was early determined that vaccinees who received vaccinia by intramuscular injection developed weaker immune responses than those vaccinated by scarification. Scarified patients that develop pox lesions develop 3-fold higher ELISA titers and 10-fold greater plaque reduction neutralization titers than those who develop no pox lesion.

Clinical Response to Vaccination

Primary vaccinees usually developed a pustule surrounded by induration 6-8 days after vaccination. This 'major reaction' was required to confer protective immunity and occurred in about 95% of primary vaccinees. All other reactions were termed 'equivocal.'

The remaining scar was usually about 1 cm in diameter. A rare but severe non-cutaneous side effect of vaccination was post-infectious encephalitis similar to post-measles encephalitis. Vaccinia provides at least three years of protection after vaccination.

Cutaneous Complications of Vaccinia

Cutaneous complications were at least 10 times more common in primary vaccinees than revaccinees. The most severe cutaneous complication, *vaccinia necrosum* (vaccinia gangrenosum, progressive vaccinia), occurred in 12.3 per million primary vaccinees. Vaccinees with cellular immunodeficiencies developed relentlessly progressive pox lesions and even metastatic lesions. Fatal cases showed no evidence of resolution, no adenopathy, and no erythema. Death occurred in 13/17 (76%) of documented cases.

Eczema vaccinatum with hundreds of pox lesions occurred in active atopic dermatitis patients who were vaccinated or merely exposed to a recent vaccinee. Mortality was 10-14%. Patients were treated with vaccinia immune globulin 0.6 cc/kg/24 hours until no new lesion appeared. Only 1.5 cases/million primary vaccinees were reported in a U.S. survey. This low rate can likely be explained by the fact that atopic dermatitis was a contraindication to vaccination.

Accidental vaccinia infection occurred among 241.5 per million primary vaccinees by autoinoculation to another body site or to another person (secondary inoculation) via intimate contact. Ocular vaccinia was one of the most troublesome forms of accidental inoculation.

Generalized vaccinia is a non-specific term applied to a vesicular eruption developing after primary vaccination. After about 7-12 days, patients developed a rash with many small vesicles on erythematous bases. Patients with generalized vaccinia are non-toxic, afebrile, and not viremic. This self-limited complication generally resolved in 6-9 days in the 38.5 per million primary vaccinees who contracted it.

Seven to twelve days after vaccination, some patients develop *erythematous urticarial eruptions* that resemble enterovirus or roseola exanthems.

Other complications may occur such as melanoma or BCC in vaccination scars. Bullous erythema multiforme, overwhelming and fatal viremia in infants, and fetal vaccinia have also been reported.

Bacterial agent—Bacillus anthracis

Bacillus anthracis is a gram-positive sporulating bacillus. The spores are resistant to heat, cold, drying, and chemical disinfection. Spores remain viable for at least several years in the top six cm of soil and in animal products. Animals that die of anthrax release massive quantities of spores into the soil which may remain for decades before being ingested again. Burying animal carcasses is probably of little use in disrupting transmission since Pasteur showed that earthworms will carry spores back to the surface! Animal carcasses should be burned, not buried, to prevent long-term environmental contamination. Anthrax is endemic in western Asia and western Africa. Disease is transmitted from infected animals or their products via skin abrasions in more than 90% of cases. Less commonly, ingestion or inhalation of spores transmits anthrax.

Gastrointestinal (GI) anthrax is exceedingly rare and has never been reported in the U.S. Patients present with ulcerative mucosal eschars that can perforate viscera thus producing abdominal pain, diarrhea, and acute infection. Secondary meningitis has occurred from primary GI disease, but any form of anthrax can progress to septicemia or meningitis.

Pulmonary anthrax, or 'wool-sorter's disease,' is an extraordinarily rare form of anthrax; only 18 cases were reported in the U.S. between 1900 and 1980. Anthrax would undoubtedly be used in this form as a BW agent. This usually fatal disease starts as a vague prodrome with fever, malaise, myalgias and cough. During the next several days, these non-specific symptoms may be rapidly followed by precordial discomfort, cyanosis, stridor, diaphoresis, moist rales, pleural effusion, and death. The initial symptoms mimic any number of influenza-like infections. The disease is difficult to diagnose in the early, treatable stage.

Inhaled spores are engulfed by alveolar macrophages and transported through lymphatics to tracheobronchial lymph nodes within four hours; they replicate in hilar nodes within 18-24 hours. The median lethal inhaled dose is 10,000 spores (range 8000-50,000 spores) that are two to five microns in diameter. The spores can retain viability in the lungs up to 100 days! Germination of spores in the hilar nodes leads to hemorrhagic mediastinitis, but not true pneumonia. A widened mediastinum on chest X-ray is diagnostically helpful. Overwhelming infection leads to uncontrolled intravascular multiplication of bacilli and fatal toxemia characterized by hypotension and hemorrhage.

Anthrax is generally sensitive to penicillin, however, rare beta-lactamase positive strains have been isolated. Ciprofloxacin, erythromycin, tetracycline, doxycycline, and chloramphenicol are alternative drugs.

Cutaneous disease begins as a small, painless, red macule that progresses to a papule that vesiculates, ruptures, ulcerates, and forms a 1-5 cm diameter brown or black eschar. Lesions usually appear within two weeks after handling sick animals or eating their meat, however, incubation periods of over eight weeks are not unknown. The black eschar gave rise to the name 'anthrax' derived from the Greek word *anthrakos* meaning 'coal.' Lesions are not purulent in the absence of superinfection. Satellite lesions and significant edema may surround the initial eschar.

Even with prompt antibiotic therapy, cutaneous lesions progress through the eschar phase. Antibiotics have no effect on the skin lesion except to sterilize it.Debridement of skin lesions is contraindicated because of the risk of spreading infection. While 80-90% of lesions heal spontaneously, 10-20% of untreated cases may progress to malignant edema, septicemia, shock, renal failure, and death. Fatalities are uncommon with therapy.

In a BW scenario, anthrax would most likely be disseminated in aerosol form because the stable spores could cause rapid death in a high percentage of those exposed. In April and May 1979, at least 66 people died during an epidemic of inhalational anthrax in Sverdlovsk, Russia following an accidental release of aerosolized spores. All victims had hemorrhagic mediastinitis. It has been estimated that the release of less than one gram of spores caused this outbreak. This accident demonstrated the silent and deadly nature of an aerosol BW attack. Larger quantities of spores released in an urban setting could be an inexpensive and effective terrorist weapon.

Anthrax spores were weaponized by Japan, the United Kingdom, and the United States in the 1940s, 1950s, and 1960s before their offensive programs were terminated. Iraq admitted to a United Nations inspection team in 1995 that they had weaponized anthrax.

Bacterial agent—Francisella tularensis

First described in 1907, *Francisella tularensis* is a gram-negative, pleomorphic coccobacillus with two serotypes: infection with type A carries a 5% mortality rate while type B causes much milder disease. The bacterium can persist for months in mud, water, and decaying animal carcasses, however, it is normally maintained in wild rabbits, squirrels, sheep, beavers, meadow voles, and muskrats. Dozens of biting and blood-sucking insects serve as vectors, and ticks pass the bacilli on to offspring trans-ovarially. *Dermacentor andersonii* (Rocky Mountain wood tick), *Dermacentor variabilis* (Pacific coast dog tick), and*Amblyomma americanum* (Lone Star tick) are the main vectors in the United States. Ticks transmit disease during spring and summer in the southwestern and central states while rabbit exposure during the winter accounts for most exposure in southeastern states.

Tularemia is highly endemic in Oklahoma, Missouri, and Arkansas. In the decade ending in 1988, 2356 cases were reported in the United States with 24 deaths (1% mortality). Each of the six clinical forms starts with sudden onset of fever, chills, headache, and generalized myalgias and arthralgias after an incubation period of 3-6 days. An ulcer is generally seen at the bite site and may persist several months as organisms spread to local lymph nodes. Untreated, mortality is 8% for all types, 4% for ulceroglandular tularemia, and 35% for the typhoidal type. With appropriate treatment, mortality is 1-2.5%. One episode usually guarantees lifelong immunity.

Skin or a mucous membrane acts as the portal of entry for tick bites, other arthropod bites, or abrasions. Rarely, inhaled or ingested organisms cause disease. At least 10^8 organisms are necessary to cause gastrointestinal disease; only 10 organisms can cause cutaneous or pulmonary infection. Local multiplication of *F. tularensis* causes a tender, red, pruritic papule that rapidly enlarges to form an ulcer with a black base. The organism then spreads to lymph nodes and causes bacteremia. Conjunctival inoculation leads to local adenopathy. Pneumonia occurs secondary to bacteremia or primarily via aerosolization. Lungs develop foci of alveolar necrosis and neutrophilic infiltrates. Chest x-ray reveals bilateral patchy infiltrates but not large areas of consolidation.

Tularemia classically presents as one of six clinical syndromes:

Ulceroglandular: the most common form of tularemia. With the glandular form, it accounts for 75-85% of naturally occurring cases. The erythematous, indurated, non-healing, punched-out ulcer lasts 1-3 weeks. Local lymph nodes may be fluctuant and drain spontaneously. Suppuration of lymph nodes may occur up to 3 weeks after treatment. The differential diagnosis of ulceroglandular tularemia includes sporotrichosis, cat scratch disease, mononucleosis, lymphangitis, lymphogranuloma venereum, plague, and *Pasteurella* infections.

Glandular: the second most common form. Glandular tularemia follows inoculation of the skin via arthropod vectors and most commonly afflicts the inguinal and femoral lymph nodes in adults and the cervical nodes in children.

Oculoglandular: Inoculation of periorbital skin or the conjunctiva by arthropod vectors or aerosols leads to the development of oculoglandular tularemia.

Oropharyngeal or gastrointestinal: This form follows ingestion of undercooked meat or direct inoculation from the hands to the mouth. Pharyngitis occurs in up to 25% of tularemia patients. The pharynx may be erythematous or may present with petechiae, ecchymoses, ulcers, and/or exudates.

Typhoidal: Only 10-50 organisms need be inhaled to cause typhoidal tularemia. While rare in the United States, it is the septicemic form of disease occurring without skin lesions or lymphadenopathy. One must suspect tularemia to make the diagnosis in time for effective treatment. The disease mortality ranges from 30-60%.

Pulmonary: Pulmonary tularemia develops in 10-30% of those with ulceroglandular disease and in 50-80% of those with typhoidal tularemia. Patients present with a non-productive cough with dyspnea or pleuritic chest pain. Chest x-rays reveal a variable parenchymal infiltrate. Up to 30% of patients die. The differential diagnosis includes Q fever, mycoplasma, psittacosis, histoplasmosis, and coccidioidomycosis.

A live-attenuated vaccine is available for individuals at risk (field or laboratory workers) and protects individuals against an aerosol challenge of *F. tularensis*. Streptomycin is the drug of choice for adults. Gentamicin, tetracycline, ceftriaxone, cefotaxime, chloramphenicol, and ceftazidime are also effective.

A chancre-like ulcer forms at the site of bacterial inoculation in 60% of patients. About 85% of patients develop enlarged lymph nodes, some of which present as fluctuant buboes. Mucous membrane lesions in the pharynx commonly accompany aerosol-induced disease. A morbilliform eruption has been reported in a minority of patients with systemic disease.

Tularemia was weaponized by the United States in the 1950s and 1960s. Other countries may have weaponized this agent for delivery by aerosol. Both typhoidal and pulmonary tularemia may result from inhalation of bacilli, and mucous membrane lesions could accompany inhalational disease. The rapid onset of action, non-specific nature of complaints in those affected, and the difficulty in identifying and culturing the organism make it a potential threat agent.

Recognising a Bliological Warefare Attack

Because the primary threat from BW agents today is from terrorists, civilians in densely populated regions would be likely targets. Therefore, civilian medical personnel need to be aware of how a BW attack would present to minimize its effects. We cannot presume that such an attack would never happen. Fortunately, the United States government has seen the need for increased education. The Federal Emergency Management Agency and local emergency responders and care givers are learning how to recognize and respond to a BW assault.

With current technology, an enemy could complete a BW attack before the local commander or medical officer would know anything had happened. Large and steadily increasing numbers of casualties would present in a shorter period than for a natural epidemic. There may be a large number of rapidly fatal cases with few recognizable signs and symptoms. Multiple diseases could present simultaneously. Vector-borne diseases will appear without natural outbreaks in animals. BW agents would likely have a high attack rate among exposed individuals, and the disease would often be unusual for the geographic area. Because most agents would be delivered in aerosol clouds, many patients would have pulmonary disease caused by agents that don't usually cause pulmonary disease.

War Crisis Management

Crisis management is an aspect or mode of strategy, not a substitute for it. This at any rate is the underlying premise of the analysis that follows. Some may worry that such an approach blurs the distinctiveness of the phenomenon of crisis management, validating simplistic approaches to the use of military force and impairing the ability or willingness of leaders to seek negotiated solutions to their security problems. Suffice it to say that strategy as used here should by no means be taken to imply a prejudice against conciliation or against diplomacy as an instrument of statecraft. Indeed, one could argue that crisis management as conceived and practiced during the Cold War was if anything *insufficiently* respectful of traditional diplomacy, while it exaggerated the value of military force when employed for directly political purposes.

Crisis management is by no means a uniquely American problem. During the Cold War itself, the Soviet Union, Britain, France, and the People's Republic of China, as well as many lesser states, experienced significant political-military crises. Israel probably belongs in a category of its own as a nation existing in a state of semi-permanent crisis. In addition, there is a rich record of well-documented crisis decision making involving the major powers of pre-1945 Europe that dates back at least to the Crimean War. With the demise of the Soviet Union and the greatly diminished threat of nuclear war, this older experience has regained much of its interest. At the same time, there is also increasing demand (or at any rate manifest need) for crisis management expertise on the part of regional and international organizations, most notably the United Nations itself, which have begun to play a much larger role in political-military crises than was the case during the Cold War.

Crises in the relations of states can be equally dramatic and demanding of attention at the highest level of government; but they can also be difficult to distinguish from the normal course of international affairs. Today, the term crisis seems to be used with ever-increasing frequency and looseness to refer to virtually any international development that reaches the front page of major newspapers: We speak of the Asian financial crisis, the Rwandan refugee crisis, the (by now long-standing) crisis in the former Yugoslavia. There has always been some vagueness in the way the term has been used both in ordinary life and in the academic literature on international affairs. But in the relatively benign international environment we currently enjoy, crisis aspects of ordinary policy making seem to get blown out of proportion. Crises are at once everywhere and nowhere. If this is so, however, a case might be made that the idea of crisis has lost its utility as a tool of policy analysis.

A special effort is therefore needed to understand the ways in which the concept and the craft of crisis management have been shaped by the matrix of the Cold War and the character of contemporary democracy. The key circumstance, of course, was the emergence of nuclear weapons as the core military capability of the United States and its principal rival, the Soviet Union. They soon gave rise to the conviction that war on a global scale could no longer be understood (in the formulation of Carl von Clausewitz) as an extension of policy by other means, or as subject to the traditional logic of strategy. This view reflected not only the increasing reach and destructiveness of the weapons themselves, but also the difficulty of defending against them. The development of ballistic missiles and bombers of intercontinental range for the first time made the American and Russian heartlands vulnerable to strategic bombardment. At the same time, the technologies supporting nuclear offensive forces greatly outpaced those available for defense against them. Eventually, defense against nuclear attack would come to be seen by many (at any rate in the West) as not only futile but dangerous, and mutual societal vulnerability as the essential precondition for deterring nuclear use and discouraging an open-ended nuclear arms race between the superpowers. This is what led a generation of thinkers to regard the dynamics of superpower crisis as *the* overriding problem of international security, eclipsing more basic strategic questions concerning the outcome of the geopolitical confrontation between the US and the USSR.

Minimizing the risk of nuclear war by preventing escalation of tensions between the superpowers entailed two distinct tasks. The first was to structure nuclear forces in such a way as to provide as few incentives as possible for either side to use them in a crisis. Success in this endeavor—achieved by unilateral decisions in nuclear force planning as well as by mutual agreement in an ongoing process of superpower arms control—was supposed to lead to a condition often called "crisis stability." The second task was to devise a system to ensure control of nuclear forces in a crisis by the highest levels of government. Only in this way, it was thought, would it be possible for governments to withstand escalatory pressures from military commanders as well as to minimize the possibility of unauthorized or accidental use of nuclear weaponry. At the same time, opportunities would be afforded for the adroit manipulation of military risk to shape the behavior of the adversary and to advance broad national interests.

McNamara's remark that "there is no longer such a thing as strategy, only crisis management" was intended to underline the importance of the handling of crisis situations by the president of the United States and his senior advisers directly rather than by a military leadership assumed to be biased toward narrowly military approaches to international questions. Implicitly, it asserted the existence of a higher-order expertise, one drawing largely on civilian perspectives drawn from business and the academy that transcended the old culture of victory and strategy that had dominated American thinking in World War II. According to this line of thinking, the Cuban Missile Crisis, the most acute and war-threatening US-Soviet confrontation of the Cold War, was paradigmatic. Features of this particular crisis—the role of secrecy and surprise in its outbreak, its very brief duration, the intensity and stress accompanying it, the decisiveness of its outcome—regularly found their way into academic definitions of crises generally. And the handling of this situation by President John F. Kennedy—with sustained involvement by officials at the highest level, sharp civilian-military disagreements, an obsession with miscalculation and inadvertent escalation, with posturing, signalling, and bargaining in the shadow of nuclear apocalypse—was to become the model for "crisis management" simply. Crisis management in this sense required an unprecedented sensitivity to and cooperation with the adversary in a situation in which both sides had more to lose than either had to gain. For this reason, managing crises required an unprecedented level of control of the military instrument by the civilian authorities, who would now wield a surgeon's scalpel rather than the bludgeon of soldierly tradition. New technologies supporting instantaneous communication helped make this kind of control possible.

While the impact of the Cuban Missile Crisis on subsequent thinking about crises and crisis management is difficult to exaggerate, in retrospect a case can certainly be made that it was exceptional, even in Cold War terms. No other US-Soviet crisis involved a truly palpable risk (or perception of risk) of nuclear war. No other US-Soviet crisis involved such a direct confrontation between the superpowers, and hence afforded a similar setting and incentives for direct crisis bargaining. Other US-Soviet crises might or might not involve surprise (even the Berlin crisis of 1948 should probably have been foreseen). Some crises, particularly the rolling Berlin crisis of the period 1958-1961, were essentially exercises in public diplomacy or psychological warfare in which surprise was not a factor, and were protracted to an extent that severely stretches the normal usage of the term.

As memories of the Cuban Missile Crisis faded and the US-Soviet relationship entered a phase of detente centering on the pursuit of strategic arms control, the crisis paradigm began to lose much of its plausibility. The crisis associated with the Arab-Israeli conflict of October 1973 was the only subsequent occasion on which the United States raised the alert level of its nuclear forces in response to threatening Soviet behavior. Meanwhile, unilateral steps (notably, improved nuclear command and control arrangements) as well as negotiated measures (such as the US-Soviet Hotline and the 1972 Agreement on Measures to Reduce the Risk of Nuclear War) helped to ease fears that crisis situations could spin out of political control and lead to unwanted escalation. Moreover, the political leadership on both sides seemed increasingly risk-averse and committed to preventing nuclear conflict at virtually any cost, while senior military ranks showed much greater sensitivity to civilian concerns on this score (and were more willing to play the arms control game) than their counterparts in 1962. In short, even the extraordinary US-Soviet nuclear relationship had become ordinary.

Nevertheless, the legacy of the Cuban crisis has shaped the meaning of the term crisis up to our own time. In spite of many variations, the term is regularly tied to a period of acute tension between states that threatens the prospect of major war. To cite one influential academic definition from the 1970s: "An international crisis is a sequence of interactions between the governments of two or more sovereign states in severe conflict, short of actual war, but involving the perception of a dangerously high probability of war." More recent attempts at a theory of crisis have largely accepted this approach, while at the same time blurring somewhat the distinctiveness of crisis and war or the use of force. A new study defines crisis as a perception by the highest level decision makers of "a threat to one or more basic values, along with an awareness of finite time for response to the value threat, and a heightened probability of involvement in military hostilities." According to this view, surprise is not a necessary component of crisis, and the time span involved is limited only very loosely (months or even a year). All that is required for a crisis is a "heightened" perception of the possibility of an armed clash, which may itself fall well short of war in any sense of the term.

Such an approach runs the risk of trivializing the idea of crisis insofar as it fails to provide criteria for distinguishing serious from less serious situations and accurate from skewered perceptions of these situations. But broadening the notion of crisis in this way is surely inevitable. Note also that the study just mentioned holds that crisis and war are not mutually exclusive. The proposition that a crisis can occur not only before but during military hostilities (an "intra-war crisis") is both plausible and useful, pointing as it does to the ineluctably *strategic* character of genuine crisis situations. War does not necessarily require the sustained engagement of a nation's political leadership. Such engagement *is* required, however, on those occasions when a major political or military development offers an unexpected opportunity or threatens catastrophic defeat. Chinese intervention in the Korean War in the fall of 1950 is a good example of such a crisis; others include major battles that mark a fundamental shift in the fortunes of the combatants, such as Stalingrad or El Alamein during World War II. The challenge of such crises lies in recognizing them as such, rather than treating them simply as part of the flow of military operations and hence not requiring special civilian scrutiny—the great American error in the Korean War.

The logic underlying the notion of intra-war crisis suggests the desirability of a further step: recognition of the crisis-like character of the climactic final stage and immediate aftermath of war. That the termination phase of a war could be, or contain, a crisis seems at first sight paradoxical, as analysts have been accustomed to understanding the dynamics of crisis in terms of escalation and deescalation. Yet it is surely a mistake to equate intensity of violence with strategic significance or policy interest. Both World War II and the Gulf War of 1990-1991 provide clear evidence of the consequences of failure on the part of an American president to recognize the point at which considerations of the shape of the international political order should take priority over the perceived requirements of the military endgame. Crises—critical turning points in a conflict, demanding the engagement or reengagement of a nation's civilian leadership in strategic decision making—occur before, during, and even after the shooting, regardless of the level of violence involved or threatened.

An additional distinction may be introduced here. In a highly original study, Yehezkal Dror develops the notion of "adversity" as a policy environment that is broader than crisis as such. Policy making in adversity is distinguished from policy making in normal or benign circumstances by the fact that the political leadership of a nation stands in greater need of external aids to decision making—information, analysis, advice, the careful coordination of a variety of instruments of statecraft. Adversity may have different faces. One of its forms is protracted conflict, of the sort experienced by the United States and the Soviet Union during the Cold War and by the Arabs and Israelis since 1947. Protracted conflict is not identical with crisis or war, but it may be described as a condition of proneness to crisis or war. Policy making in adversity, crisis and war therefore is both continuous and discrete, reflecting differences in the intensity of these environments and the demands they impose on policy makers.

The classical crisis management paradigm tends to overstate the discontinuities between crisis and non-crisis situations. While it would be going too far to say that crises exist only in the eye of the beholder, there is surely an important sense in which this is true. Crises are constituted by the perceptions of political leaders—perceptions of both an objective threat and a more or less subjective set of national and personal values and goals. For leaders who lack judgment, vision and nerve, ordinary problems balloon easily into crises. And—a point rarely remarked on—political leaders have both incentives and disincentives to identify situations as crises. Proclaiming a particular foreign threat a crisis may be politically useful in many ways; but it may also make it difficult or impossible to resolve outstanding issues through negotiation with the other party. Casual talk of crisis may make a political leader look weak if not followed by commensurate action. All of this is to suggest that identifying crises properly is a more complex exercise than seems to be generally assumed, and needs to be understood as an integral aspect of crisis management itself—or perhaps better, of policy making under adversity.

The original meaning of the (classical Greek) word *krisis* is "judgment" or "decision." A crisis in its most general sense really is a defining moment—a point in a developing series of events where significant change becomes possible, and which therefore calls for decision by those in authority. In the political arena, what distinguishes a crisis mode of policy making is the need for rapid judgment and decision by a nation's political leadership. Why this need? For two related reasons: because of the complexity of the issues raised in crises as well as the governmental instruments that handle them; and because of the consensus style of decision making that is the norm in most contemporary democracies. Direct intervention by the highest political authority is essential under such circumstances in order to make difficult tradeoffs between policy goods or evils, to coordinate recalcitrant bureaucracies, and not least, to effect a transition from a consensus to a command mode of leadership.

That crisis management so understood is a preeminently strategic function has been recognized by perceptive students of the subject. What has not been recognized adequately is the scope and complexity of this strategic function. Students of crisis management have tended to focus almost exclusively on the instruments of force and diplomacy and their competing requirements. As a result, they have both overstated the severity and inevitability of the tension between force and diplomacy, and understated the importance of other factors in crises. One need only glance at the recently declassified tapes of high-level White House meetings during the Cuban Missile Crisis to realize how prominent intelligence issues can be in crisis deliberations. A second factor is public opinion both international and domestic, and the competing demands of secrecy and publicity. The economic and financial aspects of crisis are a third factor, rarely discussed yet at least in some cases (consider the prelude to the Gulf War in the fall of 1990) exceedingly important. A fourth is law enforcement and the legal dimension generally (consider American dealings with Manuel Noriega at the time of the Panama crisis of 1989, and the burgeoning movement to create an international war crimes tribunal). Finally, there is the exercise of command as such, that is, the management of men and institutions. The Argentine junta might have won the Falklands War had it not made the fatal mistake of installing a military bureaucrat instead of a combat leader or strategist as the islands' governor. President Truman's toleration of the erratic and insubordinate behavior of Gen. Douglas MacArthur during the Korean War illustrates the opposite error. Lack of sensitivity to the importance of personality in key subordinates as well as a reluctance to discipline and if necessary relieve those who perform poorly is an obvious and yet strikingly neglected weakness of contemporary crisis management.

Several final points need to be made. Perhaps the most enduring legacy of Cold War crisis management thinking and practices is the assumption that its overriding strategic purpose is to minimize risk rather than maximize gain. This may seem a self-evident maxim for managers of nuclear "brinksmanship." At a certain point, however, crisis management so understood begins to produce diminishing returns, and slides toward appeasement. Particularly troublesome is the idea that any significant preparations for war should be avoided during a crisis because they might be misinterpreted by the other side (or even by one's own military forces) and lead to unwanted escalation. The United States entered two world wars in this century with deficiencies in military preparedness that in retrospect are virtually beyond belief. Preparation for war should be seen as a critical strategic task of crisis management, not something to be improvised at the last minute once crisis management has failed.

In a larger perspective, it is well to bear in mind this under appreciated insight: "The view that crises are undesirable neglects their positive aspects. Crises present opportunities not available in routine policy making. They provide the chance to motivate and mobilize citizens and the bureaucracy to action, to unify, to organize interest groups, and to move forward in areas where such programs might not be possible otherwise." The Chinese word for crisis contains the characters standing for both "danger" and "opportunity." As is often recognized, even (and perhaps especially) severe crises can provide an impetus to *improved* relations between the states involved (the Cuban Missile Crisis is a case in point). But crises can also afford manifold opportunities to skilled political leaders to strengthen alliances, to bolster the legitimacy of their regimes, and in other ways to advance their nation's international interests.

There is today a widespread tendency to understand crisis management as a form of "conflict resolution," in which third parties set out to prevent or end violent conflict between two other parties. One need not question the value of such efforts in principle to caution against the dangers of over optimism, over activism, and misplaced humanitarianism. Many conflicts are stubbornly resistant to mediation by outside parties, and there may well be cases (consider especially the successful Croatian offensive against Serb-controlled areas in Croatia and Bosnia in 1995) where military action is the only realistic option for advancing the prospects for a political settlement over the longer run. There are crises where the most humanitarian course for third parties may well be to let the contending sides fight it out.

This brings us to a last point. Like the larger body of strategic thought of which it was a part, traditional crisis management theory was very much affected by the axioms and aspirations of the social science of its era. Implicitly or explicitly, it accepted the notion that crises and human behavior during crises can be analyzed in terms of abstract models and a set of universally applicable rules or precepts deriving from them. Its assumption of a *homo strategicus*, engaged in fine-grained, dispassionate analysis of options and tradeoffs, was as much an artificial construct as the *homo economicus* of modern economics, and equally insensitive to the vagaries of personality and culture. Hence it tended to postulate adversaries that were mirror-images of the home team rather than enigmas of otherness that demanded careful decoding. Failure to assess systematically the processes, styles and psychology of crisis decision making in nations other than the United States is a persisting feature of crisis management theory and practice alike. Indeed, some of the most conspicuous lapses in the history of American crisis management arguably derive directly from a failure to heed one of the fundamental maxims of strategy—Sun Tzu's advice to know the enemy and know yourself.

None of this is to deny that the United States has enjoyed some successes in the crisis management business. Yet its failures are, as always, more instructive. In what follows, I will look briefly at three major political-military crises involving the United States over the past sixty years: the US-Japanese crisis of 1939-1941, the US-Soviet crisis in the fall of 1962, and the endgame of the Gulf War in the spring of 1991. These have been chosen not only to highlight the pitfalls of crisis decision making, but to illustrate the different types of crisis environments and the varying strategic problems they pose. The diversity of the opponents involved also helps bring into focus the neglected strategic-cultural dimension of crisis management.

Managing Crises: Lessons From American Practice

On December 7, 1941, a surprise assault by Japanese carrier aircraft on the American naval base at Pearl Harbor launched the United States into World War II. It is not customary to examine the events leading up to Pearl Harbor in the perspective of crisis management, in large part because of the still very generally held assumption that the Japanese action was the outcome of an inscrutable strategic calculation over which the United States had little or no influence. Pearl Harbor has tended to be treated as a failure of American intelligence, not of American policy. In fact, it is not at all clear that war was the fated outcome of the US-Japanese relationship of the late 1930s and early 1940s, or that the United States could not have managed that relationship so as to avoid hostilities on a basis consistent with its fundamental national interests. If in fact it was possible for the United States to achieve a satisfactory settlement of its long-standing dispute with Japan in order to focus its energies on the more serious Nazi threat, its failure to do so must be seen as one of the greatest strategic errors of American policy in this century, one that plunged the nation into a desperate struggle on two fronts for which it was scarcely prepared.

President Franklin Delano Roosevelt has long enjoyed a reputation as one of the greatest American presidents. A virtuoso of political maneuver, Roosevelt presided over an administration where power and responsibility were intentionally fragmented among competing officials so as to maximize his own freedom of action. In foreign affairs, Roosevelt was his own crisis manager, unsupported by any formal mechanism for interdepartmental coordination. Even with the hindsight and accumulated historical analysis of many decades, it is not easy to reconstruct Roosevelt's policy toward Japan. Some have concluded that he played a deep game, intentionally provoking the Japanese attack in order to swing an isolationist public opinion behind the war effort. While this seems highly unlikely, it is difficult to deny that from 1938 on, American policy as a whole was surprisingly provocative given the continuing weakness of the nation's defenses. The truth of the matter seems to be that Roosevelt never really pursued a consistent line toward the Japanese—that ends and means, words and deeds, never fully cohered. In an effort to satisfy one set of domestic opinions, FDR routinely attacked Japanism militarism in public speeches and applied economic pressures of increasing intensity; at the same time, to ward off criticism from other quarters, he pursued diplomatic initiatives and avoided threatening military measures. This kept the Japanese off balance and uncertain what the United States was really after. To the extent that he had an overall strategy, it seems to have been to bluff the Japanese into abandoning or delaying their course of conquest in Asia, while waiting on events elsewhere to strengthen America's hand.

Could Roosevelt have better handled the American-Japanese relationship during these critical years? There are good reasons for thinking so. In February 1939, when FDR returned the ashes of Ambassador Hiroshi Saito in an American battle cruiser, the reaction of the Japanese people was virtually a demonstration in favor of improved relations with the United States. Roosevelt sought to suppress the impact of this unintentionally effective act of public diplomacy. In August 1939, when the liberal ministry of Nobuyuki Abe assumed power in Tokyo and pressed for a renewal of the vital US-Japanese trade treaty, while fending off pressures for a deal with Hitler, Roosevelt's intransigence contributed centrally to Abe's fall in December. The wild inconsistency of which Roosevelt was capable was particularly evident in the summer of 1940, when he launched a private diplomatic feeler concerning a possible Pacific non-aggression pact and spoke approvingly in public of a (Japanese) Monroe Doctrine for Asia, only to turn around and impose a partial trade embargo on Japan in July. Even after Japanese accession to the Tripartite Pact, however, Tokyo seems to have been prepared and indeed eager to strike a bargain with the United States. Japanese councils were divided, but the ministry of Prince Konoye might well have succeeded in reconciling the Japanese army to an eventual withdrawal from China and effective neutrality in the struggle with Germany; and in fact the Japanese, in the protracted Hull-Nomura talks of 1941, came very far in the direction of these essential American desiderata. But the president's refusal to meet with Konoye at a Pacific summit, and what can only be described as the lack of seriousness in Hull's conduct of these negotiations, seem to have persuaded the Japanese that they had little to hope from diplomacy. This, coupled with the de facto oil embargo imposed by the United States in July together with the continuing weakness of American defenses in the Pacific, set the stage for Pearl Harbor, and a war the Japanese knew they were unlikely to win but thought unavoidable without a total abdication of their national honor.

The Pacific crisis of 1939-1941 is an object lesson in the dangers of an improvising and highly personalized style of crisis management.

Roosevelt's secretiveness, his chaotic management style, and his constant tactical maneuvers unconnected to any visible strategic design, confused friends and enemies alike. His use of diplomacy (including private channels that could be easily repudiated) was devious to the point of unreliability, and debased the coin of American power in ways that were particularly damaging in a time of world crisis. But perhaps the most serious flaw in Roosevelt's pre-war statecraft was his failure to understand, or to make an effort to understand, the adversary. As was sadly the case with many Americans at the time, Roosevelt had little regard for the Japanese and was inclined to see them in broad caricature. He was tone-deaf when it came to Japanese cultural sensitivities. He made no apparent effort to appreciate the delicate internal politics of the Japanese cabinet and the exposure (to assassination, among other things) of ministers who tried to accommodate American interests, much less to attempt to influence cabinet deliberations in ways favorable to the United States. And while he seems to have assumed (at least after 1940) that war with Japan was inevitable, he may well have believed the Japanese would not prove especially formidable in battle. At any rate, it is not easy to account on any other assumption for Roosevelt's seemingly relaxed view of American military requirements in the Pacific throughout the crisis.

A final point is worth emphasizing. Analysts of crisis management tend to focus on military action by the parties as the primary source of destabilizing or war-provoking behavior. The Pacific crisis is interesting as an example of a war arising from provocative economic and diplomatic activity rather than from any military measures. The fact that the critical freeze on oil imports to Japan in July 1941 was not intended by the president as a complete embargo shows that economic no less than military operations in crises may escape the control of the political leadership and lead to unwanted escalation. The lesson is particularly valuable at a time when economic sanctions seem to be taking on ever greater importance as a tool of American policy.

The US-Soviet Crisis of 1962

The Cuban Missile Crisis is the canonical case of successful crisis management in the classic Cold War mode, and in many respects contrasts favorably with American blundering prior to Pearl Harbor. The administration of John F. Kennedy was seized with the gravity of the risk and the need to handle matters deliberately and with maximum control from the top. Advice was sought and decisions communicated through multiple channels, orchestrated by a single extraordinary advisory committee in which the president himself took an active role. In contrast to Roosevelt, Kennedy was highly sensitive to the possibility of war erupting by miscalculation (he had recently read Barbara Tuchman's account of the July Crisis of 1914), and was determined this would not occur. At the same time, however, it is clear in retrospect that American management of the crisis was far from perfect.

The basic outlines of the crisis are well known. In August 1962, the Soviet Union had begun a clandestine effort to establish a major military presence in Castro's Cuba, involving significant numbers of Soviet troops and conventional armaments as well as aircraft and missiles of various kinds. In spite of assurances from Soviet leader Nikita Khrushchev as to the purely defensive intention of this buildup and a public warning by President Kennedy in September as its dimensions became clearer, American intelligence was able to report on October 16 that the Soviets were emplacing on the island nuclear-tipped medium- and intermediate-range missiles capable of striking targets virtually anywhere in the continental United States.

The crisis proper unfolded over the next thirteen days. Assisted by an ad hoc advisory group that would be designated the "Executive Committee of the National Security Council" or simply "Ex Comm," President Kennedy spent much of this period personally engaged in refining and weighing options for responding to the Soviet move. On October 21, the president settled on a naval blockade of Cuba rather than any form of direct military action, as urged by the Joint Chiefs of Staff as well as some influential civilian advisers. When the blockade was put into effect on October 24, American nuclear forces were placed at DEFCON 2, the highest alert status short of actual war—the only time this was done during the Cold War. The Soviets declined to challenge the blockade, and on October 26, faced with American warnings of imminent military action against the missiles already in place, Khrushchev sent Kennedy a message offering to withdraw the missiles in exchange for a pledge by the United States not to use force against Cuba. The day following, considerable confusion was introduced by a second Khrushchev message that upped the ante by proposing that the United States also withdraw the comparable Jupiter missiles it had recently deployed in

Turkey. In the standard version, at any rate, the president eventually decided to ignore the second message and accept the original proposal (though the missiles already deployed in Turkey and at other European sites would shortly be removed in any case). The Soviets went along, and the crisis was on its way to resolution.

Important new perspectives on the crisis have been gained, however, from Soviet records and the recollections of former high-ranking officials on both sides, as well as from recently published transcriptions of tape-recordings of Ex Comm deliberations. What emerges is a picture rather less flattering to the Kennedy administration than the familiar one. That the outcome of the crisis was a signal victory for the United States is undeniable. But it is also clear that the United States was playing a very strong hand, and against an opponent that blundered badly at critical junctures. In retrospect, what is noteworthy is not the outcome but how close the president came to snatching defeat from the jaws of victory.

Like all crises, the Cuban Missile Crisis must be evaluated in its larger strategic and political context. The abortive American-sponsored invasion of Cuba in April 1961 had revealed the hand of a president unsure of himself and overly fearful of a Soviet response. In June 1961, Kennedy met Khrushchev in Vienna, and used the opportunity to lecture the Soviet leader on the dangers of military rivalry and the need to avoid the "miscalculations" that had led the European powers into World War I. In the process, he offered the observation that "we regard...Sino-Soviet forces and the forces of the United States and Western Europe as being more or less in balance"—a gratuitous (and astonishingly inaccurate) poor-mouthing of American military capabilities. In the face of Khrushchev's intransigent posturing, Kennedy also managed to distance himself from his predecessors, admit errors in his own policies, and allude to his domestic political weakness. It is hardly surprising that Khrushchev went away from this encounter with a strong impression of the president as young, weak, overly intellectual, and "not prepared well for decision making in crisis situations." Khrushchev's actions over the next year—new threats over Berlin and the building of the Berlin Wall, the resumption of atmospheric nuclear testing, and the decision to send arms to Cuba—evidently flowed from this assessment of Kennedy's personal failings and the scope it afforded Khrushchev for a strategy of bullying and bluff.

Such a strategy was in fact nothing new. The Soviet leadership had for a number of years carried on a well-orchestrated deception campaign to inflate US perceptions of Soviet nuclear weapons capabilities, giving rise to the notion of a "missile gap" that was exploited by Kennedy against Nixon in the election of 1960. The advent of photo- reconnaissance satellites allowed American intelligence to explode the missile gap myth in the spring of 1961, but the administration as a whole seems never to have grasped or at any rate intellectually digested the actual extent of American nuclear superiority over the Soviet Union at this time, or the motives of Soviet leaders in perpetrating this apparently reckless fraud. In particular, President Kennedy himself seems to have consistently overestimated the military and political strength of the Soviet Union, while having little feel for the Leninist political style of the Soviet leadership or of Nikita Khrushchev in particular.

In the course of the Ex Comm discussions, the question of the purpose of deploying the missiles in Cuba was raised by the president himself in a way that shows he did not believe they were militarily significant; this view seems also to have been shared by Secretary of Defense McNamara. In fact, the missiles slated for deployment in Cuba would have *doubled or tripled* the number of Soviet ground-based missiles capable of reaching the United States, and because of their short flight times, would have constituted a particular threat to the American strategic bomber force as well as other critical military and civilian targets. While not providing the Soviets with anything approaching a disarming first strike capability, they would have posed for the first time a credible threat of inflicting unacceptable levels of damage on American nuclear forces and the American homeland. As such, they would have contributed in a major way to neutralizing the political if not the military effects of American nuclear superiority.

These facts make more understandable, if they do not fully justify, the bellicose reactions of most of the American military leadership during the crisis. What seems clear from the record is that the president did everything in his power to avoid using force or being placed in a situation where force might prove necessary, even at the cost of palpable strategic disadvantage, because of his underlying conviction of the unacceptable risk in any US-Soviet nuclear exchange. At the same time, Kennedy was aware that this conviction did not mirror the mood of the country (or indeed of his own advisers, and not merely those in uniform), and that a failure to react strongly to Soviet provocations could cause him grave political damage. In fact, it can be argued that the only reason the missile crisis ever occurred in the way it did is that the president felt it necessary, in a statement in early September, to draw an explicit line in the sand warning the Soviets against deployment of offensive missiles in Cuba—as a way of deflecting public criticism of the administration for its failure to react to the broader Soviet buildup there. As one of Kennedy's close aides later noted, "the President drew the line precisely where he thought the Soviets would not be....If we had known that the Soviets were putting forty missiles into Cuba, we might under this hypothesis have drawn the line at one hundred, and said with great fanfare that we would absolutely not tolerate the presence of more than one hundred missiles in Cuba." The point is that Kennedy seems to have been guided throughout the crisis not by any real strategic analysis, but by his instinct for the softest option consistent with his own and his administration's political survival.

This is strikingly confirmed by the best kept secret of the crisis—the president's use of the Jupiter missiles as a bargaining chip to ensure a Soviet retreat on Cuba. In a private meeting late on October 28 between the president's brother Robert Kennedy and Soviet ambassador Anatoly Dobrinin, assurances were given that the American Jupiters recently deployed in Turkey and Italy under NATO auspices would be withdrawn after a short interval, provided this was not publicly acknowledged as part of the settlement. Only six members of the president's inner circle were aware of this aspect of the American position. But there is almost certainly more to the story. While it remains unclear what prompted Khrushchev to send the second letter on October 28 raising the Jupiter issue, there is every reason to believe that it was in reaction to events in Washington. Ambassador Dobrinin has claimed that Robert Kennedy floated the idea of a trade in a private meeting on the evening of October 27. Word that such an idea was being actively considered in Washington had reached Khrushchev through a Walter Lippmann column of October 25, and probably as well through a report from a Soviet intelligence officer with links to Robert Kennedy.

While the Jupiter missiles were of limited military utility, their strategic and political significance for the NATO alliance was very considerable. It goes without saying that NATO and the Turks were kept in the dark about the bargain over these missiles, though their eventual withdrawal cannot but have aroused European suspicions and deepened doubts about the US nuclear guarantee to Europe that persisted throughout the Cold War. In the event, the administration was able to maintain enough secrecy surrounding the deal and to minimize the political damage it could have caused (though a contingency plan involving the United Nations was also prepared in the event it became public knowledge). But was the bargain really necessary? Were the risks it plainly involved properly weighed?

Opinions will differ on the wisdom of the president's maneuver, but it is hard to deny that it was symptomatic of larger flaws in his own performance and in the functioning of the Ex Comm throughout the crisis. Little thought seems to have been given by the president or any of his advisers to the larger issue of the American alliance system and the impact of the crisis on it. This is not surprising, however, in view of the relentlessly tactical focus of most of the Ex Comm discussions. One of the problems of the missile trade idea was that it ignored the asymmetrical requirements of nuclear deterrence and forward presence for the United States because of its commitment to the security of Western Europe. But there was very little discussion of the basics of US and Soviet nuclear strategies and force structures and their interrelationships. While it is not entirely fair to blame the president for the failure of key advisers (especially secretaries Rusk and McNamara and national security adviser McGeorge Bundy) to focus the Ex Comm discussions more effectively, he was ultimately the one responsible for a process that on close inspection plainly lacked adequate structure and discipline. Kennedy's private outburst to Rusk on October 29 over the inadequacy of State Department planning on the Turkish issue only underlines the absence of strategic focus in the Ex Comm as a whole.

But perhaps the most serious strategic error of the American side during the crisis was its cavalier dismissal of the significance of the larger Soviet military presence in Cuba and its longer term implications for the security of the western hemisphere. The administration acted as if no important concession had been made in offering a no-invasion pledge of Cuba. Yet since its beginning, the same administration had been obsessed with Fidel Castro's regime and the threat it posed to American interests throughout Latin America, and had seriously considered removing him by overt as well as covert means. Clearly, Castro's ever stronger Soviet connection only made matters worse. Quite apart from the nuclear question, Soviet military patronage of the Cubans—including the presence of large numbers of Soviet advisers and even combat troops—arguably constituted the most serious challenge to the Monroe Doctrine in its entire history. Yet the administration was prepared to wink at all of this in order to ensure a Soviet retreat on nuclear missiles. Indeed, so fixated was it on the missiles themselves that it failed to focus until awkwardly late in the crisis on the status and fate of nuclear-capable Soviet aircraft—notably, the forty-some IL-28 medium-range bombers already deployed to Cuba, which posed a threat not much inferior to the missiles themselves. Though the Soviets were finally prevailed upon to withdraw the IL-28s, the Soviet political and military commitment to Cuba not only survived the crisis but was legitimized by it.

The Crisis in the Gulf, 1990-1991

On August 2, 1990, the first elements of what would become an invasion force of some 140,000 Iraqi troops poured across the Kuwait border, surprising not only the Kuwaitis and their Arab neighbors but the United States. Contrary, apparently, to the expectations of Iraqi dictator Saddam Hussein, the United States decided to resist this act of unvarnished aggression. Over the next several months, it was able to organize a grand coalition of states under United Nations auspices, and to engineer an unprecedented buildup of American military forces in the Persian Gulf. When Saddam refused to heed an ultimatum of the UN Security Council to withdraw from Kuwait by January 15, 1991, the coalition launched a devastating air campaign against Iraqi forces as well as strategic targets throughout the country. A subsequent ground assault rolled up the Iraqi army in the Kuwait area in 100 hours, leaving allied forces astride the road to Baghdad and igniting widespread rebellion against a regime that seemed on its last legs. In the final surprise of this saga, however, Saddam Hussein was able to survive defeat, restore his regime's authority in the face of what was to become virtually a United Nations protectorate in the northern third of the country as well as severe economic sanctions, reconstitute his military power in significant part, and reemerge as a legitimate leader and a regional power broker, while the United States would become increasingly isolated and marginalized in spite of its continuing military presence in the Gulf. While the US won the battle in 1991, Saddam seemed well positioned to win the long-term war.

Though not regularly discussed in these terms, the "Desert Shield" period of the Gulf conflict (August 1990—January 1991) was nonetheless a crisis by anyone's defi- nition, and a good case can be made for considering in the same light the six months or so preceding the Iraqi invasion. There are important lessons to be drawn for crisis management from this initial period, including the run-up to the invasion itself. For our purposes, though, perhaps the most interesting aspect of the conflict as a whole is the failure of the coalition, but especially the United States, to manage effectively the war's final stage and to put its strategic imprint on the post-war Middle East.

President George Bush has deservedly won admiration as the architect of the coalition's triumph and commander-in-chief of the most formidable American expeditionary force since World War II. Under his personal leadership, the United States launched a highly effective diplomatic effort to assemble moral and material support and a regional base for opposition to Saddam, and used its growing military presence in the Gulf region first to deter a further Iraqi advance, then to pressure the Iraqis to withdraw. Yet this classic "coercive diplomacy" was never more than a sideshow in American policy, which accepted relatively early the likelihood (and strategic desirability) of a major military clash and was more concerned with preparing for war than exploring all avenues for a peaceful solution. The key challenge for the United States, and President Bush in particular, was to fend off political pressures both at home and abroad to follow the script of Cold War crisis management.

This the president succeeded in doing, but only with considerable difficulty. The administration was late and inarticulate in describing American aims in the Gulf, and came very close to losing a crucial vote in the US Senate as a result of its maladroit handling of the congressional leadership throughout the period of the buildup. These failures in the political and public relations arena were offset to a significant extent, however, by the very effective handling of media coverage of the crisis by military officers in the field and the Pentagon generally. As the first war ever covered in real time by television, the Gulf War underscored the importance of the information dimension of contemporary crises and the need for a systematic and coordinated approach to dealing with it.

If the strengths of the Bush administration were most in evidence when the Gulf conflict was at its height, its weaknesses, which have emerged with greater clarity as we gain distance from the event, can be seen especially in the initial and final phases. There can be little question that the president and other senior administration officials (notably Secretary of State James Baker) misread the situation in Iraq following the Iran-Iraq war, failed to take seriously the many indicators in early 1990 that Saddam was bent on challenging the regional status quo, and pursued an overly conciliatory policy that had the effect of persuading Saddam that the United States would under no circumstances intervene militarily to protect Kuwait. Although the horrors of his regime were hardly a secret, Saddam was not perceived by most senior American officials as qualitatively different from other Middle Eastern strongmen. In part, this reflected deficiencies in American intelligence, but more importantly, it pointed to a fundamental failure of political imagination. Bush and Baker both regarded Saddam as a man with whom they could do business, rather than as a paranoid thug who harbored dreams of a revived Babylonian Empire.

The American experience during the Gulf War well illustrates the fundamental truth that crises contain opportunity as well as danger. The Gulf War as a whole was a true "crisis" in the sense of a turning point in international affairs, affording the United States in particular manifold opportunities to strengthen its diplomatic and military position in the Middle East, complete the rehabilitation of the American armed forces as an instrument of national power in the aftermath of the Vietnam era, and lay the foundations for a "new world order" that would replace the structures and habits of the Cold War. In retrospect, it is clear that such opportunities were only partially perceived and imperfectly pursued, to the extent they were pursued at all. While certainly reflecting the particular limitations of the Bush administration, this also testifies to the persistence of a fundamentally astrategic American approach to the management of crises.

But the single greatest failure of crisis management in the Gulf conflict occurred at the end and in the immediate aftermath of coalition military operations. As argued earlier, though the notion runs contrary to the conventions of current thought, the end and immediate aftermath of wars deserve to be considered crises in the operationally precise meaning of the term, for they demand the reinvolvement of supreme civilian authority in national decision making in order to balance the requirements of the military endgame with postwar political arrangements. At the end of the Gulf War, errors on the military as well as the civilian side compounded American decision making failure and laid the groundwork for the flawed strategic outcome of that conflict that has become increasingly obvious in the intervening years.

The outlook of the American military leadership at this time, as articulated especially by the Chairman of the Joint Chiefs of Staff, Gen. Colin Powell, was decisively shaped by the experience of failure in the war in Vietnam. The lessons of Vietnam were thought to be, first, that any application of force by the United States should be massive rather than limited or incremental, geared to overwhelming the enemy and bringing the conflict to a rapid conclusion; and second, that wars should be run by the uniformed military—better, by the commander on the spot—without second-guessing or micromanagement by higher authority. This thinking, which was accepted with few reservations by the Bush administration as a whole, was faithfully reflected in the preparations for and conduct of the Gulf War, and seemed to be vindicated by the outcome. The theater commander, Gen. Norman Schwartzkopf, had unusual freedom to plan and execute overall US military strategy in the region, with results that exceeded virtually all expectations. Unfortunately, both Schwartzkopf and his superiors in Washington failed to recognize the point at which military considerations should have taken second place to larger requirements of US policy.

The self-imposed ceasefire, fixed (in part for dubious symbolic reasons) at one hundred hours from the beginning of the ground campaign, was the first major mistake. While this decision was not solely a military one (it reflected high-level administration concern that pursuit of fleeing Iraqi troops along the "highway of death" was turning into a public relations debacle), it was driven in great measure by the desire of the military leadership to declare victory and disengage before being drawn into a Vietnam-like "quagmire" of low-intensity conflict. The immediate effect of the ceasefire was to prevent American field commanders from closing the ring on the Iraqi Republican Guard divisions, the mainstay of Saddam's regime and the core of his military strength, whose destruction had been a key coalition objective. More broadly, the ceasefire deprived the United States of the option of ratcheting up the pressure on Saddam's regime and threatening his personal tenure in office by advancing on major Iraqi population centers, particularly Baghdad and Basra. It also confirmed that the coalition had little interest in active support of the revolts in Kurdistan and the Shi'ite region of southern Iraq, then in full swing in no small measure because of words of encouragement pronounced by the president himself.

The second major error had to do with the ceasefire talks between Gen. Schwartzkopf and senior Iraqi commanders held shortly thereafter at the town of Safwan. Lacking any instructions from Washington and with no civilian presence on his delegation, Schwartzkopf treated his Iraqi opposites with a chivalry and forebearance that was at best absurdly inappropriate. He threw away whatever leverage the coalition presence in Iraq might have been able to exert by promising unilaterally an immediate withdrawal from all Iraqi territory; and his casual and gratuitous exemption of helicopters from a ban he imposed on the use of Iraqi military aircraft led directly to their employment in the suppression of Saddam's internal enemies.

There is surely a legitimate argument to be made in favor of the broad strategy the US pursued at the end of the Gulf War. Even if Baghdad had been threatened, it is not certain that Saddam's regime would have fallen; and there were strong political constraints imposed on US action not only by the fragility of the coalition (its Arab members in particular had little stomach for an intrusive or semi-permanent US military presence in Iraq) but by the formal mandate bestowed by the United Nations Security Council. In addition, the implications of a breakup of the Iraqi state for the stability of the region could not safely be ignored, and the Saudis in particular were intensely concerned over the potential for a greatly expanded Iranian role. Still, it is hard not to conclude that the US squandered significant opportunities in the aftermath of the coalition victory. The US military bowed out of the conflict before any real pressures were brought to bear to halt military operations, and the American push for a military ceasefire prior to the resolution of any of the political issues raised by the war has to be considered a classic case of crisis mismanagement. While no one knows whether added coalition pressure would have led to the downfall of Saddam Hussein, it is certain that the failure of the American government during this critical period to look beyond the crisis contributed importantly not only to the survival of Saddam's regime but to the contraction of the political space for American diplomacy throughout the region in succeeding years.

Crisis Management After the Cold War

There is a broad continuity in the requirements for intelligent crisis management. Crises require the sustained attention of the national leadership, a working mastery of an array of instruments of statecraft, orderly processes of information gathering and analysis, an unprejudiced and probing review of available options, sensitivity to the opponent, timely decisions, and careful coordination and control of their implementation. Above all else, though, they require strategic vision and political competence. It was argued earlier that the peculiar circumstances of the Cold War served in a number of ways to distort the idea of crisis management. The nuclear allergy encouraged the belief that the prevention of war is the overriding purpose of crisis management generally and that political and military operational needs in crises are necessarily in tension. It further encouraged the identification of crises generally with situations involving a risk of nuclear war, emphasizing thereby the discontinuities between crisis environments and ordinary policy making and the centrality of the military component of crisis decision making.

Crises today, to repeat what was said at the outset, are everywhere and nowhere. For the major powers at any rate, the relative decline in external threats of all sorts, coupled with the increasing demands of multilateral political-military operations, create what one might call an environment of pseudo-crises, in which governments are constantly agitated by events but lack sufficient incentives for rapid and strategically coherent decision making.

Much of the change in the contemporary strategic environment has to do with the greatly enhanced role of the Western (but particularly the American) media in defining crisis situations and forcing governments to react to them. As indicated earlier, the psychological-political dimension of crises has always been an important one—more important, in fact, than has been generally recognized in classic crisis management theory. Public statements by government officials have usually figured prominently in the handling of crises, and independent news media have served as a crucial source of factual information as well as an interpreter of crisis-related events. In the current era, the psychological-political dimension of international conflict is even more central than it was in the strategic environment of the Cold War. New technologies and global media organizations such as CNN have revolutionized not only the reporting of international crises but the interactions of governments in crises. The Kurdish exodus from Iraq at the end of the Gulf War and the Somali famine and civil war of 1992-1994 are classic instances of humanitarian "crises" driven and indeed defined primarily by media pressure. And the Gulf War itself well illustrates the challenges involved in waging the kind of limited or constrained warfare that is likely to be the rule in coming decades—warfare undertaken in a glare of publicity in which unaccustomed factors such as human rights outrages and environmental concerns can unexpectedly assume great political importance. In such an environment, it is harder than ever for governments to maintain a strategic perspective.

The problem of the post-Cold War security environment from the perspective of crisis management may be said to be the relaxed level of tensions between all the major powers. The effect of this is to widen the gap between normal and crisis modes of national security decision making, making it more difficult both to anticipate crises and to take them seriously as they develop. A related problem has to do with the relatively diminished level of strategic-cultural knowledge of potential opponents in a world in which real conflict seems increasingly remote. In spite of a certain proneness to mirror-imaging analysis, the American preoccupation with understanding the Soviet adversary during the Cold War was intense, and Americans and Soviets both gained valuable experience over the years in dealing with one another in crisis-related situations. With much lowered incentives, the United States cannot be expected to bring to bear the same level of intelligence attention or comparably sophisticated strategic assessments against the hypothetical adversaries of today. The extent to which American intelligence was surprised by the Indian nuclear tests of spring 1998 shows how little can now be taken for granted in this regard. More importantly, our current political leaders cannot be expected to play the same central role in international crises as their predecessors. Indeed, given their preparation and proclivities, they probably ought not to be encouraged to even if they were so inclined.

What all of this seems to point to is the need for carefully staffed and structured crisis management mechanisms that can operate to some extent independently of top government leaders, yet at the same time be more closely integrated with national policy and strategic decision making generally. Such mechanisms should take full advantage of the ongoing revolution in computer and communications technologies to develop sophisticated data bases that can improve crisis prediction, identification and analysis as well as the operational aspects of crisis management; and they should be designed to couple core staffs as tightly as possible with responsible agency officials, operators in the field, comparable units in other governments and nongovernmental organizations, and experts and other resources in the private sector. While it is obviously unworkable and undesirable to have wholly autonomous crisis management capabilities in governments (or anywhere else), the American experience shows that there are also penalties to be paid in thrusting senior policy officials into the crisis management role, given the virtually inevitable lack of real preparation one should expect in such individuals and the steepness of the learning curve. The key requirement is to devise doctrine and procedures that will integrate political, strategic, and operational/crisis perspectives while preserving an appropriate balance among them.

It was only at a late stage in the Cold War that the United States approached having a system of the sort just described. In the early postwar years, crisis management in the White House was relatively informal and for the most part quite distinct from the process of national strategic planning carried out under the auspices of the National Security Council (NSC). With the sharp decline in the importance of the NSC system in the Kennedy-Johnson era, political and operational perspectives tended to dominate crisis management. In the Nixon administration, a crisis management committee (the "Washington Special Actions Group") was established within a revived NSC system in order to address what were seen to be serious deficiencies in US government performance in this area, and proved to be reasonably effective. However, it was not until the first Reagan administration that an effort was made to create a dedicated crisis management organization in the White House. What eventually became the Crisis Management Center (CMC) was an innovative undertaking intended to integrate intelligence, policy, and operational concerns from the vantage point of presidential decision making, utilizing for the first time advanced information processing and communications capabilities that were to be fully linked with key agencies and information resources throughout the US government. The CMC, with a substantial staff of its own but closely integrated with the staff and operations of the National Security Council, became fully functional in mid-1983 and played an important role in a number of crises over the next several years. Unfortunately, it never succeeded in carving out a secure bureaucratic niche, and eventually fell victim to the Iran-Contra scandal, which caused the White House to pull back from anything that could be perceived as an "operational" role in national security decision making.

In more recent years, the pendulum has begun to reverse direction in response to widely felt deficiencies in American policy and operations during the protracted crises in Somalia and Bosnia, with the NSC staff reasserting a central role in managing the interagency decision process in what are now often referred to as "complex contingencies." Nevertheless, all of this falls well short of a national crisis management capability of the kind the United States possessed briefly in the 1980s.

At the operational level, the great challenge for crisis management remains the disciplined and rapid coordination and integration of diverse governmental functions. The post Cold War strategic environment has if anything—contrary to what one might at first suppose—*sharpened* the problem of interagency coordination in crises, precisely by reducing the salience of crisis issues for political leaders and central administrative staffs. Under such circumstances, agencies tend to be left alone to operate according to bureaucratic imperatives and routine procedures. This is particularly true of military organizations, which tend to be especially jealous of their organizational integrity. But in an environment in which force can no longer be assumed to be *the* crucial instrument of crisis management, one in which military units are frequently expected to operate in subordinate roles in unfamiliar civilian contexts, crisis operations must increasingly involve not only the coordination but the active *integration* of civilian and military personnel and functions. Yet who is to do the integration, and more importantly, by what criteria?

The history of UN and NATO intervention in the Bosnian conflict is a clear demonstration of the continuing inadequacy of multilateral crisis operations in this vital area. While ad hoc efforts (particularly in and after the Gulf War as well as in Somalia) to foster civil-military integration have had some success, there is as yet insufficient awareness of the fundamental character of the problem. Unfortunately, the downsizing experienced by most Western military establishments over the last decade has all too often resulted in a drastic reduction in just those capabilities—special forces, foreign area and language qualified officers, civil affairs specialists, and the like—that are most needed and best suited for contemporary crisis operations. The example of highly effective organizations such as the Kuwait Task Force of 1990-1991 shows that hybrid civil-military structures can work well under the pressure of circumstances. What is needed now is a systematic effort on the part of the United States as well as its multilateral partners to develop interagency doctrine and associated command and control arrangements that would permit their routine use in post Cold War crises.

It must again be emphasized, however, that non-military factors will almost certainly continue to gain in importance in the management of contemporary crises. Domestic politics and public relations, public diplomacy, economics, and law-enforcement will likely all require increased attention in the handling of crises in the emerging security environment. Ways will have to be devised not only to better integrate these functions operationally with the more traditional instruments of statecraft, but also—and more importantly—to recast them in a more *strategic* form than they generally assume in the routine world of government bureaucracy. This is a challenge that should not be underestimated.

That crisis management is preeminently a mode of strategy, not an alternative to it, has been a major theme of the argument developed here. A fully adequate account of crisis management in the contemporary world would have to address an array of fundamental strategic issues which have been treated here only in passing if at all. Perhaps the most important practical lesson emerging from the foregoing analysis is the need for crisis management to be seen and to function as an extension of national strategic decision making processes rather than as an improvised substitute for them.

References

Alibek, K. and S. Handelman. (2000). *Biohazard: The Chilling True Story of the Largest Covert Biological Weapons Program in the World– Told from Inside by the Man Who Ran it*. Delta.

Appel, J. M. (2009). Is all fair in biological warfare? The controversy over genetically engineered biological weapons, *Journal of Medical Ethics*, Volume 35, pp. 429–432.

Adams, S. & Crawford, A. (2000). *World War II.* First edition. Printed in association with the Imperial War Museum. Eyewitness Books series. New York, Doring Kindersley Limited.

Barton A.H. (1969). *Communities in Disaster. A Sociological Analysis of Collective Stress Situations*. SI: Ward Lock

Chomsky, Noam. (2001). *Prospects for Peace in the Middle East*, page 2. Lecture.

Mikiso Hane. (2001). *Modern Japan: A Historical Survey*. Westview Press.

7

Managing Nuclear and Radiation Accidents

A nuclear and radiation accident is defined by the International Atomic Energy Agency as "an event that has led to significant consequences to people, the environment or the facility. Examples include lethal effects to individuals, large radioactivity release to the environment, or reactor core melt." The prime example of a "major nuclear accident" is one in which a reactor core is damaged and significant amounts of radiation are released, such as in the Chernobyl Disaster in 1986.

The impact of nuclear accidents has been a topic of debate practically since the first nuclear reactors were constructed. It has also been a key factor in public concern about nuclear facilities. Some technical measures to reduce the risk of accidents or to minimize the amount of radioactivity released to the environment have been adopted. Despite the use of such measures, "there have been many accidents with varying impacts as well near misses and incidents".

Benjamin K. Sovacool has reported that worldwide there have been 99 accidents at nuclear power plants. Fifty-seven accidents have occurred since the Chernobyl disaster, and 57% (56 out of 99) of all nuclear-related accidents have occurred in the USA. Serious nuclear power plant accidents include the Fukushima Daiichi nuclear disaster (2011), Chernobyl disaster (1986), Three Mile Island accident (1979), and the SL-1 accident (1961). Stuart Arm states, "apart from Chernobyl, no nuclear workers or members of the public have ever died as a result of exposure to radiation due to a commercial nuclear reactor incident."

Nuclear-powered submarine mishaps include the K-19 reactor accident (1961), the K-27 reactor accident (1968), and the K-431 reactor accident (1985). Serious radiation accidents include the Kyshtym disaster, Windscale fire, radiotherapy accident in Costa Rica, radiotherapy accident in Zaragoza, radiation accident in Morocco, Goiania accident, radiation accident in Mexico City, radiotherapy unit accident in Thailand, and the Mayapuri radiological accident in India

One of the worst nuclear accidents to date was the Chernobyl disaster which occurred in 1986 in Ukraine. That accident killed 30 people directly, as well as damaging approximately $7 billion of property. A study published in 2005 estimates that there will eventually be up to 4,000 additional cancer deaths related to the accident among those exposed to significant radiation levels. Radioactive fallout from the accident was concentrated in areas of Belarus, Ukraine and Russia. Approximately 350,000 people were forcibly resettled away from these areas soon after the accident.

Benjamin K. Sovacool has reported that worldwide there have been 99 accidents at nuclear power plants from 1952 to 2009 (defined as incidents that either resulted in the loss of human life or more than US$50,000 of property damage, the amount the US federal government uses to define major energy accidents that must be reported), totaling US$20.5 billion in property damages. Fifty-seven accidents have occurred since the Chernobyl disaster, and almost two-thirds (56 out of 99) of all nuclear-related accidents have occurred in the USA. There have been comparatively few fatalities associated with nuclear power plant accidents.

Accident Types

Criticality Accidents

A criticality accident (also sometimes referred to as an "excursion" or "power excursion") occurs when a nuclear chain reaction is accidentally allowed to occur in fissile material, such as enriched uranium or plutonium. The Chernobyl accident is an example of a criticality accident. This accident destroyed a reactor at the plant and left a large geographic area uninhabitable. In a smaller scale accident at Sarov a technician working with highly enriched uranium was irradiated while preparing an experiment involving a sphere of fissile material. The Sarov accident is interesting because the system remained critical for many days before it could be stopped, though safely located in a shielded experimental hall. This is an example of a limited scope accident where only a few people can be harmed, while no release of radioactivity into the environment occurred. A criticality accident with limited off site release of both radiation (gamma and neutron) and a very small release of radioactivity occurred at Tokaimura in 1999 during the production of enriched uranium fuel. Two workers died, a third was permanently injured, and 350 citizens were exposed to radiation.

Decay Heat

Decay heat accidents are where the heat generated by the radioactive decay causes harm. In a large nuclear reactor, a loss of coolant accident can damage the core: for example, at Three Mile Island a recently shutdown (SCRAMed) PWR reactor was left for a length of time without cooling water. As a result the nuclear fuel was damaged, and the core partially melted. The removal of the decay heat is a significant reactor safety concern, especially shortly after shutdown. Failure to remove decay heat may cause the reactor core temperature to rise to dangerous levels and has caused nuclear accidents. The heat removal is usually achieved through several redundant and diverse systems, and the heat is often dissipated to an 'ultimate heat sink' which has a large capacity and requires no active power, though this method is typically used after decay heat has reduced to a very small value. However, the main cause of release of radioactivity in the Three Mile Island accident was a pilot-operated relief valve on the primary loop which stuck in the open position. This caused the overflow tank into which it drained to rupture and release large amounts of radioactive cooling water into the containment building. In 2011, an earthquake and tsunami caused a loss of power to two plants in Fukushima, Japan, crippling the reactor as decay heat caused 90% of the fuel rods in the core of the Daiichi Unit 3 reactor to become uncovered. As of May 30, 2011, the removal of decay heat is still a cause for concern.

Transport

Transport accidents can cause a release of radioactivity resulting in contamination or shielding to be damaged resulting in direct irradiation. In Cochabamba a defective gamma radiography set was transported in a passenger bus as cargo. The gamma source was outside the shielding, and it irradiated some bus passengers. In the United Kingdom, it was revealed in a court case that in March 2002 a radiotherapy source was transported from Leeds to Sellafield with defective shielding. The shielding had a gap on the underside. It is thought that no human has been seriously harmed by the escaping radiation.

Equipment Failure

Equipment failure is one possible type of accident, recently at Bialystok in Poland the electronics associated with a particle accelerator used for the treatment of cancer suffered a malfunction. This then led to the overexposure of at least one patient. While the initial failure was the simple failure of a semiconductor diode, it set in motion a series of events which led to a radiation injury.A related cause of accidents is failure of control software, as in the cases involving the Therac-25 medical radiotherapy equipment: the elimination of a hardware safety interlock in a new design model exposed a previously undetected bug in the control software, which could lead to patients receiving massive overdoses under a specific set of conditions.

Human Error

Many of the major nuclear accidents have been directly attributable to operator or human error. This was obviously the case in the analysis of both the Chernobyl and TMI-2 accidents. At Chernobyl, a test procedure was being conducted prior to the accident. The leaders of the test permitted operators to disable and ignore key protection circuits and warnings that would have normally shut the reactor down. At TMI-2, operators permitted thousands of gallons of water to escape from the reactor plant before observing that the coolant pumps were behaving abnormally. The coolant pumps were thus turned off to protect the pumps, which in turn led to the destruction of the reactor itself as cooling was completely lost within the core.

A detailed investigation into SL-1 determined that one operator (perhaps inadvertently) manually pulled the 84-pound (38 kg) central control rod out about 26 inches rather than the maintenance procedure's intention of about 4 inches.

An assessment conducted by the Commissariat à l'Énergie Atomique (CEA) in France concluded that no amount of technical innovation can eliminate the risk of human-induced errors associated with the operation of nuclear power plants. Two types of mistakes were deemed most serious: errors committed during field operations, such as maintenance and testing, that can cause an accident; and human errors made during small accidents that cascade to complete failure.

In 1946 Canadian Manhattan Project physicist Louis Slotin performed a risky experiment known as "tickling the dragon's tail" which involved two hemispheres of neutron-reflective beryllium being brought together around a plutonium core to bring it to criticality. Against operating procedures, the hemispheres were separated only by a screwdriver. The screwdriver slipped and set off a chain reaction criticality accident filling the room with harmful radiation and a flash of blue light (caused by excited, ionized air particles returning to their unexcited states). Slotin reflexively separated the hemispheres in reaction to the heat flash and blue light, preventing further irradiation of several co-workers present in the room. However Slotin absorbed a lethal dose of the radiation and died nine days afterwards. The infamous plutonium mass used in the experiment was referred to as the demon core.

Lost Source

Lost source accidents, also referred to as an orphan source are incidents in which a radioactive source is lost, stolen or abandoned. The source then might cause harm to humans. For example, in 1996 sources were left behind by the Soviet army in Lilo, Georgia. Another case occurred at Yanango where a radiography source was lost, also at Samut Prakarn a phosphorus teletherapy source was lost and at Gilan in Iran a radiography source harmed a welder. The best known example of this type of event is the Goiânia accident which occurred in Brazil.

The International Atomic Energy Agency has provided guides for scrap metal collectors on what a sealed source might look like. The scrap metal industry is the one where lost sources are most likely to be found.

Trafficking in Radioactive and Nuclear Materials

Information reported to the International Atomic Energy Agency (IAEA) shows "a persistent problem with the illicit trafficking in nuclear and other radioactive materials, thefts, losses and other unauthorized activities". From 1993 to 2006, the IAEA confirmed 1080 illicit trafficking incidents reported by participating countries. Of the 1080 confirmed incidents, 275 incidents involved unauthorized possession and related criminal activity, 332 incidents involved theft or loss of nuclear or other radioactive materials, 398 incidents involved other unauthorized activities, and in 75 incidents the reported information was not sufficient to determine the category of incident. Several hundred additional incidents have been reported in various open sources, but are not yet confirmed.

Nuclear Safety

Nuclear safety covers the actions taken to prevent nuclear and radiation accidents or to limit their consequences. This covers nuclear power plants as well as all other nuclear facilities, the transportation of nuclear materials, and the use and storage of nuclear materials for medical, power, industry, and military uses.

The nuclear power industry has improved the safety and performance of reactors, and has proposed new safer (but generally untested) reactor designs but there is no guarantee that the reactors will be designed, built and operated correctly. Mistakes do occur and the designers of reactors at Fukushima in Japan did not anticipate that a tsunami generated by an earthquake would disable the backup systems that were supposed to stabilize the reactor after the earthquake. According to UBS AG, the Fukushima I nuclear accidents have cast doubt on whether even an advanced economy like Japan can master nuclear safety. Catastrophic scenarios involving terrorist attacks are also conceivable.

An interdisciplinary team from MIT have estimated that given the expected growth of nuclear power from 2005 – 2055, at least four serious nuclear accidents would be expected in that period. To date, there have been five serious accidents (core damage) in the world since 1970 (one at Three Mile Island in 1979; one at Chernobyl in 1986; and three at Fukushima-Daiichi in 2011), corresponding to the beginning of the operation of generation II reactors. This leads to on average one serious accident happening every eight years worldwide. Nuclear weapon safety, as well as the safety of military research involving nuclear materials, is generally handled by agencies different from those that oversee civilian safety, for various reasons, including secrecy. There are ongoing concerns about terrorist groups acquiring nuclear bomb-making material.

Strategies for Nuclear Emergency Management

As India's nuclear energy programme grows in both the power and non-power sectors, the nuclear emergency management approach in the country will be so formulated that the radiation exposure to occupational workers and the public and the release into the environment are not significantly beyond the permissible limits. Towards this goal, the existing nuclear emergency management approach in the country will be periodically reviewed and strengthened, as necessary, based on the following four-pronged strategy.

i) Support the nuclear emergency management framework on some prominent mainstays of strength like prevention, mitigation, compliance with regulatory requirements, capacity building, etc. The existing DAE framework, needs to be further strengthened, wherever necessary, and established in all future facilities in line with the guidelines being issued in this document.

ii) Strengthen the existing legal framework through various legal and regulatory means.

iii) Institutionalise the DM framework by identifying the various agencies with their respective responsibilities in a people-centric, bottom-up approach.

iv) Implement the nuclear emergency management framework through close monitoring of the existing action plans or those to bc prepared at the national, state and district levels in the country for future facilities in line with the guidelines being issued.

NUCLEAR EMERGENCY MANAGEMENT FRAMEWORK

The existing nuclear emergency management framework will be periodically reviewed and further strengthened by the following strategic supports, where highest priority is assigned to the prevention of nuclear emergency at any level in the country.

Prevention of Nuclear Emergencies

To prevent the occurrence of a nuclear emergency in the facilities, all engineered systems are built and operated by adopting the best available technologies and practices during the various phases of the life cycle of the facilities, viz., siting, design, construction, commissioning, operation and decommissioning. Following the defence-in-depth approach, all safety systems are built with adequate redundancy and diverse working principles.

Nuclear power plants/facilities in India have been built on the basis of the above approach. However, sustained efforts will continue to improve the situation further through the induction of improved safety systems and state-of-the-art technologies.

Emphasis on Prevention (Risk Reduction) and Mitigation Measures

Prevention (Risk Reduction)

This strategic pillar aims at reducing the frequency of occurrence of nuclear emergencies in general, and ensuring that nuclear incidents/ accidents do not escalate to a disaster level, in particular. Nuclear technology has continuously endeavoured to improve such features. Risk reduction calls for the implementation of transparent, comprehensive, efficient and effective risk management strategies to take care of, inter alia, the health and environmental effects along with the social and economic factors.

Mitigation measures

While the design and operating conditions of nuclear power plants ensure that the likelihood of malfunctions/failures leading to unsafe conditions is very small, yet such conditions are postulated and safety systems provided to minimise the impact of these failures.

Inbuilt safety measures, including biological shields, safety systems and interlocks, safety audits, adherence to a safety culture combined with operational and administrative safety procedures prevent the chances of radiation accidents in the nuclear facilities in India and mitigate the impact in the event of an accident, if any.

However, efforts will continue for further improvement of safety measures in reactor systems.

Compliance with Regulatory Requirements

The prevention or mitigation of the impact of a nuclear emergency must be ensured by compliance with the applicable rules, standards and codes in all the activities involved in nuclear fuel cycle facilities as well as the organisations/ units using radioisotopes or radiation sources in any form, so that the use of ionising radiation and nuclear technology in India causes neither undue risk to the health of occupational workers and the public nor any adverse impact on the environment.

The AERB is the nuclear regulatory authority in India which, as per the legal framework of Atomic Energy Act, 1962, has the mandate for issuance of licenses to nuclear and radiation facilities upon ensuring compliance with the applicable standards and codes.The AERB issues a large number of standards, codes and guides for various practices which must be strictly adhered to, for the prevention or mitigation of the impacts of any nuclear/radiological emergency. The codes issued by the AERB for various applications provide for a graded approach for regulatory control of a facility depending on the level of radiological hazard involved.

Nuclear Emergency Preparedness

Preparedness is 'getting ready' to respond to an emergency and it encompasses all DM activities, viz., planning, developing, training, exercising, maintaining capacity, etc., prior to the emergency that are essential to ensure a fast and effective response capability in the event of an actual emergency situation. It envisages the development and maintenance of such a capability in a well-structured and well-rehearsed fashion with seamless coordination among the various agencies involved. It does not have the pressure of time and stress associated with responding in an actual emergency.

The development of a preparedness programme for responding to nuclear emergencies is very essential even for these 'very low probability' emergency situations. It is recognised that an emergency preparedness and response system is in place, but its adequacy will be reviewed periodically.

Similarly, radiological emergencies arising in the country due to accidents involving radioactive sources are to be minimised by having strict administrative control. This ensures safety and security of the sources.

However, with the increasing use of a large number of radioactive sources in various applications or during their transportation, it is recognised that the adequacy of an emergency preparedness and response system will be reviewed periodically to counter the new threats.

The country should be prepared for responding to any of the five major categories of nuclear emergencies, viz., (i) accident in nuclear facilities, (ii) 'criticality' accident, (iii) accident during transportation of radioactive materials, (iv) emergency arising out of an RDD and (v) nuclear attack (which has been dealt with separately).

Capacity Development

Capacity development is an important component in the preparedness of nuclear/ radiological emergencies and it entails all those activities which are necessary to build and sustain the performance, across all domains of DM continuum, to ensure an effective emergency response. This includes a variety of time-bound programmes that would need to be taken up by all stakeholders for all-round development of the community and infrastructure in terms of trained manpower, knowledge enhancement, state-of-the-art monitoring systems and protective gear, communication, transport including technical upgradation of all those concerned with the management of nuclear/radiological emergencies/disasters.

Nuclear Emergency Response

Any action taken to mitigate the consequences during an actual emergency situation is termed as response. It always takes place under pressure of time with associated stress for the emergency responders. Even though an efficient response system would centre around effective utilisation of all available and mobilised resources by well-informed, well-trained and well-equipped responders for any given type of nuclear/radiological emergency, the response will be commensurate with the severity of the event.

Legal and Regulatory Means

Legal Framework of the Atomic Energy Act, 1962

The Atomic Energy Act, 1962 is the main Nuclear Legislation in India. It was enacted to provide for the development, control and use of atomic energy for the welfare of the people of India and for other peaceful purposes and for matters connected therewith. The Act and the rules framed thereunder, provide the main legislative and regulatory framework pertaining to atomic energy. The DAE implements the provisions of the Atomic Energy Act, 1962 and controls the use of atomic energy in the country. The AERB regulates the safety provision envisaged in the Atomic Energy Act to ensure that the use of ionising radiations and nuclear energy in India does not cause undue risk to public health and the environment.

Private Participation in Future Nuclear Power Programmes

In the future, private entrepreneurs may play an important role in India's nuclear power programme. The utilisation of nuclear science and technology being quite complex and multi-disciplinary in nature, calls for the availability of a strong technological base with a large pool of highly skilled and experienced professionals to design, construct and operate any nuclear facility as per the stipulated safety standards of the AERB. Accordingly, while considering the proposal for private participation in India's growing nuclear energy programme, the AERB will evaluate, as is being done in the case of the Nuclear Power Corporation of India Ltd. (NPCIL) and BHAVINI, the suitability or otherwise of all such proposals by detailed and careful assessment of the party in terms of its techno-legal considerations right at the preliminary stage so as to ensure not only its technical capability for design and construction as per the codes and standards but also its capability for compliance with the safety rules and regulations stipulated by the AERB during the entire lifetime of the nuclear power plant.

Strengthening Disaster Management through Legislation in Parliament

To replace the erstwhile reactive and response-centric approach with a proactive and holistic DM in the country, the Government of India, backed by the unanimous support of all the political parties in Parliament, took a path-breaking decision by promulgating a new Disaster Management Act in December 2005 that has provided DM activities in India a statutory backing. This DM Act ushers in a paradigm shift in the DM framework in the country by adopting a holistic approach where prevention, mitigation and preparedness activities are to be addressed to as multi-disciplinary tasks spanning all sectors of development along with further improvement of response systems through well-trained, fully rehearsed and better equipped responders. Broadly, the enactment of the DM Act has stressed on the following:

i) Mainstreaming the disaster concerns into the development planning process.

ii) Promoting a culture of prevention and preparedness by centre staging DM as an overriding priority at all levels of development activity.

iii) Ensuring mitigation measures based on state-of-the-art technologies that are also environment friendly.

iv) Ensuring prompt and efficient rescue and relief operations through a caring approach towards the needs of the vulnerable sections of the society.

v) Undertaking all reconstruction activities as opportunities to build back better which will go a long way in establishing disaster resilience in the society.

Institutionalisation of Nuclear Emergency Framework

For the success of a nuclear emergency management programme, in addition to the task of identifying the agencies at different levels, it is essential to dovetail their respective responsibilities into the DM framework.

For handling any type of disaster in the country, the following four types of organisations have been instituted by the Act to support, interact, coordinate and complement each other at all levels of operations.

i) The creation of the NDMA at the national level under the chairmanship of the Prime Minister of India.

ii) The creation of State Disaster Management Authorities (SDMAs) at the state level under the chairmanship of the chief ministers.

iii) The creation of District Disaster Management Authorities (DDMAs) at the district level under the chairmanship of district magistrates/collectors with the elected representative as the co-chairperson.

iv) The creation of Local Authorities for mitigation and response.

NDMA, as the apex body, is responsible for each of the three phases of the DM continuum with eight major responsibilities, viz., pre-disaster (prevention, mitigation and preparedness), during the disaster (response, rescue and relief) that have been delegated to be carried out by the NCMC/National Executive Committee (NEC) on its behalf and post-disaster (rehabilitation and reconstruction) scenarios. NDMA will be assisted by NEC, as per the provision of the DM Act, as the implementing agency for the plans/programmes of NDMA.

The national guidelines are to be implemented through establishing appropriate DM plans at all levels of administration. NEC, with technical support from DAE (the nodal technical agency for nuclear/radiological emergency/disaster), will prepare the detailed national plan for management of nuclear emergencies in consultation with the various stakeholders. The most crucial stakeholder is the community at large, which is affected by any nuclear emergency/disaster.

All the central ministries will make their own DM plans, which are to be approved by NDMA. Similarly, all the states/Union Territories (UTs) will make their own DM plans in consultation with the district authorities. These plans will be based on the NDMA guidelines and in accordance with the national DM policy and plan.

Monitoring the Implementation of Action Plans

Planning, execution, monitoring and evaluation are the four steps of the comprehensive implementation cycle of the various action plans to be prepared on the basis of the guidelines being issued. While the nuclear emergency management framework for NPPs and transportation accidents are already in place, similar plans are to be prepared at different levels of administration in the country through an extensive consultative process for other possible scenarios in the public domain.

The detailed documents prepared will also specify the various indicators of progress to be adopted for enabling transparent monitoring for an objective and independent review of the implementation of nuclear/radiological emergency action plans. Specialists in Nuclear Science and Technology will be inducted at all levels of administration for formulation of the plans and their effective monitoring during implementation. In particular, implementing the National Disaster Management Guidelines: Management of Nuclear and Radiological Emergencies (NDMG-NRE) activities can be smooth and successful if a single window system is adopted for execution and documentation of each of the above four phases, i.e., by having one person accountable for each of the above four phases of NDMG-NRE activities at each of the stakeholder ministries, departments, state governments, related agencies and organisations.

Highlights

Some of the highlights are given below:

i) The existing nuclear emergency management framework will be periodically reviewed and further strengthened by some strategic supports, where the highest priority is assigned to the prevention of a nuclear emergency at any level in the country.

ii) While the design and operating conditions of nuclear power plants ensure that the likelihood of malfunctions/failures leading to unsafe conditions is very small, yet such conditions are postulated and safety systems provided to minimise the impact of these failures.

vi) interlocks, safety audits, adherence to a safety culture combined with operational and administrative safety procedures prevent the chances of radiation accidents in the nuclear facilities in India and mitigate the impact in the event of an accident, if any.

iii) The prevention or mitigation of the impact of a nuclear emergency must be ensured by compliance with the applicable rules, standards and codes in all the activities involved in nuclear fuel cycle facilities as well as the organisations/units using radioisotopes or radiation sources in any form, so that the use of ionising radiation and nuclear technology in India causes neither undue risk to the health of the occupational workers and the public nor any adverse impact on the environment.

iv) The country will be prepared for responding to any of the five major categories of nuclear emergencies, viz., (a) accident in nuclear facilities, (b) 'criticality' accident, (c) accident during transportation of radioactive materials, (d) emergency arising out of an RDD and (e) nuclear attack (which has been dealt with separately) to ensure an effective emergency response.

v) Capacity development is an important component in the preparedness of nuclear/radiological emergencies and this includes a variety of time-bound programmes for the all-round development of the community and infrastructure in terms of trained manpower, knowledge enhancement, state-of-the-art monitoring systems and protective gear, communication, transport including technical upgradation of all those concerned with the management of nuclear/radiological emergencies/disasters.

vi) The national guidelines are to be implemented by preparing appropriate DM plans at all levels of administration. NEC, with the technical support of DAE (the nodal technical agency for nuclear/ radiological emergency/disaster), will prepare the detailed national plan for management of nuclear emergency in consultation with the various stakeholders.

All the central ministries will make their own DM plans, which are to be approved by NDMA. Similarly, all the states/UTs will make their own DM plans in consultation with the district authorities. These plans will be based on the NDMA guidelines and in accordance with the national DM policy and plan.

vii) Planning, execution, monitoring and evaluation are the four steps of a comprehensive implementation cycle of the various action plans to be prepared on the basis of the guidelines being issued. While the nuclear emergency management framework for NPPs and for transportation accidents are already in place, similar plans are to be prepared at different levels of administration in the country through an extensive consultative process for other possible scenarios in the public domain.

Emergency Structure

The Government of India has identified DAE as the nodal agency for providing the necessary technical inputs to the national or local authorities for responding to any nuclear or radiological emergency in the public domain. The Ministry of Home Affairs (MHA) is the nodal ministry in such emergencies. For this purpose, a Crisis Management Group (CMG) has been functioning since 1987 at DAE. This Group is chaired by the Additional Secretary, DAE, and has on board expert members from different units of DAE and AERB. Each member has an alternate member and CMG is backed by resource agencies of various units of DAE. These resource agencies are expected to provide advice and assistance in the areas of radiation protection and measurement, medical assistance to persons exposed to high radiation doses, communication support, seismological inputs and help in the dissemination of information to the public.

In the event of any nuclear/radiological emergency in the public domain, CMG is immediately activated and it coordinates with the local authority in the affected area and all the concerning authorities at the centre (NCMC/ NEC/NDMA) to ensure that the necessary technical inputs are available to respond to the nuclear/radiological emergency.

Regulatory Body

The basic regulatory framework for safety of all activities related to the atomic energy programme and the use of ionising radiation in India is derived from Sections 3 (e) (i), (ii) and (iii), 16, 17 and 23 of the Atomic Energy Act, 1962. The AERB carries out certain regulatory and safety functions under these Sections of the Act. The mandate for AERB, inter alia, includes:

i) Powers to lay down safety standards and frame rules and regulations with regard to the regulatory and safety requirements envisaged under the Atomic Energy Act, 1962.

ii) Powers of a Competent Authority to enforce the rules and regulations framed under the Atomic Energy Act, 1962 for radiation safety in the country.

iii) Authority to administer the provisions of the Factories Act, 1948 for ensuring industrial safety of the units of DAE as per Section 23 of the Atomic Energy Act, 1962 and enforce the rules and regulations promulgated there under.

Under the given mandate, the AERB carries out, inter alia, the following functions:

i) Develop safety policies in nuclear, radiological and industrial safety areas.

ii) Develop safety codes, guides and standards for siting, designing, construction, commissioning, operation and decommissioning of different types of nuclear and radiological facilities.

iii) Grant consent for siting, constructing, commissioning and decommissioning after appropriate safety review and assessment, for the nuclear and radiological facilities.

iv) Ensure compliance with the regulatory requirements during all stages of consenting through a system of review and assessment, regulatory inspection and enforcement.

v) Prescribe the recommended limits of radiation exposure to occupational workers and members of the public and approve acceptable limits of environmental releases of radioactive substances.

vi) Review the emergency preparedness plans for nuclear and radiological facilities and transportation of large radioactive sources, irradiated fuel and fissile material.

vii) Review the training programmes, qualifications and licensing policies for personnel of nuclear and radiological facilities and prescribe the syllabi for training of personnel in safety aspects at all levels.

viii) Take such steps as necessary to keep the public informed of major issues of radiological safety significance.

ix) Promote research and development efforts in the areas of safety.

x) Maintain liaison with statutory bodies in the country as well as abroad, regarding safety measures.

It is emphasised that the AERB, which oversees nuclear and radiological safety in the country, has the powers to not only licence the operation of a facility but also the power to order partial or full shutdown of any facility that violates its guidelines.

The AERB has been playing a very crucial role in the prevention of nuclear/radiological accidents by ensuring that proper safety design features and operating procedures in all nuclear and radiation facilities are in place.

On-Site and Off-Site Preparedness

Elaborate and reliable safety systems are in place in all the nuclear facilities in India which are functional during the lifetime of the facility. As a matter of abundant caution, even though highly unlikely, certain 'beyond design basis accidents' are also postulated, which can lead to a radiation emergency in the public domain. Accordingly, while preparing the response plans to handle local emergencies within the plant, plans have also been drawn up for handling emergencies in the public domain, i.e., 'Off-site Emergencies'.

Based on the radiological conditions and their consequences, emergencies at nuclear facilities are categorised as emergency standby, personnel emergency, plant emergency, on-site emergency and off-site emergency. For the first three types of emergencies, in the order of severity which are foreseen as possible, though with very low probability, detailed plant-specific emergency response plans are already in place. In all these situations, the consequences of the accident are expected to be limited to the plant only.

Similarly, for the next higher level, viz., on-site emergency, where the consequences of an accident are not likely to cross the site boundary, a detailed response plan does exist. This emergency does not lead to any radiation release in the public domain.

The last type of emergency scenario, even though with a very low possibility of radioactive releases in the public domain, is off-site emergency for which detailed response plans are put in place by the district magistrate/ collector of the area in coordination with the plant authorities.

Each nuclear power station of the present generation has an Exclusion Zone surrounding the power station in which no habitation is permitted and this area is under the administrative control of the plant authority. An area of larger radius outside the Exclusion Zone is declared as the Sterilised Zone where growth and development is restricted. The Emergency Planning Zone (EPZ) extends further beyond the Sterilised Zone.

It has been made mandatory by the AERB for all nuclear power plant operators to have comprehensive and well laid out plans to deal with all the above types of emergencies. It may be mentioned that the AERB does not permit the operation of a new power plant until preparedness plans are in place for the postulated emergency scenarios. Barring the off-site emergency response plan, the other plans fall within the domain of responsibility of the facility operator and the AERB has to approve these plans.

As per statutory requirements, the local district administration is responsible for drawing up and rehearsing the off-site emergency plan in coordination with the facility operator. It is also mandatory for the power plant operators to periodically rehearse these plans by way of exercises and based on the feedback and experience, take corrective measures. As the first stage of the trigger mechanism, CMG, DAE, and the resource agencies are alerted even when a plant or site emergency exercise is conducted.

During off-site emergency exercises, which are conducted as per international norms once in two years at all nuclear power plant sites, all the members and alternate members of CMG, along with other key DAE officials in Mumbai, are alerted. In addition, the Secretary (Security) in the Cabinet Secretariat who is the contact person for DAE with NCMC, and the Secretary, Ministry of Environment and Forests, are also alerted during the off-site emergency exercises. In these exercises, the district administration is the key participant and the reports of the independent observers (from the AERB, NPCIL and CMG) are used as a feedback for further improvement of the emergency response system.

Emergency Plans at Radiation Facilities

All radiation facilities which have a potential for high exposures, depending upon the envisaged emergency scenarios, have emergency plans in place which include response actions and details of other agencies whose assistance will be sought. The competent authority (AERB), prior to issuance of licence, reviews these emergency plans of the facility. Barring the case of a loss of radioactive source, other scenarios do not have the potential to result in radiation exposures in the public domain. In case of any loss of source, the facility is required to immediately inform the AERB, CMG and the police.

The AERB has also laid down guidelines for the safe use of sources and safe operation of facilities which are to be adopted and followed by all the facilities using radioisotopes/radiation sources. These include safe design of the equipment used, its operation within the permissible range of parameters and availability of a suitably qualified Radiological Safety Officer (RSO) who is responsible for ensuring safe practices. The prescribed procedures also describe what will be done in the event of any radiation emergency—the precautions to be taken, the agencies to be notified, etc. The CMG, DAE, would also be available to direct the technical resources of DAE to the accident site and to assist the local authorities in handling the emergency situation.

Emergency Plans to Respond to Transportation Accidents

The AERB has laid down guidelines to be adopted for the transport of radioactive materials and emergency response plans for accidents during their transportation. The consignor of the material is responsible for ensuring that the prescribed safety procedures are followed. The AERB's safety code covers the design of the transport container, its handling and loading, procedures for transporting and unloading, including the procedures to handle any accident en-route. The SOPs also indicate what will be done in the event of any radiation emergency—the precautions to be taken, the agencies to be notified, etc. The CMG, DAE, will also be available to direct the technical resources of DAE to any location and to assist the transporters/ local authorities in responding to the emergency situation.

Medical Preparedness for Nuclear Emergencies

In each constituent unit of DAE, a few doctors have been dedicated and given the necessary training in the medical management of radiation emergencies. All nuclear power plants and the Bhabha Atomic Research Centre (BARC) are equipped with radiation monitoring instruments, have personnel decontamination centres and the necessary stock of antidote medicines and specific de-corporation agents for typical radioisotopes.

A few hospitals in the country are also equipped with the facilities required for bone marrow transplantation, which will be useful in managing cases of acute whole body irradiation. Further, doctors from various defence units and other organisations in the country are also to be trained in the medical management of nuclear emergencies.

Emergency Response Teams

In addition to the basic training for teams of the National Disaster Response Force (NDRF), the training of 'First Responders' and Training of the

Trainers (TOT) are being imparted by BARC. Further, BARC is also providing active help in imparting training to Quick Reaction Teams (QRTs) of the paramilitary forces. It has also been regularly conducting week-long training courses on Planning and Preparedness for Response to Radiological Emergencies (PPRRE) since 1999 at the College of Military Engineering (CME), Pune, for defence Chemical, Biological, Radiological and Nuclear (CBRN) officers, during which the participants are also trained in aerial survey for quick assessment of radiological impact in case of a nuclear/ radiological emergency. Some units of the Defence Research and Development Establishment (DRDE) are also imparting training to these personnel in nuclear emergency preparedness.

Emergency Response Centres

As a basic regulatory requirement, emergency preparedness exists at all nuclear and radiation facilities to respond to any on-site or off-site emergency in their areas. But to handle radiological emergencies arising from a transport accident or from the movement/ handling of 'orphan sources' (radioactive sources that have lost regulatory control are called 'orphan sources') or due to malevolent acts like explosion of an RDD, Radiation Exposure Device (RED) or IND any time or anywhere in the country, a network of 18 units of Emergency Response Centres (ERCs) has been established by BARC, DAE. This number is far too inadequate and will be enhanced. This network is basically meant for responding to such emergencies and also providing timely advice and guidance to first responders at the state and national levels. These ERCs are equipped with radiation monitoring instruments, protective gear and other supporting infrastructure. Many units of nuclear Emergency Response Teams (ERTs), consisting of personnel from different DAE units, are also being raised. The centralised agency, called the CMG, at DAE coordinates the nuclear/radiological emergency management activities not only by activating these ERCs and ERTs but also by mobilising resources from all DAE facilities at the time of crises.

Monitoring and Protective Equipment

A variety of hardware for radiation monitoring along with impact assessment software for the management of nuclear disasters have been developed at BARC. Similarly, a number of smart radiation monitoring systems like Environmental Radiation Monitor with Navigational Aid (ERMNA), Aerial Gamma Spectrometry System (AGSS), Mobile Gamma Spectrometry

System (MGSS), Indian Environmental Radiation Monitoring Network (IERMON), Compact Aerial Radiation Monitoring System (CARMS), Indian Real-time On-line Decision Support System (IRODOS), etc., have also been developed. Some of these systems can quickly monitor and scan a contaminated area, process the data and present it in a colour-coded graphical format [superimposed on a Geographic Information System (GIS) map of the affected area] to help the decision-making process.

For procurement of essential radiation monitoring and protective gear for NDRF, civil defence agencies and other defence forces, BARC is assisting in preparing the technical specifications. The instruments/protective gear so procured will help these agencies in building up their capacity as 'first responders' to any nuclear/radiological emergency in the public domain.

Based on the utilisation of various types of detectors, the Defence Research and Development Organisation (DRDO) has also developed a number of instruments, like the high-range radiation monitor for field use, personal dose monitor, etc. They have also developed mobile systems like nuclear field laboratory, CBRN reconnaissance vehicle and reconnaissance laboratory.

Public Awareness

Public awareness plays a key role in the emergency preparedness and response plans for any type of emergency/disaster where the participation/ role of the public is of prime importance. The fact that one cannot see, feel or smell the presence of radiation, coupled with a general lack of credible and authentic information to the public at large about radiation and radiation emergencies and the wide publicity given to any nuclear/radiation-related incident, has resulted in several erroneous perceptions about nuclear technology. Not surprisingly, most people perceive that any small nuclear/ radiation-related incident will lead to a situation like Hiroshima or Nagasaki, or the Chernobyl accident.

To educate the people about the beneficial aspects of nuclear radiation and to remove their misgivings about it, the authorities of nuclear fuel cycle facilities in general, and that of nuclear power stations in particular, are actively involved in carrying out regular public awareness programmes for people living in the vicinity of these facilities. People are invited and taken on guided tours of the nuclear power stations, made conversant with the basics of radiation protection, safety limits, safety practices, and the dos and don'ts during a nuclear emergency. The station authorities also make visits to the surrounding villages and population centres to create awareness of the same. Good coordination is also maintained with the district officials. Prior to any off-site emergency exercise, awareness programmes are specially conducted for the public officials, making them conversant with their responsibilities during any off-site emergency.

DAE also participates in many exhibitions in the country, and puts up stalls and interactive models to create awareness among the public about the benefits and safety aspects of the nuclear energy programme.

Research and Development

Research and development related to radiation effects on health and on the environment has been continuing in various research wings of DAE, DRDO and certain universities in the country. Considerable fundamental knowledge has been gained and certain technologies have been developed for radiation detection and measurement.

Research on the development of anticancer drugs and radio-protectors is in progress at various institutions in the country. Nuclear establishments have put in place dosimetry procedures and regulatory standards for safe operation of nuclear facilities. R&D needs to be continued in the area of processing and disposal of high-level radioactive wastes.

Education and Knowledge Management

At present, practically no education is imparted at any level on nuclear/ radiological emergencies in the national educational system. It goes against one of the basic concepts of good emergency response, which envisages that the culture of preparedness has to be imbibed right from childhood in all sections of the society. The basics of radiation, radioactivity and the use of nuclear radiation in day-to-day life (with its beneficial aspects) should be taught in schools and colleges. Once people are sensitised about this subject, it will help in removing prejudices/misconceptions of the general public about nuclear radiation/ programmes and they will treat a nuclear/ radiological emergency like any other type of natural or man-made emergency.

Further, presently there is no mechanism for maintaining a knowledge base or case studies in the public domain on the events of previous emergencies and their consequences. As a result, the lessons that should have been learnt from the handlings of those emergencies have been lost sight of.

Enhancing Public Awareness

In general, there is very limited public awareness about radiation emergencies. Even the intelligentsia have misconceptions about nuclear energy in general. Ever since the reactor accidents at Three Mile Island and Chernobyl, any news of a nuclear/radiological emergency has always been of great interest that generates misconceptions in the minds of the public. The sensationalisation of such news by the media has also erroneously caused a perception that any radiation or nuclear emergency will result in cancer or death.

Such lack of public awareness is a major constraint in handling and objectively responding to these emergencies. To overcome this, sincere and concerted efforts are needed to create awareness amongst the general public with the target audience of school and college students, teachers, technocrats and government officials.

The fear in the minds of the public that even a small accident in nuclear facilities will lead to a situation like Hiroshima/Nagasaki, can be removed only through proper awareness generation and training programmes.

People living in the vicinity of nuclear power plants, and particularly the student community, have been trained on these aspects to some extent. The existing atmosphere of openness and transparency will be continued and promoted further around the nuclear facilities covering a larger segment of the population.

Training of Stakeholders

There is much work to be done with regard to the training of all the agencies involved in the management of radiation emergencies. These include education of senior public functionaries like the district or state-level officials who would manage a radiation emergency as well as the first responders. This would also include RSOs, civil defence personnel and home guards, police and fire and emergency services personnel and medical professionals.

Strengthening the Institutional Frameworks

It is well known that effective coordination mechanisms amongst the different agencies involved is the key to an efficient emergency response mechanism. This requires formal institutional frameworks and linkages, with the necessary statutory backing. Some of these issues pertain to the implementation of a regulatory and enforcement mechanism by the AERB and a coordination mechanism between DAE and the local/district officials who would be responding to any radiation emergency in the public domain.

Regulatory and Enforcement Issues

The AERB, the national regulatory authority, has been regulating the nuclear and radiation facilities in the country very effectively and has, over the years, issued a large number of codes, standards and guides. These cover the various activities relating to the nuclear fuel cycle as well as for radiation applications in medicine, industry, agriculture and research.

Till now, all activities pertaining to the nuclear fuel cycle (controlled and operated by DAE) have been handled by DAE in a safe manner because of the sharing of a common safety culture among the various units of DAE.

High-strength radioactive sources are extensively used in industry and hospitals in India. In the case of industry, these sources are mainly used for radiography, where there is a high potential of loss of sources. In this area, there is an urgent need to further strengthen the regulatory and security aspects by the AERB.

In the event of the private sector getting involved in the nuclear power programme, it might be required of the regulatory authority to ensure that the necessary knowledge base exists in the concerned private industry for building and operating the nuclear facility as per the stipulated safety standards of the AERB.

Formalising the Coordination Mechanism with Public Authorities

While DAE, as the nodal technical agency, has a system in place to respond to requests for assistance to any radiological/nuclear event in the public domain, the coordination mechanism of DAE with each state is yet to be formalised (the formal linkages of the state/ district administration with CMG, DAE, and the nearest ERC, need to be strengthened significantly). Similarly, there is also a need to establish the linkages of SDMAs/DDMAs with the nearest NDRF battalion. This would require the state/district administration to develop their respective emergency plans and link up with the ERCs of DAE and NDRF battalions in the neighbourhood. Presently the empowerment of local administrative authorities is not adequate.

Action Levels in Radiological Dispersal Device

In case of a large-scale nuclear disaster from, say a nuclear attack, the population will be exposed to the effects of blast (shock) wave, burns and fires along with effects of prompt as well as delayed radiations. As a result of all these effects, rescue and relief measures will be highly demanding in terms of the availability of adequate trained manpower as well as advanced instruments/ equipment. It is important to note that the nature of relief measures would be different in many ways from those carried out in natural disasters like fire, floods, earthquakes, etc. In a nuclear emergency/disaster, however, the persons carrying out the relief work are also likely to be exposed to both high doses of radiation and/or high levels of contamination which, if not controlled, may affect their health as well as their potential to carry out the relief work effectively.

In the light of the above, a question that is frequently asked is about the radiation dose levels at which intervention is required for various actions (like sheltering, iodine prophylaxis, evacuation, etc.) in the case of nuclear disasters. The availability of this information on the averatable dose level is important not only for the public but also for the rescue and relief workers. In addition to the intervention levels, the action levels that will be needed to control the consumption of contaminated food items in the affected areas is another issue. These values are presently not available either for an RDD or a nuclear disaster and are needed to be generated because these are essential in respect of both (i) the members of the relief and rescue teams, and (ii) the public.

Strengthening the Infrastructure

Network of Emergency Response Centres

At present, 18 ERCs of BARC are available for giving the necessary technical support to local authorities for responding to any radiation emergency. For a large and densely populated country like India, this is not considered adequate.In fact, several major metros and other vulnerable locations will need to have ERCs established in their areas. Local civil defence, police, fire brigade, hospitals and other agencies also need to develop liaison with these ERCs. Some of the major functions of ERCs are:

i) To detect any radiation-related abnormal situation in a suspected area by detection and monitoring the radiation and to continuously assess the situation.

ii) To keep an inventory of radiation monitoring instruments and Personal Protective Gear (PPG).

iii) To provide training to first responders, administrative staff of SDMAs/ DDMAs and the technical staff of government agencies in handling nuclear/radiological emergencies.

iv) To provide technical advice to first responders and the concerned local authorities in handling a nuclear/ radiological emergency; to guide them further in resource mobilisation and in the optimum utilisation of available manpower and equipment in case of a nuclear/radiological emergency.

Enhancing Security Systems

Strengthening Border Controls

There can always be a possibility of some radioactive sources going 'out of control' in some country and from there entering country, either inadvertently or deliberately. Instances of the first type have occurred in the past in the form of the sources being present in the scrap imported by certain domestic steel foundries in country. Such unnoticed entry has the potential of the end products of the steel mills being contaminated or, in the worst scenario, the source being used in an RDD. Hence the strengthening of border controls will need to be addressed on priority by MHA.In addition, there is also the potential that radioactive materials might be smuggled into the country by antisocial elements, terrorist organisations and state-sponsored activists. Presently, there is no monitoring system in place at the entry points to prevent such events.

Creating a Pool of Radiological Safety Officers at the National Level

An RSO is a trained and qualified radiation protection professional who is certified by the AERB for assisting in the area of radiological protection. A nationwide capability for utilisation of the services of a large number of RSOs for managing both RDD related scenarios and large-scale nuclear disasters will be considered on priority. At present, no formal system exists in this regard.

Strengthening the Medical Preparedness and Response Mechanism

Due to the absence of any significant number of nuclear/radiation related incidents, there have been very few instances of radiation-related injuries.

However, it is essential that the medical community is educated and kept informed about the management of radiation injuries.

Presently, there is no network of hospitals in the country which can handle radiation-induced injuries on a large scale. The establishment of such a network is essential for handling nuclear emergencies/disasters. There should also be a dedicated and reliable communication facility among hospitals so that they can pool their resources when required.

Role of the Police, Civil Defence and Home Guards

In any type of disaster, the community will be the first to respond, but by and large the community is an unskilled force for nuclear/ radiological emergencies. Therefore, skilled 'first responders' will generally be the fire service personnel, the police force and medical professionals as well as the NDRF, which is being specially trained for such situations.

In the context of large-scale radiation disasters, the involvement of civil defence personnel and home guards is usually considered highly desirable.

Role of the Armed Forces

Because of their preoccupation with defending the nation from external threats, the armed forces are normally not always available to respond to a nuclear disaster scenario. However, for any major nuclear accident where the situation is beyond the coping capability of the civil administration, the services of the armed forces may be called for to take over several critical operations related to response (i.e., rescue and relief); rehabilitation (i.e., evacuation and sheltering) and reconstruction activities, including the immediate restoration of essential infrastructures like communication, electrical power, transportation, etc. For such operations, specially trained teams in the armed forces will always be available from within their existing sources. Civil-military coordination will be developed for such purposes so that specially trained and rehearsed teams of the Army can be inducted to assist the civil administration as and when called for and are available.

Prevention of Accidents at Nuclear Plants

A unique feature of the application of nuclear/radiation technology in India, as is the case the world over, is the concept of ensuring safety by incorporating design features to prevent any incident or accident which will lead to a nuclear or radiological emergency. This concept is applied equally to nuclear power plants, nuclear facilities and even in smaller applications like the use of radiation sources in laboratories.

Design Philosophy for Accident Prevention

The inherent safety philosophy in design features, adoption of best available manufacturing/fabrication procedures, best operating practices and stringent regulatory measures are practiced to ensure prevention of unlikely accidents in nuclear power plants.

A reactor accident is prevented by the design philosophy of defence-in-depth, where several levels of protection and multiple barriers are provided to prevent the release of radioactive materials, and to ensure that failures or combinations of failures that might lead to radiological consequences are of very low probability.

It may be noted that all Indian nuclear power plants have all the five levels of defence incorporated in their plants.

Unique Features in the Design of Nuclear Reactor Systems

To ensure a very high level of reactor safety, the present generation of nuclear reactors in India are designed, as followed worldwide, on the basis of some unique features that ensure the following:

i) *Reliability:* To achieve a high level of reliability of safety and safety-related systems by implementing the principles of diversity, redundancy and independence.

ii) *Adoption of a fail-safe design:* To ensure that the plant comes to a safe shutdown state in the event of any failure of safety related components.

iii) *Resistance to natural disasters:* Structures, systems and components necessary to assure capability for shutdown, decay heat removal and confinement of radioactive material are designed to remain functional throughout the plant's life, even in the event of natural disasters like earthquakes, cyclones, floods, etc.

    In the light of the impact of the tsunami, as experienced on 26 December 2004 in the Indian Ocean, the location and design aspects of nuclear installations are required to take this natural hazard also into account.

iv) *Seismic qualification:* The plant is designed for Operating Basis Earthquake (OBE), which is the maximum ground motion that can be reasonably expected to be experienced at the site area once, with an estimated return period of about 100 years.

The design also takes into account another higher level of earthquake called Safe Shutdown Earthquake (SSE), which is the maximum level of ground motion expected to occur once in 10,000 years.

v) *Safety analysis:* Safety analyses are carried out for postulated initiating events as per the standard design codes and guides of the AERB to demonstrate the safety of a plant.

Safety Considerations for Accident Prevention

Well-established safety criteria are used during siting, designing, construction, commissioning, operations and decommissioning of nuclear plants.

i) *Siting:* The site for a nuclear power plant is selected through a detailed study of the site to ensure the requirements laid down by the AERB in such a manner that its operation has no adverse impact on the environment.

ii) *Design and Construction:* To prevent accidents caused by faulty design, it is ensured that the technologies incorporated are state-of-the-art and proven and the man-machine interface is considered in all stages of designing.

iii) *Commissioning Programme:* The commissioning programme confirms that the installation, as constructed, is consistent with design and safety requirements. Operating procedures are validated as part of the commissioning programme.

iv) *Operation:* During operation, it is ensured that the plant is always operated within the safe boundaries as identified by safety analyses. Further, all the important functions, viz., operations, inspection, testing, maintenance and support functions are conducted by a sufficient number of properly trained and authorised personnel in accordance with the approved procedures.

v) *ALARA Principle:* During all the stages of the life of a nuclear plant, starting from design to decommissioning, radiation exposure to both the occupational workers as well as members of the public are kept As Low As Reasonably Achievable (ALARA).

vi) *Management:* The managing authority assigns the highest priority to safety standards and ensures that safety policies are implemented with a clear division of responsibility and a well-defined protocol of communication.

vii) *Decommissioning:* The decommissioning aspect is to be taken into account in such a manner that the radioactive wastes generated during decommissioning are handled with care. It must be ensured that (i) it does not add to excessive exposure of the plant's personnel and members of the public after decommissioning is completed and (ii) even after a long period of time, it does not get into the local environment or get mixed up with the water table.

Safety Approach for Future Reactors

The current nuclear energy systems are designed, constructed and operated to meet stringent safety criteria, as laid down in various national regulatory (AERB) requirements and corresponding industry standards, codes, rules, guides and other documents. The main thrust of this approach is to prevent the occurrence of accidents. Features are to be incorporated in the design and construction of nuclear facilities in the future, based on the best engineering codes and standards available at that point of time.

The safety approach of future reactors will be periodically reviewed, to meet the emerging safety standards to be laid down by the AERB.

Prevention of 'Criticality' Accidents

'Criticality' control is a risk management issue unique to nuclear fuel cycle facilities and other activities involving high-grade fissile materials. It calls for a detailed safety analysis of the system and incorporation of various technical and administrative measures to prevent a 'criticality' situation under all possible scenarios. To prevent 'criticality' accidents in fuel cycle facilities, licensees must ensure that 'criticality' is prevented through proper design and quality assurance programmes on the following parameters which affect 'criticality', viz., mass, density, geometry, interaction, moderator, poison, reflector, etc.

Prevention of Accidents during Transportation of Radioactive Materials

As regards the transportation of radioactive materials, there are regulatory guidelines which specify the design of the container as well as the manner in which they should be handled and transported.

The containers used for transportation of high-strength radioactive materials like nuclear spent fuel, are designed to withstand severe shock, fire, drop from a height, etc. These containers are certified by actual tests carried out with a scaled-down model. Additionally, restrictions are imposed on the speed of the transport vehicle along with adequate physical protection by security forces to take care of any threat from misguided elements.

Prevention of Radiological Emergencies

The user has the primary responsibility for the safe use and control of radioactive materials/ radioisotopes. Every industry using radioactive materials/radioisotopes will have an inventory of all radioactive sources and access control to prevent the loss of such sources/nuclear materials. Radiological accidents could take place at locations where radiation or radioactive sources are used, e.g., in industry, medicine, agriculture and research. Accidents could also take place during the transportation of radioactive materials.

The regulatory guidelines require that all the applications conform to the specified safety standards. These, in turn, are covered by the design, fabrication, testing and operation of various equipment as well as standard operating procedures to ensure safety. This also involves strict administrative control and security of the radioactive sources.

Prevention of Radiological Dispersal Device and Improvised Nuclear Device Incidents

The best available physical protection systems using state-of-the-art surveillance and monitoring systems will be provided at all nuclear/ radiological facilities. Similarly, by implementing appropriate safety and security measures, strict accounting procedures and quick detection/ identification devices, the plant authorities will strengthen the prevention of (i) illicit trafficking of radioactive sources and Special Nuclear Materials (SNMs) and (ii) their falling into the hands of unlawful elements and/or terrorists. These measures will also prevent a radioactive source from being lost, stolen or abandoned (leading to what is termed an 'orphan source').

The first step to counter RDD is to ensure security for all radioactive sources in the country. In this regard, regulatory requirements regarding the security and safety of radioactive sources should be enforced across the country. This will be backed by measures to prevent the smuggling or illicit trafficking of radioactive materials, especially fissile materials. The controlling of such activities calls for setting up a comprehensive national/ international security system, auditing and a detecting and monitoring methodology for such materials. Nuclear materials must have material protection, control and accounting, and should have coverage of vigilance and intelligence.

Highly sensitive detectors/dirty bomb detectors capable of detecting the smuggling of radioactive sources or explosives will be installed by MHA at all entry and exit gates of the various possible routes to prevent radiological terrorism. On detection of radioactive materials, these detector systems will generate an alarm on real time basis. All nuclear facilities will also have monitoring systems installed at the entry and exit gates to detect any unauthorised movement of radioactive materials. Police patrolling vehicles will also be provided with portable radiation monitors to detect the presence of unauthorised sources in the public domain.

Compliance with the Regulatory Framework

So far as man-made disasters are concerned, if proper safety design features and operating procedures are in place, the probability of an accident can be very low. In this regard, the regulatory authority plays a crucial role in the prevention of such emergencies/disasters. Globally, the nuclear industry has given formal recognition to this basic principle by giving utmost importance to the role of the national radiation safety regulator. This has resulted in setting up functionally independent and robust regulatory authorities in many countries, including India, which have nuclear fuel cycle facilities. These independent authorities assign utmost priority to the safe operation of any nuclear or radiation related facility so that radiation exposure of the occupational workers is well below the permissible limits and there is no radiation hazard to the general public. Countries are required to give statutory authority to their regulatory authorities who, in turn, issue formal standards, codes, rules, guides and manuals which follow internationally accepted safety criteria. In India, this role of national radiation safety regulator is performed by the AERB. To achieve its objectives, the AERB ensures compliance with the various rules applicable for:

i) Radiation protection.

ii) Disposal of radioactive wastes.

iii) Food irradiation.

iv) Work in mines and mills.

By virtue of its stringent regulatory measures implemented through a large team of highly competent professionals, the AERB has succeeded in establishing world-class safety standards in the nuclear plants/facilities in India.

Mitigation Measures

The main objective of risk reduction is to minimise the risk to human health and the environment, including the ecosystem and the constituent parts thereof (that are identified to be fragile, in the proximity of a nuclear installation/facility), which are to be protected during nuclear/radiological emergencies. This may call for the promotion and support of the development of better and safer alternate technologies.

The accident mitigation measures for a plant are engineered safety features and accident management procedures which are aimed at minimising the impact with the objective of keeping the release of radioactivity into the environment as low as possible.

Defence-in-depth helps to ensure that the three basic safety functions, viz: controlling the power, cooling the fuel and confining the radioactive material, are preserved and that even in case of an emergency, radioactive materials do not reach the public or the environment. The defence-in-depth concept is centred around several levels of protection, including successive barriers, preventing the release of radioactive materials into the environment.

While the design and operation principles of nuclear power plants ensure that the likelihood of an accident is very small, still such failures are postulated and engineered safety systems for reducing damage and confinement of radioactivity are provided to minimise the impact of these failures. The measures incorporated in the present generation of nuclear reactors in India include:

Engineered Safety Features

i) *Emergency core cooling systems:* To ensure emergency core cooling and thereby limiting core damage in case of an emergency or loss of fuel cooling and, hence, limiting the release of radioactivity within the containment.

ii) *Containment and associated systems:* While the inherent safety features, design provisions and safety system mentioned above will reduce the chances of an accident to a very low probability, an added level of safety is provided by the double containment and associated systems. The primary containment of pre-stressed concrete envelopes the reactor and other nuclear systems to act as a barrier to the release of radioactivity during an accident. The secondary containment of reinforced concrete limits the ground release of radioactivity.

Accident Management

The possible accident scenarios are to be identified before the start of a plant's operation. For each identified accident, structured procedures are developed along with its Emergency Operating Procedures (EOPs). These EOPs define the expected progression of an event and guidelines for the plant's management for managing accidents. These EOPs also help in mitigating the impact of such an event.

General Mitigation Features

For nuclear facilities, the inbuilt safety measures, including biological shields, safety systems and interlocks, safety audits combined with operations and administrative safety procedures, mitigate the consequences of accidents.

Periodic regulatory inspections by the AERB and surveillance by plant safety personnel are carried out to ensure that a mitigation mechanism is in place.

Engineered Safety Features in Nuclear Power Plants

The following are the other engineered safety systems provided in some of India's existing nuclear power plants for mitigating the consequences of an accident:

i) Vapour Suppression System to limit the peak pressure of containment during a loss of coolant accident condition.
ii) Liquid Poison Injection System for long-term sub-criticality of reactors.
iii) Reactor Building Coolers to bring down the primary containment pressure during an accident condition.
iv) Secondary Containment Recirculation System to reduce activity release, using multi-pass filtering by recirculation.

However, such systems are evolutionary in nature and future nuclear power plants are likely to induct the upgraded version of these systems or entirely new ones.For any unlikely event of release of radioactivity in the public domain or loss of a radioactive source, the emergency response system of DAE can be activated any time through its 24x7 emergency communication system. To ensure their effectiveness, the emergency preparedness plans are rehearsed periodically.

Goals of Preparedness

The probability of a major accident at nuclear facilities leading to the release of large quantities of radioactivity into the environment is always ensured to be negligibly small. However, even in the event of a major release into the environment, the prompt and effective implementation of countermeasures can reduce the radiological consequences for the public.

The practical goals of nuclear emergency preparedness are:

i) To reduce radiation-induced health effects by preventing, to the extent possible, the occurrence of severe deterministic effects in workers and in the public.

ii) To limit, to the extent practicable, the occurrence of stochastic effects in the population. It should be borne in mind that actions to reduce the risk of stochastic effects beyond a point (e.g., relocation from an area with insignificant levels of dose or contamination) will sometimes do more harm than good. Taking protective action significantly below the generic international guidelines for intervention and actions for protective measures levels could do more harm than good.

The level of preparedness for response will be commensurate with the severity of the nuclear/radiological hazard potential.

The handling of nuclear emergencies requires coordination among different service groups of the nuclear facility. In the event of potential radiological consequences in the public domain, all the authorities at the three levels, i.e., district, state and central, will play a vital role.

Major Responsibilities of Nuclear Power Plant Operators

This includes the arrangements required to promptly classify an emergency, mitigate the emergency, notify and recommend protective actions off the site consistent with international guidelines, protect those on site, obtain off-site assistance, conduct environmental monitoring of the affected area and assist off-site officials in keeping the public informed.

Major Responsibilities of Off-Site Officials

This includes the arrangements required to promptly implement protective actions and countermeasures in the affected area.

Emergency Preparedness for Nuclear Power Plants

Since the proper implementation of countermeasures can significantly reduce the consequences of an emergency situation, it is mandatory for all nuclear facilities that there must be a comprehensive emergency preparedness plan. Prior to the issuance of a license for the operation of a nuclear facility, the AERB ensures that the facility has the Emergency Response Manuals for the three main types of emergencies, viz., plant, on-site and off-site, and that the plans are in place to handle these types of emergencies. The operators of nuclear facilities must make an assessment of the type and quantum of release of radioactivity under various accident conditions and the extent to which it can spread into the environment.

The response actions within the site boundary of the nuclear facility are the responsibility of the management of the nuclear facility whereas the implementation of the emergency response plan in the public domain is the responsibility of the concerned district authority. In the event an off-site emergency having the potential for trans-boundary effects, necessary action is taken by DAE in accordance with the country's international obligations.

The operating authorities of nuclear facilities in India already have an emergency response plan in place to be invoked in the event of an emergency, which is tested during periodic exercises as per international practice.

Handling a Plant Emergency

When the radiological consequences of an abnormal situation are expected to remain confined to the plant boundary or a section of the plant, it is described as a plant emergency. Nuclear facilities in the country already have the following provisions for the detection, classification, notification and mitigation of any emergency situation:

i) Emergency operating procedures for the assessment of an emergency condition and its mitigation.

ii) Pre-identification of any facility-specific, abnormal situation for classification of a plant and site emergency.

iii) Facility-specific, approved nuclear emergency response plans specifying the jobs of all the functionaries who have assigned roles during the emergency.

iv) Alerting the plant personnel by sounding the emergency siren and making an emergency announcement.

v) Adequate means for communicating a notification to the emergency response organisations at the facility, the district and state authorities, CMG of DAE and the central government authorities.

vi) Identified assembly locations for plant personnel and casual visitors for their accounting, and assessment of persons trapped in the radiological areas.

vii) Formation of rescue teams and activation of a treatment area and decontamination centre.

viii) Radiation survey around the plant and outside the plant and site boundaries.

ix) Assessment of wind speed, wind direction and the affected sector around the nuclear facility.

x) Whenever required, the nuclear facility is able to mobilise the services of the ambulance and paramedical staff at its site.

xi) Equipment and materials for handling a nuclear emergency are kept at a designated place of the nuclear facility and ERC.

Handling On-Site Emergencies

An accidental release of radioactivity or the potential of release of activity extending beyond the plant, but confined to the site boundary, constitutes a site emergency condition.

In addition to all the provisions applicable in a plant emergency, the following additional provisions are ensured:

i) Extensive radiological survey for an assessment of the radiological conditions within the site boundary of the nuclear facility.

ii) Suitable prophylaxis to be made available at all assembly areas for administration to plant personnel, in case the situation demands.

iii) Identification of temporary shelters within the facility/site for shifting plant personnel, in case required.

iv) Provision of a fleet of vehicles for evacuation of plant personnel from the site to a safer place.

v) Provision of fixed and portable contamination monitors to check contaminated personnel/vehicles leaving the site.

vi) On sensing the potential of release of radioactivity which can transgress into the public domain, the concerned district authorities are alerted to be on standby for emergency operations in the public domain.

vii) Radiological monitoring of the environment in the EPZ (16 km radius around the plant).

Handling Off-Site Emergencies

On recognising the potential for an uncontrolled release of radioactivity into the public domain, the concerned district authorities are alerted to be on standby for emergency response operations.

In addition to all the provisions applicable in plant emergency and site emergency, the following additional provisions are to be ensured for handling a nuclear emergency in the public domain:

i) Pre-identification of plant conditions which can lead to an emergency in the public domain.

ii) An assessment of the radiological status at the site boundary and in the public domain.

An Off-site Emergency Response Plan has already been drawn up by the local administration in consultation with the concerned plant authority. It identifies the role of each response agency in a clear and unambiguous manner. After obtaining concurrence from the AERB, detailed emergency response plans and procedures for handling off-site emergencies are approved by the Chairman, SEC, of the respective state where the nuclear facility is located. Finally, procedures are also in place to carry out drills/ exercises to rehearse these plans which, in turn, are periodically reviewed and revised/updated based on the lessons learnt from past exercises.

For handling of an off-site emergency condition in an NPP, there is an off-site emergency committee headed by the district magistrate of the concerned district and supported by the district subcommittee, which include chiefs of all public service departments relevant to emergency management in the district and also the Head of the Site Emergency Committee of the nuclear facility for technical advice. This committee takes decisions pertaining to the handling of a nuclear emergency outside the site boundary and ensures implementation of countermeasures such as sheltering, prophylaxis and evacuation and resettlement, including maintenance of law and order and civil amenities. All the activities pertaining to the handling of an off-site emergency are guided and coordinated from a pre-designated emergency response centre located outside the boundary of the nuclear facility. The information and broadcasting department of the district, in association with an authorised information officer, ensures the smooth flow of information to the media to avoid panic and spreading of rumours.

Raising Specialised Response Teams

Specialised response teams will be raised, specially trained for a nuclear/radiological emergency/disaster and fully equipped at the state as well as central levels. In this context, it is to be noted that four battalions of NDRF are being specially trained by NDMA with assistance from DAE/DRDO (for detecting and monitoring radiation, for their own protection during response actions, decontamination and triage operation, etc.) to provide specialised response during a nuclear/radiological emergency/disaster.

Since the response actions during CBRN disaster scenarios are quite different from those needed for natural and other man-made disasters, CBRN-trained battalions of NDRF (presently located at Greater Noida, Kolkata, Talegaon in Pune and Arakonam in Chennai) must always be available on an emergent basis.

Role of Civil Defence

Civil defence organisations near existing NPPs are provided training on emergency preparedness. Their volunteers also participate in off-site emergency exercises. Civil defence is expected to play a significant role in future nuclear emergency/disaster scenarios arising from facilities other than NPPs. Civil defence personnel are normally trained in handling natural calamities. Therefore, selected civil defence personnel will be trained extensively in the subjects of radiation, radioactivity, radiation protection, use of monitoring instruments, use of protective gear, shielding, decontamination, waste disposal, etc.

A revamping of the civil defence set-up has been proposed in which it will be made district-centric in order to cover all the districts of the country in two phases. In the first phase, 241 multi-hazard districts will be covered.

Of these, 37 districts which are cyclone prone already have civil defence set-ups in their major towns.

In the meanwhile, the civil defence set-up already existing in the country will be immediately utilised to train the community for disaster response in the concerned districts of the towns already activated. The Director General of Civil Defence in each state will work out training modules for DM covering awareness generation, first aid and rescue drills. Selected civil defence personnel will be trained for CBRN emergencies and will be closely involved in assisting all the response agencies. Other civil defence personnel will support response agencies for the management of CBRN emergencies. The National Institute of Disaster Management (NIDM) will prepare a comprehensive training module simultaneously and circulate it, which will be incorporated in the ongoing training programme.

The civil defence authorities will work out their overall mechanism for responding to various disasters and take the assistance of DAE/DRDO as well as CBRN-trained NDRF staff in training and equipping their personnel with regard to handling radiation emergencies/ disasters.

Instruments, equipment and protective gear for response teams

The standard list of instruments, equipment and protective gear necessary for the various response teams will be drawn up in consultation with DAE, with full technical specifications and procured by the concerned SDMAs and DDMAs in advance for the response action. These will be procured for the specialised response teams, medical teams, and civil defence personnel. An adequate stock of specified clothing will be procured for use by the affected people.

Role of the Armed Forces

While the central and state governments must aim to develop suitable response capabilities to meet the perceived nuclear emergency/disaster threat scenario; such response efforts might require to be augmented by the armed forces. To ensure optimum synergy, it is imperative that there is proper interaction between the civil authorities and the armed forces during all stages of planning, preparedness and response.

While NDMA and MHA have co-opted suitable members from the Ministry of Defence in all the committees, similar action must be taken by the state governments and district authorities at their respective locations.

The armed forces will also gear up their nuclear disaster preparedness so that they can be inducted in the event of nuclear disasters.

Training of Stakeholders, Periodic Exercises and Mock Drills

Training plays an important role in the proper implementation of various emergency response activities. It focuses on roles and responsibilities, resource identification, use of equipment, understanding the effects of radiation on human beings, animals and the environment. The required emergency preparedness is maintained by organising various training courses for on-site and off-site personnel at regular intervals. Appropriate training is imparted to employees of the facility at all levels at regular intervals to familiarise them with the required actions during an emergency. Similar training courses are organised round the year for various public authorities and state government officials in view of the routine turnovers.

The adequacy of emergency response arrangements at a nuclear facility is evaluated through the audit and review of plans, procedures and infrastructure. The ability to carry out the required emergency actions is assessed, in general, through audit and reviews of past performance. However, a primary evaluation of the same is based on the feedback of designated observers for the periodic mock exercises. The preparation, conduct and evaluation of these exercises shall involve the coordination of all functionaries within the facility, the district authorities and the CMG of DAE. These drills for plant, on-site, and off-site emergencies will preferably be conducted quarterly, annually and once in two years, respectively; however, the frequency of the actual exercise will depend on the type of nuclear facility.

The nuclear facility will have proper media management to minimise possible negative impacts of the exercise on the public psyche.

The evaluation of an exercise will identify areas of emergency plans and preparedness that may need to be improved or enhanced. It will be the responsibility of the nuclear facility and the district authority to review the evaluation report and ensure implementation of the corrective measures recommended by the evaluators.

A large number of organisations/agencies have to be fully integrated by SDMAs, SECs, and DDMAs with assistance from DAE, DRDO, NIDM, and NDMA into the nuclear/radiological emergency programmes at the district and state levels. These organisations/agencies include (i) CBRN-specialised teams of the four battalions of NDRF; fire and emergency services personnel and the police force as the first responders along with medicos, paramedics, (including the staff from rural/primary health centres); Non-Governmental Organisations (NGOs), Community Based Organisations (CBOs); the civil defence staff and home guards; (ii) designated specialists from the hospitals of DAE units; elected officials; public information officers and academicians as resource personnel to educate the public; and teachers and students from schools, colleges and universities.

The procedures and actions for the various response agencies will be evolved and regularly rehearsed so as to use their services as and when required. SOPs will need to be laid down for first responders, who will also be trained and empowered to carry out their assigned tasks.

References

Arm, Stuart T. (2010). "Nuclear Energy: A Vital Component of Our Energy Future". *Chemical Engineering Progress*. New York, NY: American Institute of Chemical Engineers.

Benjamin K. Sovacool (2011). *Contesting the Future of Nuclear Power: A Critical Global Assessment of Atomic Energy*, World Scientific, p. 192.

Hugh Gusterson (16 March 2011). "The lessons of Fukushima". *Bulletin of the Atomic Scientists*.

James C. Oskins, Michael H. Maggelet (2008). *Broken Arrow — The Declassified History of U.S. Nuclear Weapons Accidents*. lulu.com. I

Johnston, Robert (September 23, 2007). "Deadliest radiation accidents and other events causing radiation casualties". Database of Radiological Incidents and Related Events.

Staff, IAEA, AEN/NEA (in Technical English). *International Nuclear and Radiological Events Scale Users' Manual, 2008 Edition*. Vienna, Austria: International Atomic Energy Agency. p. 184. Retrieved 2010-07-26.

8

Disaster Mitigation: Tools and Techniques

Mitigation and prevention are used as synonyms. Some prefer to drop the term Mitigation and use only Prevention. The term Mitigation can be comprised in the term Prevention. Mitigation means to reduce the severity of the human and material damage caused by the disaster. Prevention is to ensure that human action or natural phenomena do not result in disaster or emergency. Primary prevention is to reduce -avert- avoid the risk of the event occurring, by getting rid of the hazard or vulnerability, e.g. to avoid overcrowding, deforestation and to provide services. Healthier people in a healthy environment will be less vulnerable to most hazards. E.g. immunizing people against smallpox made them less vulnerable to the virus, and slowly eradicated the disease. Secondary prevention means to recognise promptly the event and to reduce its effects, e.g. by staying alert to possible displacements of population; by being ready to provide immunisation, food, clean water, sanitation and health care to refugees. Healthier people in a healthy environment will also be more capable to overcome the emergency.

The objective of prevention is to reduce the risk of being affected by a disaster. Even if the hazard cannot be removed, vulnerability can be decreased and in case of an impact, the capacity to withstand, to respond and to recover will be stronger.

Mitigation is the ongoing effort to lessen the impact of natural disasters on people and property. Mitigation is the cornerstone of emergency management. The best response to natural disaster is to proactively prevent or diminish its impact. Disaster mitigation measures eliminate or reduce the impacts and risks of hazards through proactive measures taken before an emergency or disaster occurs. One of the best known examples of investment in disaster mitigation is the Red River Floodway. The building of the Floodway was a joint provincial/federal undertaking to protect the City of Winnipeg and reduce the impact of flooding in the Red River Basin. It cost $60 million to build in the 1960s. Since then, the floodway has been used over 20 times. Its use during the 1997 Red River Flood alone saved an estimated $6 billion.

Disaster mitigation measures may be structural (e.g. flood dikes) or non-structural (e.g. land use zoning). Mitigation activities should incorporate the measurement and assessment of the evolving risk environment. Activities may include the creation of comprehensive, pro-active tools that help decide where to focus funding and efforts in risk reduction.

Other examples of mitigation measures include:

- Hazard mapping
- Adoption and enforcement of land use and zoning practices
- Implementing and enforcing building codes
- Flood plain mapping
- Reinforced tornado safe rooms
- Burying of electrical cables to prevent ice build-up
- Raising of homes in flood-prone areas
- Disaster mitigation public awareness programs
- Insurance programs

Disaster mitigation requires rapid and efficient search and rescue of survivors. The goal of search and rescue is to locate and access injured or trapped victims, stabilize the emergency situation, and transport the patients to safety. Relief workers need to speedily find the trapped survivors in collapsed buildings and crumbled structures in the aftermath of disasters. Otherwise the likelihood of finding victims alive could be negligible.

The search-and-rescue operations in the aftermath of disasters commonly employ many traditional methods and techniques which have been evolved over a long period of time. Modern technology has also provided vital inputs to their evolution, and these techniques are still being widely used by disaster rescue workers. Newer and advanced technologies and equipment have recently made an impact in search-and-rescue operations, making them easier and quicker, while improving a missing or injured person's chance of survival.

Technology Options

The choice of search-and-rescue tools and methods depends on their availability and the needs of the situation. For example, storm and earthquake wreckage may require tools for lifting debris whereas flood damage may require boats and ropes. Different scenarios require differing technology options for disaster search and rescue. These are summarized below:

- Improved real-time data access.
- The ability to accurately and non-invasively locate survivors following structural collapse—the ability to "see" through walls, smoke, debris, and obstacles.
- The ability to communicate (transmit signals) through/around obstacles.
- Lighter, more efficient power sources (batteries, fuel cells, or other technologies able to power multiple systems for longer periods of time).
- Improved monitoring systems (i.e. atmospheric, biomedical, personnel accountability, etc.)—realtime, portable, multi-function devices that expand on existing detection capabilities.
- Improved personal protective equipment—lightweight, comfortable, and rugged equipment that provides enhanced worker protection against multiple hazards.
- Improved breaching, shoring, and debris removal systems—portable, lightweight, longer life, stronger materials and equipment.
- Reliable non-human, non-canine search-and-rescue systems—robust systems that combine enhanced canine/human search-and-rescue capabilities without existing weaknesses (i.e. robots).

Tools and Equipment

The tools and equipment for disaster search-and-rescue operations include cutting equipment; diving equipment; forcible entry tools; jacks (hydraulic/ pneumatic); life rafts; lighting (torch, lamps, searchlights); location beacons; night vision equipment; pneumatic/ hydraulic equipment and tools; rescue equipment; rescue tools; rope rescue systems; rescue belts; safety equipment; search equipment; spreading tools; thermal imaging equipment; water rescue equipment; winches; robotic systems; etc.

Concrete saw

A concrete saw (often known as a consaw or road saw) is a power tool used for cutting concrete, masonry, brick, asphalt, and other solid materials. Concrete saws are powered by petrol, hydraulic, pnuematic, or electrical motors. The significant friction generated in cutting hard substances such as concrete means that the blades need to be cooled to prolong their life and reduce dust. Blades are either abrasive or diamond-tipped.

Jackhammer

A pneumatic drill or jackhammer is a portable, percussive drill, powered by compressed air. It is used to drill rock and break up pavement, among other applications. It works in a manner similar to a hammer and chisel: by jabbing with its bit, not rotating it.

Drill

A drill (from Dutch drillen) is a tool with a rotating drill bit, used for drilling holes in various materials. Drills are commonly used in woodworking and metalworking. Thc drill bit is gripped by a chuck at one end of the drill, and is pressed against the target material and rotated.

Of the many types of drills, some are powered manually and others use electricity or compressed air as the motive power. Drills with a percussive action are usually used for hard materials such as masonry and rock.

Air-lifting bags

Three types of lifting bags are generally sold and used for rescue or heavy recovery work: high-pressure, medium-pressure, and low-pressure systems.

Low-pressure bag systems are essentially high-lift bags which operate at 7¼ psi maximum working pressure. These low-pressure cushions provide vertical lift over a large surface area and work especially well on thin-skinned, light-walled vehicles such as aluminum truck trailers, tankers, buses, and aircraft. The construction of low-pressure bags utilizes seven-ply strong, reinforced fabric material for the top and bottom surfaces. The internal structure is designed with nylon strapping supports. The cushion itself is constructed of a simple canvas of Kevlar which is impregnated and bonded to neoprene.

Medium-pressure bag systems are designed to operate at 15 psi and are not very common. Most tasks can be accomplished with 8-12 psi. These bags are designed to function at 15 psi, but register bursting pressures between 58 psi and 100 psi, depending on the size and style manufactured. Generally, medium-pressure bags have thicker sidewalls than low-pressure bags.

High-pressure bag systems are the type most commonly found on rigs today. High-pressure air-lifting bags generally operate with inflation pressures of 90 psi-145 psi. With a high-pressure system, a direct relationship is evident between lifting capacity and inflation height.

Emergency rescue shoring

Emergency shoring operations for urban search-and-rescue incidents are defined as the temporary stabilization or re-support of any part of, or section of, structural element that is physically damaged, missing, or where the structure is partially or totally collapsed or in danger of collapsing. Such an exercise is conducted in order to secure a safe and efficient atmosphere while conducting search-and-rescue operations of trapped victims at a collapse incident where the risk conditions are relatively safe and reduced for the victims as well as the concerned trained rescue team. The work includes the stabilization of any adjacent structure or object that may be affected by the initial incident.

For a shore to work properly and be considered a system, it must generally have four main parts: a header or top plate, one or more posts or struts, a bottom plate or sole plate, and finally, a lateral or diagonal bracing system. Each of these constituents is important for the success of the shoring system. The key to all the shores is to collect the loads from a damaged area, funnel it through the post system, and redistribute the load to the ground or other suitable structural elements.

Hydraulic rescue tools

Hydraulic rescue tools are used by emergency rescue personnel to assist vehicle extrication of crash victims, as well as other rescues from small spaces. These tools include cutters, spreaders, and rams. Hydraulic rescue tools are powered by a hydraulic pump, which can be hand-, foot-, or engine-powered, or even built into the tool itself. These tools may be either single-acting, where hydraulic pressure will move the cylinder in only one direction; and the return to starting position is accomplished by using a pressure-relief valve and spring set-up; or it is dual-acting, i.e. hydraulic pressure is used to both open and close the suzzette cylinder.

Spreader-cutters

In operation, the tips of the spreader-cutter's blades are wedged into a seam or gap—for example, around a vehicle door—and the device engaged. The hydraulic pump, attached to the tool or as a separate unit, powers a piston which pushes the blades apart with great force and spreads the seam. Once the seam has been spread, the now-open blades can be repositioned around the metal. The device is engaged in reverse and the blades close, cutting through the metal. Repeating this process allows a rescuer to quickly open a gap wide enough to pull free a trapped victim. The blades can spread or cut with a force of several tons or kilonewtons, with the tips of the blades spreading up to a metre. This operation can also be performed by dedicated spreading and cutting tools, which are designed especially for their own operations and may be required for some rescues.

Rams

Rams are used far less than spreader-cutters in auto rescues; nonetheless, they serve an important purpose. There are many types and sizes, including single-piston, dual-piston, and telescopic rams. Sizes commonly vary from 20" to 70". As rams use more hydraulic fluid during operation than spreader-cutters, it is essential that the pump being used have enough capacity to allow the ram to reach full extension.

Rescue craft

Inflatable life rafts are lowered from small aircraft during marine rescues. Jet rescue boats, and later inflatable jet boats, assisting in close-to-shore rescues, are also widely used. Their advantage is that they can be launched anywhere.

Planes and helicopters

Aircraft help to spot missing people in land searches. Light planes are also used in coastal searches, and have proved even more successful than seaborne craft in finding lost boats. Helicopters have also revolutionized both land and marine search-and-rescue missions, as they can reach people in remote places and take them quickly to safety.

Communications equipment

Communications equipment relays information to and from searchers. Today, HF and VHF radio are used and, where appropriate, satellite phones and cellphones. In cave rescues, Michie phones are useful. An insulated wire is attached to a receiver at the cave entrance and strung into the cave. Underground search teams can puncture the wire to use a handset and talk to those aboveground. Increasingly, emergency beacons are being carried by passenger aircraft and boats, and marine radio has become more sophisticated. Emergency beacons equipped with GPS have helped to speed up the rescue of victims. In 2007, analogue beacons were replaced by digital beacons linked to a satellite system, making for quicker and more efficient rescues.

Laser light

Sophisticated laser light signaling instruments may be a promising new option over conventional light systems. Waterproof and simple to use, laser light devices emit light that can be seen for up to 20 miles. They can be used for both sending signals to lost parties and detecting reflective materials to locate a lost person. Laser light is stronger and more directional than conventional light systems and produces an unmistakable brilliant red flash which can be easily seen by the lost party. When the light is reflected by some object on the lost person, the search party will see a bright red flashback.

Infrared surveillance

A new airborne surveillance technology, the Infrared Eye, is a promising viewing system that will enhance airborne spotting-and-searching techniques. The Infrared Eye accomplishes this task by duplicating the mechanics of the human eye and simultaneously using two fields of view. This includes a wide overall field with high sensitivity but low resolution for situation awareness and detection, and a narrow field of view with very high resolution which can be easily directed to objects of interest in the wide field, tracking the operator's line-of-sight.

Robots

Robots can bypass any existing danger and expedite the search for victims immediately after a collapse. For the robots to handle these tasks, appropriate mobile bases need to be developed which can crawl through unstructured terrain, heavy rubble, and confined spaces. Some hardware platforms such as small robots, shape-shifting robots, and flexible snake robots already exist. So, both robot mechanisms and software are the current focus of development for urban search-and-rescue robots.

This technology can assist rescue workers in four ways: (1) reduce the personal risk to workers by entering unstable structures; (2) increase the speed of response by accessing ordinarily inaccessible voids; (3) increase efficiency and reliability by methodically searching areas with multiple sensors, using algorithms guaranteed to provide a complete search in three dimensions; and (4) extend the reach of specialists to go places that were otherwise inaccessible.

Latest technologies for Disaster Mitigation

Wireless Network for Disaster Rescue

The Asian Institute of Technology in Bangkok, Thailand, has unveiled a state-of-the-art mobile wireless network which can be used to establish communication for emergency workers after a disaster. The network, developed with groups in France, Japan, and other countries, will allow rescue teams at a disaster site to communicate even if conventional forms of communication break down.

The new network allows emergency workers to set up a mobile satellite station which creates a wireless network for laptop computers or personal digital assistants (PDA). Each laptop or PDA is then able to act as a node that can transmit the wireless signal to other devices further out in the field and extend the network into hard-to-reach areas.

The project aims to turn any ordinary device into a wireless node without having to acquire special hardware. Users on the network could use video, SMS, or e-mail to communicate with others on the network or over the internet.

High-tech Tool for Disaster Rescue

The Responding to Crises and Unexpected Events (RESCUE) project is working to transform how communities and first responders plan for and respond to both natural and man-made disasters by turning new technologies and cutting-edge research into practical tools for emergency planners and responders. Funded by the National Science Foundation (NSF), RESCUE's goal is to dramatically improve the ability of emergency responders to gather, process, and disseminate information with each other and the general public. Led by the University of California, Irvine, RESCUE brings together researchers from around the country who work in a variety of academic fields, creating a unique perspective to the understanding of disaster responses. Scientists have provided risk communication models and insight into how humans perceive and react to risk communication. Engineers helped the team understand how tools such as early warning systems could impact evacuation routes and other concerns. The result has been new approaches to risk communication which are being put into practice.

Another tool being developed by RESCUE researchers is a complex disaster simulation platform called MetaSim. This computer system allows researchers to merge different types of simulations at once in order to provide planners with a more accurate picture of what conditions may be like during and after a disaster, as also provide researchers with a way to test and validate how new technology concepts could help a response effort.

Wearable technology to aid disaster relief

Wearable, interactive 3-D technology being developed by the University of South Australia will be able to transfer people into "mobile augmented reality (AR) systems". Weighing 7 kg, the technology is composed of a computer which can be carried in a backpack, virtual reality goggles, and an attached video camera which can convey information to a control room via wireless, LAN, and 3-G networks.

Professor Bruce Thomas, director of the wearable computer laboratory at the university, said the technology has the potential to dramatically improve the effectiveness of disaster relief operations. The control centre can also create 3-D maps and images for field personnel to view through their goggles. The project is composed of three components: the indoor visualization control room, the outdoor wearable AR system, and collaboration between the indoor and outdoor systems.

Canine search-and-rescue technology

Computer Science Associate Professor Dr. Alex Ferworn heads a team of Ryerson researchers who are improving the communication between trained search-and-rescue dogs and their handlers. Equipping man's best friend with top-notch sensory gear can increase the effectiveness of search-and-rescue missions, according to Ryerson University researchers.

Under the leadership of Associate Professor Dr. Alex Ferworn, the team has developed two new products for trained search dogs: Canine Augmentation Technology II (CAT II) and Canine Remote Deployment

System (CRDS). Employing existing off-the-shelf components from the realms of wireless communication, canine care, computer science, and search and rescue, the team has created an integrated system that is customized to the needs of the search-and-rescue community.

Dr. Ferworn's research uses custom camera, and audio and communication harnesses which enable wireless transmission of information to a receiver carried by the handler to another responder, or to a receiver located in the site command post. Rescue teams are able to receive real-time video of the disaster site from a dog's-eye view, as well as two-way audio. The new CAT technologies also enable search dogs to deliver equipment or supplies to a trapped victim long before emergency personnel can reach them.

Mechanical mole

A digging robot inspired by the mole is being built by UK researchers, who hope it will one day 'swim' through rubble at disaster sites to help find survivors. Robin Scott and Robert Richardson at the University of Manchester, UK, assert that a robot that digs would be most useful in an emergency. The pair has already built a new digging mechanism that can shove aside relatively light objects, such as bricks and furniture.

The digging robot was inspired by the European mole, which uses its spade-like front paws in a digging motion similar to a swimmer's breast-stroke. The first part of the 'stroke' drags earth in front of the animal to the side and pushes it to the rear. The return stroke brings the forelegs to the front again, keeping them close to the mole's body to avoid pushing already-moved earth forward again.

To duplicate the mole's digging motion, the researchers used a tried-and-tested design called a four-bar mechanism which is similar to the arrangement that drives car windscreen wipers. The new mole-style digging arm links two of these four-bar mechanisms. This arrangement makes it possible to create a molelike digging motion from two normal rotary electric motors that never need to run in reverse. That should make for low maintenance, according to the researchers. In preliminary tests, the digging arm has successfully moved aside bricks and other debris. The design is now being mounted onto a robot chassis for more comprehensive tests. Richardson estimates that an actual search-and-rescue robot based on the design might be ready in two years.

Role of Energy and Power Technologies

Power supply is generally the first casualty when a natural disaster strikes an area. Grid failure often follows immediately after major disasters such as earthquakes, cyclones, and floods. The utility grid, a highly centralized and complex system, is inherently vulnerable to disaster-related disruptions. In such an eventuality, lights fail, and furnaces, refrigerators, and other electrical appliances stop working. Further, the drinking water supply, sewage treatment, and conventional communication systems are also disrupted. Emergency response teams therefore need a reliable source of electric power, even to begin to deal with the crisis situation.

The services needed for disaster relief, particularly in the reconstruction phase, require energy. Some of the time, traditional energy systems are appropriate; at other times, renewable energy systems serve the purpose. The potential for renewable energy technologies to support disaster relief is significant. The concept of using on-site renewable energy systems to mitigate the crippling impact of power shortage during disasters has been successfully introduced in many instances. Solar, wind, and hydroelectric systems are notable examples, providing enough power to meet the basic needs of the disaster-affected population. Biomass can also be used to generate electricity or as an emergency fuel source for heating and cooking.

Many renewable energy technologies can provide base-load power, and others are suitable for providing power on a distributed grid basis. This can be either in the form of heat or electricity.

Depending on the sources of energy, disaster situations require mainly two groups of technologies. These are:

— *Conventional energy:* electrical generators, lighting equipment, fuel for cooking; and

— *Renewable energy:* portable solar PV systems, PV-powered generators, solar water heaters (SWH), solar lanterns, solar cookers, solar stills, solar batteries, and micro wind generators.

Conventional Energy Technologies

Electrical Generators

Emergency generators are very popular after disasters. They can help preserve food in freezers and refrigerators, but they may also be dangerous if not used with due care. Standby generators are powered by tractors or engines and may be either portable or stationary. Engine-driven units may have an automatic or start and are powered by gasoline, LP gas, or diesel fuel. The generators must provide the same type of power, at the same voltage and frequency as that supplied by power lines.

A full-load system handles an entire farmstead's energy needs. An automatic, engine-powered, full-load system begins to furnish power immediately or within 30 seconds after power is off. A smaller, less expensive part-load system may be enough to handle essential equipment during an emergency. Power take-off (PTO) generators cost about half as much as engine-driven units and can be trailer-mounted. A part-load system operates only the most essential equipment at a time.

Renewable Energy Technologies

The availability of fuel supplies is a constant anxiety to those who rely on fossil-fuel-powered generators during an emergency. Not only do renewable energy systems eliminate that worry, but they also work without producing the overbearing noise and noxious fumes that accompany gasoline and diesel generators. Because they can be designed to continue working even when the utility grid fails, renewable energy systems can actually prevent power outages — keeping homes and businesses functioning during black-outs, or amid the chaos following natural disasters. A key benefit of renewable energy systems for emergency use is their self-sufficiency. They require no fuel and minimal maintenance, yet provide reliable power for as long as needed.

— Two types of renewable energy systems are generally used for meeting the energy requirements of disaster management: fixed and portable. Fixed systems tap the renewable resource most appropriate for specific locations, be it solar, wind, hydro, or biomass. These systems function constantly, supplementing utility power during normal times and providing back-up power during outages. Portable systems, on the other hand, are deployed following disasters to assist response crews and victims. Solar electricity is the most appropriate renewable energy source for such applications because the systems are relatively easy to transport, and solar energy is plentiful in many regions. Portable photovoltaic (PV) systems are best suited for meeting smaller-scale needs which require only a few kW or less.

The applications for renewable energy equipment for disaster relief, reconstruction, and development are:

— emergency relief;
— lighting (portable lighting, street lighting);
— water supply (water pumping and distribution, water purification);
— healthcare (field hospital, morgues, medical refrigerators);
— refrigeration (individual power kits);
— food preparation (cooking);
— communication (radios, satellite communication systems, laptop and mobile charging systems); and
— security and safety (alarm systems, lighting).

PV-powered Generators

Powered by the sun, the PV-powered gensets make use of a solar electric panel to produce electricity. The electric energy produced by these gensets can be used immediately or stored in batteries for later use. These gensets have many advantages: they are virtually silent, safe to operate, environmentally benign, and seldom a fire hazard; they are also extremely rugged, having been designed to withstand the impact of hailstones; they can be made mobile for transporting from place to place by truck.

Solar Lighting

Solar PV lighting can replace typical flame-based lanterns, providing better quality light with greatly improved safety, while also avoiding refueling needs. A solar lantern pack has a small solar PV module for daytime charging to provide three or more hours of light at night. PV modules for solar lanterns may be permanently mounted on a pole or roof of a shelter for convenience.

Power Requirements of Medical Services

Power requirements for medical services in disaster-affected areas are mainly in the following areas:

— power for medical services;
— supply of clean water;
— water heating (sterilization, personal hygiene); and
— cooking.

Maintenance of the cold chain is critical for the preservation of vaccines. In the aftermath of a disaster when there is no reliable electricity supply, highly efficient, well-insulated vaccine refrigerators connected to a gas or kerosene-powered system or a battery bank, and a solar PV or small wind energy system are useful. Solar PV-powered vaccine refrigerators are robust and have low maintenance requirements. They do not depend on fossil fuel supplies, and can be designed to provide additional electricity for lighting, minor operations, and health workers' residences in disaster-affected areas.

Similarly, solar PV, or small wind generators, can support lighting for medical facilities, extending the effective operating hours of hospitals and clinics. The power demands of communication networks and other systems required for effective health centre operations may also be readily achieved with small-scale renewables. Depending on the scale of the operations, a wide range of power needs may be met—from relatively simple, small-scale systems, comprising only a few solar modules and a small battery bank, to power a few lights and a refrigerator, to a fully contained PV/diesel hybrid unit capable of delivering grid-quality power for multiple lights, fans, oxygen concentrators, nebulisers, microscopes, and other vital medical equipment.

Transportation Aids and Warning Signals

Transportation aids, along with PV-powered emergency telephone call boxes, flashing barricade lights, and other warning signals, are extremely handy not only during times of crisis, but also for day-to-day use. The signs and barricades inform motorists about road construction projects, and highway call boxes play an important safety role. PV cells also power warning signals on Coast Guard buoys and navigational beacons; solar heat energizes railroad signals, aircraft warning lights, and road crossing lights, enabling these public safety systems to continue functioning when a disaster disables the utility grid.

Battery Charging

Another potential use for PV in the disaster response area is for charging batteries. When rechargeable batteries are used to power items such as hand-held radios and cellular phones, they sometimes lose their power before the workers can return to the base camp to recharge them. Work crews are often transported by bus to work sites where they lack the vehicular chargers they can rely on at home. When their battery packs run down, their communication line is cut until someone can bring a charged one or they themselves return to camp.

Another PV-battery charging option would be to equip a mobile unit with PV panels. It could be parked at a remote site to recharge an entire bank of cellular phones, or radio battery packs, simultaneously. Search cameras and high-tech listening devices used to locate trapped victims also operate on DC batteries which could possibly be recharged by using PV panels. However, all of these potential battery-charging applications require field testing to determine their need and feasibility.

Portable PV power

Portable PV power systems are especially well-suited for meeting long-term emergency power needs at small-scale, isolated sites. These systems could be used to provide electricity for relief operations centres, and to operate vaccine refrigerators, lights, fans, medical equipment, and small radios and televisions. Solar power is especially ideal at clinic locations, because it protects patients from prolonged exposure to the noise and fumes of portable generators. It also aids in the operation of medical instruments (stethoscopes, for example) that require a quiet environment for proper use.

Portable units that arrive on the scene ready to go, with little user interaction, are essential to the expanded use of PV generators in disaster response. During a crisis, there is no time for careful installation of delicate equipment. Rescue workers must also be educated on the proper use of PV before the disaster occurs, as they are not in the proper frame of mind to learn new technologies in the disaster response environment.

At some locations, PV systems eliminate the need for portable generators, and at others, solar power significantly reduces the use of generators. The systems enable workers to turn off the generators at night without having to handle dry ice for the vaccine refrigerators, thereby lessening anxiety in respect of fuel supply.

Outdoor Lighting

PV-powered outdoor security lights are useful for disaster-affected areas. Though they are low-power systems as compared with traditional street lights (30W versus 250W), the light they provide greatly raises the comfort level in times of total darkness. Solar-powered lanterns also help in disaster relief efforts when certain outdoor emergency lighting needs are too large to be met with PV systems.

In less-populated but very dark areas, PV outdoor lights are ideal. They represent yet another PV application that works well not only during emergencies, but also all the time. They can be found illuminating parking lots, highway signs, parks, trails, and bus shelters. In many cases, the use of solar power is more economical and expedient than extending utility service to these locations.

Technologies for Food Supply, Storage and Safety

In the aftermath of natural disasters, such as earthquakes, floods, cyclones, and tsunamis, food in distress areas may become a scarce commodity. The available food may also become contaminated and consequently lead to outbreaks of food-borne diseases, including diarrhoea, dysentery, cholera, hepatitis A, and typhoid fever. The lack of suitable conditions for preparing food, coupled with poor sanitation, including inadequate safe water and toilet facilities in disaster-affected areas, has led to outbreaks of food-borne diseases.

Storage, safety, and distribution of food in disaster-prone and disaster-affected areas require a package of best practices, technical know-how, technologies, equipment, and devices. Disaster management practitioners could make use of the best possible options that are available at hand;

- preventive food safety measures;
- safe and hygienic warehouse management;
- safe food handling during food distribution and preparation;
- inspecting and salvaging food;
- food storage—refrigerated and frozen foods, canning of food;
- cooking stoves;
- solar cookers; and
- food supply and delivery systems—mobile canteens, mobile kitchens, and mobile feeding units.

Food Safety Measures

While contamination can occur at any point of the food chain, inadequate washing, handling, and cooking of food just before consumption is still a prime cause of food-borne diseases. Many infections are preventable by observing simple, hygienic rules during food preparation whether in family settings or large food-catering facilities.

Under most conditions, the threats posed by polluted water and contaminated food are interrelated and cannot be separated. Therefore, water should be treated as a contaminated food and should be boiled, or otherwise purified, before it is consumed or used as an ingredient in food. The World Health Organization (WHO) has prepared guidelines for public health authorities and other related bodies on the key food safety measures to be observed in disaster situations. This includes a reminder that authorities maintain existing support for food safety and improve their vigilance against new food-borne risks posed by disasters..

Safe and Hygienic Warehouse Management

Large-scale storage and warehousing facilities for food are a necessity in disaster-stricken areas. The warehousing structures and food storage practices are critical to the safety of food that is stored in the aftermath of natural disasters. The practices adopted for safe and hygienic warehouse management in disaster-affected areas include:

— Storage structures should have good roofs and ventilation. Products should be kept away from walls and off the floor. Pallets, boards, heavy branches, bricks, plastic bags, or sheets should be placed underneath them for protection. Bags should be piled two-by-two, cross-wise to permit ventilation.

— Spilled food should be swept up and disposed of promptly to discourage rats.

— Fuel, pesticides, bleach, and other chemical stocks should never be stored together with food.

— If spray operations for pest control are needed, they should be carried out by qualified technical staff, under close supervision of the national authority. The operators should wear protective gear to reduce their exposure to toxic chemicals in the sprays.

Safe Food Handling

Emergency response operations often include large-scale distribution of imported or locally-purchased food items as well as mass preparation of cooked food. In this context, special attention must be given to the following:

— All foods used in food distribution and mass feeding programmes must be fit for human consumption. The quality and safety of all items should be controlled before importation or local purchase, and any unfit items should be rejected.

— Stocks should be regularly inspected, and any suspect stocks should be separated from other stocks, and samples be sent to a suitable laboratory for analysis; in the interim they should not be used.

— Kitchen supervisors, cooks, and ancillary personnel should be taught personal hygiene and the principles of safe food preparation. Their implementation of these healthy norms should be regularly monitored.

— Kitchen supervisors should be trained to recognize potential hazards and apply appropriate food safety measures.

— Employees and volunteers preparing food should not be suffering from any of the following ailments: jaundice, diarrhoea, vomiting, fever, sore throat, visibly infected skin lesions, or discharge from the ears, eyes, or nose.

— Staff should be employed to ensure that the kitchen and surrounding areas are clean; they should be properly trained in this basic exercise and their work supervised..

— Adequate facilities for waste disposal are essential.

— Water and soap must be provided for personal cleanliness, and detergent for cleaning utensils and surfaces which should also be sanitized with boiling water or a sanitizing agent, e.g. bleach solution.

— Hot and/or cold holding of food may have to be improvised.

Inspecting and Salvaging Food

In disaster situations, food items available from the market, storage depots, and warehouses should be of high quality. The available food and its source entities should be under constant inspection and quality surveillance for safe supply and distribution to the affected population. This process should conform to the following norms:

— Food industries, slaughterhouses, markets, and catering establishments should be inspected to ensure their safe operation. Particular attention should be given to those handling perishable products, such as milk. Steps should be taken to bar the marketing of foods that have been adversely affected.

— When salvaged foods are fit for consumption and sold, they should be labelled accordingly, and consumers should be clearly informed of measures they need to take to render them safe.

— In areas that have been flooded, those foods that have remained intact should be moved to a dry place, preferably away from the walls and off the floor.

— Any foodstuff found to be unfit for human consumption must be disposed of, used for animal feed or industrial purposes or destroyed, depending on the assessment of the food safety authorities. Condemned food may be marked with a harmless dye, such as gentian violet, to ensure that the item is not used for human consumption.

— When salvaged foods are deemed fit for consumption and sold, they should be labelled accordingly. If necessary, consumers should be clearly informed of measures they need to take to render them safe.

Assessing and using Salvaged Pre-packaged Food

— Discard canned foods with broken seams, dents, or leaks as also jars with cracks.

— Undamaged canned goods and commercial glass jars of food are likely to be safe. However, if possible, containers should be sanitized before being opened. To do this, the jars and cans need to be washed thoroughly. As this may result in the loss of labels, it is advisable to write the contents on the lid of the can/jar with indelible ink before washing. Finally, the containers need to be immersed for 15 minutes in a solution of 2 teaspoons of chlorine bleach per quart of room temperature water and air-dried before opening.

Foods that are exposed to chemicals should be dumped, as the chemicals generally cannot be washed off the food. This includes foods stored in permeable containers such as cardboard and screw-top jars and bottles which are difficult to clean.

Assessing and Using Salvaged Refrigerated Food

— Inspect refrigerators to determine if their functioning is affected by the lack of electricity or by flood waters. Where refrigerators and cold food have not been directly affected, they may be a suitable source of safe food.

— Where power is not available, try to use refrigerated food—especially meat, fish, poultry, and milk -before it is held in the danger zone (5-60°C) for more than two hours,,

— To avoid the loss of meat, fish, poultry, and milk, these may be placed in a freezer immediately if they have not reached the danger zone. They may also be cooked and frozen in case they are to be kept longer.

— Some foods normally stored in the refrigerator can be kept in the danger zone for longer than others. Under emergency conditions, it is possible that foods such as butter, margarine, fresh fruits, and vegetables, open jars of concentrates and sauces, and hard and processed cheeses can be kept and used for a longer period; but they should definitely be discarded if they show signs of spoilage.

— To prevent warm air from entering the refrigerator, open it only when necessary.

Assessing and Using Salvaged Dry Stores of Food

— Check all food for physical hazards (such as glass) that may have been introduced during the earthquake.

— The likelihood of mould growth on stored dried vegetables, fruits, and cereals is greater in a humid environment and where food has become wet. Mould growth can be associated with chemical toxins.

— Intact food should be moved to a dry place, away from the walls and off the floor. Bags must not lie directly on the floor—pallets, boards, heavy branches, bricks, plastic bags, or sheets should be placed underneath them for protection. Bags should be piled two-by-two, cross-wise to permit ventilation.

— Wet bags should be allowed to dry in the sun before storage.

— Damaged bags should be replaced and stored apart from undamaged ones. A reserve of good-quality empty bags should be kept for this purpose.

— Spilled food should be swept up and disposed of promptly to discourage rats.

Technologies for the Healthcare of Disaster Victims

Medicine and healthcare are critical considerations in disaster preparedness and mitigation of all types of diseases. In the immediate aftermath of disasters, the distraught population is in dire need of medicines and healthcare. This has always been a major challenge for administrative authorities. Any delay or laxity in the supply of medicines and appropriate healthcare aid could multiply the number of casualties among the victims. Hence, providing an adequate supply of disaster medicine and medical relief always remains a top priority for disaster management personnel.

In preparing for a disaster such as an earthquake, storm, or power outage, people with special medical problems need special attention. Technology plays a crucial role in meeting the many challenges faced in providing the requisite medicine and healthcare in disaster times. Modern healthcare management systems and equipment could provide vital support to the medical personnel engaged in post-disaster areas. The technological solutions considered helpful for disaster healthcare managers would include the following:

— diagnostic equipment;
— equipment for critical care;
— equipment for disaster health kits: basic, first-aid items; intravenous (IV) and feeding tube equipment; oxygen and breathing equipment; electrically-powered medical equipment;
— disaster relief response: robot-assisted medical reachback; telemonitoring; patient tracking systems;
— pre-hospital management systems;
— relief medical equipment vans;
— post-response rehabilitation systems;
— tele-medicine: disease surveillance systems; web-based tele-medicine; personal digital assistants; wearable computing; advanced sensors and medical monitoring; DICOM network services; and e-Film Video; and
— advanced systems for disaster medicine and medical relief.

The following sections provide an overview of the technological inputs required for disaster medicine and healthcare management.

General Equipment

— Large commercial or general-purpose military canvas tents
— Generators and associated power distribution systems

— Lighting
— Water purification systems
— Water
— Fuel
— Food (normally, ready-to-eat meals)
— Latrines
— Showers and sinks
— Safety, communications, and computer equipment
— Medical equipment
— Monitor defibrillators
— Ventilators
— Portable ECG machines
— Pulse oximeters
— Small point-of-service laboratory analysers
— Minor surgical kits
— Wound and orthopaedic stations
— Intravenous set-ups
— Minor care stations
— Observation unit supplies
— Large cache of medical disposable supplies
— Associated housekeeping equipment

Diagnostic Equipment

The diagnostic equipment needed in disaster situations are a small ultrasound device, and point-of-care laboratory testing and portable bronchoscopy. Other useful apparatus includes monitoring devices, infusion pumps, and ventilators.

Equipment for Critical Care

Equipment for critical care components, especially retrieval, should include monitoring technologies that overcome the limitations of noise. This includes automated blood pressure monitors, oxygen saturations, end tidal carbon dioxide, limited electrocardiography, and ventilators with variable minute volumes over a wide range of barometric pressures. Infusion devices must be compact and robust with extended battery life.. Point-of-care laboratory testing is needed. And the drugs available must include those that can meet the critical needs of analgesia, sedation, vasoconstriction, inotropic support, vasodilation, and neuromuscular blockade.

Disaster Health Kits

A well-stocked health kit could be very useful to disaster victims. However, such a kit should be readied well before crisis strikes. Several modern apparatus and devices are included in the disaster health kits which, besides the basic first-aid items, include: medications, intravenous (IV) and feeding tube equipment, oxygen and breathing equipment, and electrically-powered medical equipment.

Medications

- At least a three-day supply of all prescribed medications.
- All medications stored in one place in their original containers.
- A complete list of all prescribed medications: name of medication, dose, frequency, and doctor's name.

Medical Supplies

- If medical supplies such as bandages or syringes are being used, an extra three-day supply should be available.

Intravenous (IV) and Feeding Tube Equipment

- If an infusion pump is being used, one needs to ascertain that it has battery back-up, and how long it would last in an emergency.
- Instructions from the home-care provider a anual infusion techniques in case of a power outage are often useful.
- Written operating instructions should be attached to all equipment.

Oxygen and Breathing Equipment

- If oxygen is being used, an emergency supply (for three days or more) is recommended.
- Oxygen tanks should be securely braced to ensure they do not fall over. The bracing instructions should be checked in advance with the medical supplier.

— If breathing equipment is being used, a three-day supply or more of tubing, solutions, medications, etc is advisable.

Electrically-powered Medical Equipment

— For all medical equipment requiring electrical power—for instance, beds, breathing equipment, infusion pumps -, one needs to check with the medical supplier for details on a back-up power source, e.g. a battery or a generator.

— A helpful precaution is to check in advance with one's local utility company to ascertain that backup equipment is properly installed.

Emergency Bag

In the event one needs to leave home at short notice, an emergency bag should always be packed with:

— a medication list;

— medical supplies for three days;

— copies of vital medical papers such as insurance cards, Advanced Directive, Power of Attorney, etc;

— refrigerated medications and solutions.

Medical Relief

In disaster-affected areas, medical relief requires a wide range of technological back-up and support systems for meeting the complex challenges. The requirements vary at different stages of the disaster management process, namely, relief response, pre-hospital management, and post-disaster response; rehabilitation.

Relief Response

— Robot-assisted medical reach-back

  — Access to the victim during the 4-10 hrs of extrication.

  — All functions below depths of 10-30 metres in rubble.

— Tele-monitoring

  — Critically ill patient—sensors nodes.

  — During triage.

— Patient tracking systems

— Bar coding and mobile wireless data acquisition to individually identify and track victims of Pre-hospital Management disasters.

— Bar coding has been piloted and tested in Europe.

Relief Medical Equipment Vans

In India, Accident Relief Medical Equipment (ARME) vans and Accident Relief Trains (ART), including a few self-propelled vehicles, are positioned at strategic locations for rushing to an accident site on top priority, along with doctors, paramedical staff, rescue workers, and engineers. The medical team attends to injured passengers, and the seriously wounded are transported to nearby hospitals. ARME vans are equipped with medicines, resuscitation machines, dressings, disposables, etc for use in emergencies and also have an operation theatre with facilities for conducting minor surgeries. These vans are so located as to cover an area within a distance of 150-200 km, normally in two-to-three hours. ARME vans may take up to four hours to reach a remote accident site.

Tele-medicine

Tele-medicine refers to the utilization of telecommunication technology for medical diagnosis, treatment, and patient care. A tele-medicine system is composed of customized medical software integrated with computer hardware, along with medical diagnostic instruments connected to the commercial VSAT (Very Small Aperture Terminal) at each location on fiber optics.Tele-medicine enables a physician or specialist at one site to provide healthcare, diagnose patients, treat and monitor them, give intra-operative assistance, administer therapy, and consult with another physician or paramedical personnel at a remote site, thereby ensuring convenient, site-independent access to expert advice and patient information. Transmission modalities include direct hard-wired connections over standard phone lines and specialized data lines (single/twisted pairs of metallic wires, coaxial lines, fiber optic cable) and "wireless" communications, using infrared, radio, television, microwave, and satellite-based linkages. Improved space-and ground-based technologies now form a communications infrastructure well suited to addressing ongoing disaster management needs.

Disease Surveillance Systems

Some of the existing (or in the process of being developed) disease surveillance systems are as follows:

— Electronic Disease Reporting and Management System (EDRMS)
— Real-time Outbreak and Disease Surveillance (RODS)
— Lightweight Epidemiological Advanced Detection and Emergency Response system (LEADERS)

Web-based Tele-medicine

The Web provides an efficient platform for medical education, access to medical knowledge, and tele-medicine consultations. An ideal Web-based tele-medicine system would integrate existing technologies, providing access to diverse application programs and utilizing multimedia modalities. It would also deliver information to a single access point, independent of hardware platform (e.g. desktop PC, portable laptop computer, or pocket-sized computer), and be protocol-driven, with store-and-forward or real-time tele-consultancy capability. The system would promote cost-efficient transfer and sharing of clinical information throughout the world, even in remote areas.

Personal Digital Assistants

Recent computer miniaturization has produced pocket-sized personal digital assistants (PDAs) with personalized interfaces. These small computers can support keyboard, pen, touch, and voice inputs and provide information management, portability, connectivity and, to varying degrees, e-mail, fax, graphics, digital photography, and voice recording capabilities. The ability to use a single small communicator to transmit different types of information anywhere in the world would be ideal for the disaster field worker. A small "pocket tele-medicine" unit, equipped with Web-browsing capability, a digital camera, telephone, and computer, could be used to conduct on-site, real-time consultations whenever necessary.

Wearable Computing

Miniaturization of components has enabled the development of personal computer systems that are lightweight, unobtrusive, and wearable. Both the military and civilian sectors are investigating such systems which allow hands-free operation, enhanced mobility, access to information, and shared visual experiences. Early prototypes for wearable wireless computers utilized video images sent to a remote supercomputing facility over a high-quality microwave communication link. The computing facility sent back the processed image over ultra-high frequency communication links. Newer versions incorporate commercial head-mounted displays and cellular communications.Wearable computing will, in the future, incorporate the advantages of a PDA but in a more compact, hands-free form which allows the worker to communicate while helping disaster victims. This will become the ultimate wireless-communication support system for the disaster responder.

Advanced Sensors and Medical Monitoring

Innovative applications for advanced sensors and smart materials currently being developed for combat soldiers in the USA could act as potential telemedicine devices. The Personnel Status Monitor (PSM), a miniaturized device resembling a wristwatch, is being designed to be worn by the soldiers. It combines advanced environmental sensors and non-intrusive physiologic sensors with a CPU, geo-positioning receiver, and low-power wireless radio. The PSM will monitor the soldier's vital signs continuously. The monitor is programmed to remain passive until queried, when it replies with the soldier's geographic location and vital signs. However, if the soldier's vital signs alter significantly from established norms, the PSM would promptly transmit the location and vital signs until it is shut down by a medic.

DICOM Network Services

The DICOM network services are based on the client/server concept. Before two DICOM applications can exchange information, they must establish a connection and agree on the following parameters: (a) Who is the client and who is the server? (b) Which DICOM services are to be used? (c) Which format is to be used for data transmission?

E-Film

Organizations often have equipment that does not support the DICOM standard or provide the means of outputting digital images. e-Film Video is a system that captures still images and video streams from analog medical image acquisition devices (with analog outputs) and converts them to the industry standard DICOM 3.0 format. Promoting integrated digital medical imaging, e-Film Video images and video loops can be sent to DICOM-compliant devices for display and processing.

Life Support for Trauma and Transport (LSTAT)

The LSTAT is the result of a joint effort of Northrop Grumman Corp (Los Angeles, California) and various military medical services in the USA. The

LSTAT is a self-contained, stretcher-type platform designed to aid in field stabilization and transport of severely injured patients. It incorporates a number of on-board devices for ongoing treatment, which include monitors for basic vital signs and blood chemistry; mechanical ventilation and oxygen supplementation for patients requiring endo-tracheal intubation; a self-contained, battery-powered infusion pump to deliver intravenous fluids; and a self-contained, battery-powered suction pump. An automated external defibrillator is also built into each of the LSTAT units. All patient medical data that is monitored by the on-board devices of the LSTAT can be data-linked to the receiving medical facility while the patient is being transported by air or ground ambulance.

Mobile Medical Communication Technology

Telemedicus owns the exclusive rights to an innovative breakthrough in rapid medical emergency response and communications technology called "Disaster Relief and Emergency Medical Services (DREAMS™)", jointly developed by the University of Texas Health Science Center in Houston, led by Dr. Red Duke, and the Texas A&M University, led by Dr. Richard Ewing.

DREAMS™ is the latest generation of mobile medical communication technology that allows a doctor to be "virtually on board" the ambulance or medi-flight as the patient is transported to the hospital or at the scene of an accident or at a remote location where traditional medical treatment is impractical.

New Technology for Hospital Readiness for Disasters

In the USA emergency medicine specialists from Johns Hopkins have developed a tool to help hospitals prepare for disasters with the potential to overwhelm services. The Electronic Mass Casualty Assessment & Planning Scenarios (EMCAPS) computer program calculates the impact of such crises as a flu epidemic, bio-terrorist attack, flood, and plane crash, accounting for such elements as the number of victims, wind direction, available medical resources, bacterial incubation periods, and bomb size. Written by members of the Johns Hopkins Critical Event Preparedness and Response (CEPAR) office and the Johns Hopkins University Applied Physics Laboratory (APL), the program depends heavily on population density estimates to derive 'plausible estimates' of what hospitals may expect in the initial minutes or hours of a disaster.

Deployable Tele-medicine Kit

AMD Telemedicine, the world leader in developing, marketing, and providing training for tele-medicine equipment, has created a Deployable Tele-medicine Kit and is working to identify disaster organizations, first-responder teams, and medical facilities around the world that would be able to deploy and/or utilize this type of medical equipment in the event of a disaster. With this kit, healthcare providers in the field would have the ability to send photo images of the inner ear/nose/throat; of any trauma to extremities; of soft tissue injuries; of captured ultrasound scans; and of digital 12-lead electrocardiograms, digital lung capacity reports, and heart or lung sounds. The specialist in the field would then send this data to a medical specialist via satellite, internet, or Integrated Services Digital Networks (ISDN), providing an evaluation and/or consultation for these remote victims by using live videoconferencing or store-and-forward applications.

The new transportable, tele-medicine kit includes:

— AMD-2500s General Examination Camera, a powerful general examination camera, which is the first analog camera to combine power zoom, auto focus, freeze frame capture, and electronic image polarization in one diagnostic device.

— AMD-3550 SmartSteth Digital Electronic Stethoscope, permitting the recording, analysis, and transmission of high quality lung and heart sounds.

— AMD-2015 ENT/Otoscope for comprehensive ear, nose, and throat (ENT) examinations, combining the functionality of a high performance otoscope, a short sinus scope, and an oral exam scope in a single diagnostic device.

— AMD-3920 Digital Spirometer for PC, the PC-based digital spirometer that supports a full range of diagnostic cardiac and pulmonary applications, including expiratory reserve volume (REV), relaxed vital capacity (VC), forced vital capacity (FVC), forced expiratory volume (FEV), peak expiratory flow (PEF), and maximal voluntary ventilation (MVV). Fully compliant with the strict requirements of the American Thoracic Society (ATS).

— AMD-2020 Direct Opthalmoscope, the video version of a diagnostic direct ophthalmoscope which enables viewing and illumination of retina, head of optic nerve, retinal arteries, vitreous humor, through an undilated pupil.

— AMD-5500 SmartProbe™ Ultrasound,-the system on a chip provides true 128 channel resolution in a laptop PC, with all the functionality of the most expensive ultrasound systems.

— AMD-3875 12 Lead Interpretive ECG for PC, when connected to the serial port of a PC, converts any Windows® 98/NT platform to a real-time 12 Lead ECG machine with Interpretation.

— The AMD Image Management System—a quick and efficient software program to organize individual patients, conditions, and screenshots while at the emergency scene.

References

Comfort, L. K., ed. (1988). *Managing Disaster: Strategies and Policy Perspectives.* Durham, NC: Duke University Press.

Constantine, G. Ted. (1995). *Intelligence Support to Humanitarian-Disaster Relief Operations, An Intelligence Monograph.* Washington, DC: CSI 95-005, December.

Garshnek, Victoria and Burkle, Frederick M., Jr. (1999). Applications of Telemedicine and Telecommunications to Disaster Medicine: Historical and Future Perspectives, *J Am Med Inform Assoc,* Jan-Feb 6(1): 26–37. 7.

Wong, James, Robinson, Cassandra et al. (2004). *Urban Search and Rescue Technology Needs: Identification of Needs.* Savannah River National Laboratory, November.

9

Managing Disaster Information

Disasters show little regard for existing boundaries, whether geographical, political, or professional. When a disaster strikes, everyone needs to make informed decisions about what to do to protect their families, their businesses, and their community. Disaster managers and responders suddenly become very important, but so do emergency responders such as physicians, firefighters, and law enforcement personnel. As rebuilding proceeds, architects, engineers, financiers, construction workers, building inspectors, and many others play critical roles. Thus, much of the disaster management community is involved full time, while many of those affected are involved only part time. Disasters involve the public and private sectors, government and business, professionals and volunteers, practitioners, academia, and the research community.

A comprehensive approach to disaster management involves four basic phases: mitigation, preparedness, response, and recovery. In times of disaster, people are preoccupied with response and then with recovery. The greatest potential for loss reduction, though, is typically during the mitigation phase, when communities can be made more disaster resistant.

The largest share of costs, however, are directed toward the recovery phase, where good mitigation principles also need to be put into practice rather than just rebuilding only to face a similar disaster in the future. Lessons learned or information gathered during one phase are often valuable when put into practice in other phases. Such interrelationships argue not only for a comprehensive approach to disaster management, but also a comprehensive approach to managing disaster information.

The challenge for a disaster information system is to meet the widely varying needs of a very broad spectrum of users during all four phases of disaster management. In addition to the needs for basic situational awareness and resource management information, there are needs for information to make critical decisions, needs for training, and needs for communication among people with similar responsibilities or interests. The disaster management community throughout the world must continually be improved and benefit from technical assistance, training, and the latest technologies so that it is ready to take crisis preparation and mitigation actions.

The need to integrate across many boundaries, all phases of disasters, and the many different user requirements make designing a Disaster Information Network a formidable task.

Conceptual Flow of Disaster-Related Information

Disaster information involves more than just data. Several interconnecting steps are typically required to generate the types of action-oriented products needed by the disaster management community. The exact steps taken depend on the disaster phase and how time critical the need is. The following describes each step in the product generation process:

Problem

Define the problem, event, or phenomena to be studied. For instance, an ability to measure the health of vegetation is critical for land managers to determine fire-prone areas within their jurisdiction. The underlying conditions leading to disaster events must be well understood in order to determine which data need to be collected.

Requirement

Decide what is required to study the problem. By knowing the driving forces behind the measurements, one can commit the right resources, coordinate the activities, determine how to best manage the collection and analysis methodologies, and judge how best to distribute the eventual information products. Knowing what is needed and how to get it is fundamental to every disaster-related action.

Supporting Data

Know which information sources are available to meet disaster manager needs. Because there is an increasing amount of source material available and because varying disaster events require different data sets, the optimal toolset is an up-to-date knowledge base.

Data Exploitation

Analyse data to generate products. This includes the processing of digital data, image integration, feature classification and attribution, classification output, accuracy assessments, and post processing operations. It is the most technically challenging step in the process and probably best performed at exploitation centers where there is resident expertise.

Decision Support

Provide ways for decision-makers to visualize and merge data and products. This phase essentially involves the synthesis of the data types in order to generate data layers (e.g., soils, vegetation, terrain) along with the models and simulation techniques that stem from use of the data layers.

Product and Actions

Produce products that lead to actions to save lives and reduce damage. Actionable information can be defined as a tangible product that supports these activities such as the delineation of evacuation routes and damage assessments.

Delivery Process

Communicate and disseminate information through all the disaster management stages. This means that the communications and dissemination infrastructure must work in a timely and effective manner.

Understanding this broad conceptual flow of information sets the stage for the required breadth of a disaster information network developed.

Disaster Information: User Needs

The Disaster Information Task Force had to develop a fundamental understanding of the needs that exist within the U.S. disaster management community. This phase of the DITF process was initiated through analysis of existing and requested information from within the DM community.

To better understand the needs of the DM community, therefore, the GDIN User Working Group conducted a DM requirements assessment in which the following user communities were represented:

— Federal, state, and local governments, including all those engaged in disaster management

— The private sector, including critical infrastructure services

— Scientific and engineering research and systems development communities

— Non-profit organizations, private volunteer organizations, and the public at large, including populations with special needs.

In addition to identifying the importance of information sharing and communication among these entities, discussions helped define the relationship between the DM community, the information provider community, and the community of technologists tasked with identifying communication requirements.

The DM community is undergoing rapid transformation as it assimilates critical technologies to improve direction and control, operational readiness, and situational awareness. It is among the most interdisciplinary public-service professions. The disaster manager coordinates the plans and actions of engineers and scientists as well as public health, law enforcement, communications, and transportation professionals, among other disciplines. The disaster manager must understand the roles and responsibilities of multiple agencies and must coordinate preparedness and mitigation efforts to inspire readiness through drills, exercises, planning, and training. Emergence of a nascent emergency information infrastructure and aggressive efforts in implementing professional standards through certification programs, such as that of the National Coordinating Council on Emergency Management (NCCEM), have contributed to a synthesis of DM skills and experience and a convergence of tools and techniques.

Guidance

The DITF defined its strategy for the user information needs analysis through a concise fact-finding and evaluation effort.

Survey

The User Working Group developed a survey as a first step to organize and communicate user community requirements. In order to accurately and comprehensively represent the user base—from first responders to national program planners—the User Working Group pursued a multidimensional investigation of needs.

The diversity of resources, research, and source material employed in the user needs analysis and requirements synthesis activity is illustrated below. The DITF endeavoured to recognize, amplify, and complement the findings and activities of the SNDR, NRC, and other distinguished bodies involved in strategic planning and assessment of the DM enterprise worldwide.

Synthesis Activity

The hundreds of survey responses and user input forms were aggregated by the DITF. The data set was then evaluated, and themes, clusters, and commonalities were identified. A compilation of user requirements, referred to as the "Synthesis of User Requirements for GDIN Working Group Evaluation (SURGE)," was developed for evaluation by the User, Provider, Disseminator, Pre-Event, Post-Event, and Hazard-Specific Teams comprising the DITF. These expert teams then derived DM information findings. These findings express composite DM requirements that would translate into appropriate provider and disseminator technical solutions.

GDIN is built on a foundation of detailed user requirements. This rigor is required to ensure that solutions proposed in a future GDIN are responsive to unmet needs and provide a pathway for cooperation among participants.

Current Environment

Utilization of the distributed national information infrastructure is increasing within the DM community. Innovative intranet implementations based on emergency support functions within the U.S. Federal Response Plan illustrate how the Internet model can successfully mesh with the functional mission of the FRP partners. The initial GDIN user needs analysis suggests a similar model can address the full life cycle of DM, encompassing mitigation, preparedness, response, and recovery activities. The following paragraphs are a distillation of the DITF-identified needs of the DM community and the various technologies that are emerging to support them.

Connectivity

The universality of the WWW offers unprecedented portability for the disaster manager on the scene or in the Emergency Operations Center. In addition, services such as the Asynchronous Transfer Mode, modems, and hand-held personal computers (HPCs) with integral GPS and GIS capabilities provide increased secure bandwidth to fulfil the goal of full service to the last mile of connectivity.

The National Academy of Public Administration (NAPA) reports that in 22 states the state emergency management office reports to the Adjutant General, effectively placing both the National Guard and the DM office within the same organization. This legacy of close cooperation between state Emergency Operations Centers (EOCs) and the National Guard facilities creates a unique opportunity for exploitation of the emergent GuardNet XXI services supporting Federal and state connectivity. Commercial carriers are implementing usage-based cost structures for the National Guard that promise a more efficient balance between fixed costs and costs associated with surge scenarios.

Data Dependencies

DM users want to identify, import, condition, and integrate data from geographically disparate data sources and warehouses. The geospatial referencing capability provided by the GPS has greatly improved data quality and GIS, models, and other analytical tools available to the disaster manager. The data/information provider community is responding to calls for organizing an emerging state and national spatial data infrastructure through easy-to-access clearing house services. Widely adopted geospatial data standards are expected to facilitate interoperability across complex systems and networks.

Products derived from high-resolution, space-based imagery offer new insights into environmental behaviour and processes. These derived products—fused with baseline environmental, socioeconomic, and critical infrastructure data in modelling and simulation processes—offer the promise of enhanced precision and more effective predictive capability for the DM community. The disaster manager who understands the process of capturing data and turning that data into information and decision support products will better address DM issues.

Broadcast Services

The DM community needs global broadcast services to provide wide-area dissemination of warnings, information products such as earthquake damage maps or loss estimation data, and situation reports. Both users and providers recognize the services such as the Emergency Management Weather Information Network (EMWIN) and NOAA Weather Radio as important components of the existing infrastructure; however, these services do not reach many end users. The planned constellations of orbiting satellites form the backbone of emergent global cellular services. These systems suggest wide-bandwidth alternatives to terrestrial wireless networks and are anticipated to be operational within 1 to 4 years. Unlike terrestrial networks—which are vulnerable to earthquake, flood, fire, or other catastrophic events—the new global services can provide critical alternative communication pipelines during localized service outages.

Service Priority

Users stressed the need for prioritization for disaster preparation and national security use within these global wireless services, consistent perhaps with the current practice of the Government Emergency Telecommunications Service (GETS) Program managed by the National Communications System (NCS). This requirement will take on a higher profile as the GDIN pursues international cooperation. The need to ensure a quality or class of service was frequently mentioned by both users and providers. Thus, the GDIN will require congestion control during high-stress usage. Secure information capabilities—exemplified in practice by the Defense Information System Agency's Secure Internet Protocol Router Network (SIPRnet) and the Defense Message System (DMS)—have been cited as important attributes for Federal agency nodes linking headquarters, regional, and disaster field offices.

Service Delivery Demands on the GDIN

The DITF survey results suggest that we need an effective dissemination network in order to realize the full potential of the existing data and infrastructure.

The public service challenge for the GDIN is to effectively utilize Federal data resources to fortify state and local decision-making readiness in all phases of the comprehensive DM cycle. The Federal sector can provide key preparation information ranging from base maps to critical infrastructure overlays for response and recovery damage estimation and assessment to mitigation planning for disaster-resistant communities. The importance of information portraying both natural and built environments is perhaps most obvious for preparation and mitigation. Mitigation actions range from structural engineering modifications to community relocation programs, and the need for data/information exists across the spectrum of mitigation actions. Preparedness also requires data/information to improve understanding of existing hazards and features of the natural and built environments, and simulation tools to support plans, exercises, and training—the crucial ingredients of readiness.

Information Resources

The emergency Information Infrastructure (EII) would include best available environmental, socioeconomic, and infrastructure information with coverage of the area of interest, as well as metadata identifying government, research community, and related commercial data. The information might be organized around any number of schema, ranging from the traditional FRP emergency support functions to taxonomy initiatives such as that of the National Emergency Response Information Network (NERIN). Regardless how information resources are arrayed at key nodes, they will be built around existing legacy database management systems and catalogs and must leverage the substantial institutional investment. The continuum of information needs across the comprehensive DM cycle is shown above. This is the framework within which the GDIN can supplement current support functions. The GDIN can make a critical contribution to the DM community, supporting the definition, identification, and availability of essential information for community resilience. With this objective, the GDIN will enhance information preparation and delivery with improved access to and transport of refined content for the DM community. It offers a building-block approach of robust, agile services for disseminators and information providers to meet user needs for accurate capability assessment and fortification of community resilience.

Experts' Virtual Forum

The GDIN should support technology currently available for a rapid virtual conference capability. An experts' virtual forum would serve to assimilate on-site conditions from first responders in order to launch models and simulation tools; this permits furnishing mitigation and prediction analysis and damage estimation output products to users in need of rapid situation assessment. It would empower the DM community with unparalleled reachback to geographically dispersed technical or scientific expertise to augment both strategic planning and on-the-scene and EOC decision-making.

The enhancement GDIN could offer, in both communications infrastructure and actionable information data and decision support tools, is perhaps best characterized by a user vision that was articulated during the user needs analysis.

Imagine decision-makers with the ability to view the three-dimensional environment; to point-and-click on various rainfall scenarios; to watch the progression of a flood through communities at risk; to select various mitigation actions such as levee breaks, sandbagging, and dam releases; and to view in fly-through mode the impacts of their decisions on natural resources (crops, livestock, timber), on the built environment (commercial and residential properties, transportation infrastructure, other lifelines), and on the population, including those with special needs.

The profound insight and foresight such a tool could provide would be an invaluable asset in the portfolio of the DM community. Indeed, many of the features are now in operation or in advanced stages of development. The NIMA fly-through visualization experience, NTM-derived products, the virtual reality assets of NASA, and DoD—these are but a few of the building blocks currently available. GDIN can motivate and facilitate the DM future.

User Community Vision

A systems approach needs to be developed that can serve as a resource multiplier offering improved access to and assured transport of refined and derived data and other actionable information products. The GDIN should be defined and designed within the context of operational assumptions about the DM user community. A sampling of operational assumptions shaping the vision of the Emergency Information Infrastructure (EII) include:

Remote execution of simulation tools

For timely decision support, emergency managers need access to simulation tools (e.g., chemical release models; earthquake ground failure, liquefaction, and landslide models; nuclear plant release models; flood inundation models) maintained by distant institutions or operations centers.

Wireless interfaces

Unrestricted access to on-scene commanders and first responders will be needed to support the transfer of imagery and overlays to portray a composite picture of areas impacted by an event. Such access extends situational awareness of the EOC to the field in the response and recovery phases.

For improved user capability throughout the comprehensive disaster management cycle, the disaster manager must be a full partner with both the information provider and the network and communication technologists. All-source data fusion, image analysis techniques, and simulation and modelling are among the currently available and emerging resources that would benefit the DM community.

In addition, the burgeoning use of networks and increasing complexity of communication systems present barriers to interoperability. Further, since this diversity of systems, methods, and protocols results in disparate formats, there is need for data compatibility and comprehensive metadata—information about the data—that enables data interoperability. Information assurance must be maintained across all open, restricted, and classified levels of transmission and processing. For effectiveness, coordination to ensure timely information delivery is critical in all phases of the DM cycle. Finally, the information infrastructure for disaster management must be capable of supporting a variety of user knowledge, skills, and experience. Thus, an important function of an end-to-end capability, such as that envisioned for GDIN, is to establish stronger interagency cooperation to improve the capability of the user community throughout the comprehensive DM cycle. A systems approach needs to be established and sustained, serving as a resource multiplier improving access to and assuring transport of refined and derived data and other actionable information.

Responsibilities of Information Provider Community

A multifaceted community of providers supports disaster information needs. Providers include organizations responsible for acquiring in situ and remotely sensed data, exploiting these data, generating information products, and developing projections and forecasts that convey dynamics associated with a disaster event. The disaster information industry prepares information under the most stressful situations during crisis response and recovery. It also develops and maintains vital baseline data used during earlier stages of disaster mitigation and preparedness.

During times of crisis, emergency response teams depend on providers for event-related information such as maps that delineate affected areas and detail critical infrastructure, identification of people at risk, estimates of projected inundation, and weather reports. To support crisis management, as well as planning and mitigation efforts during non-crisis periods, emergency managers rely on providers for baseline information such as land cover, topography, housing and public infrastructure, volcanic or earthquake activity, or snow pack.

The line is often blurred between information provider and information user. Most organizations responsible for generating information products act as information intermediaries, enhancing supplied data into forms needed by disaster managers now or information providers in the future. For the disaster manager, these products form the basis for developing a plan of action to mitigate against, prepare for, respond to, or recover from a disaster event. The need for such "actionable information products" often creates a complex chain of events involving several organizations.

The availability of advanced measurement systems—such as space and airborne remote sensing instrumentation, the GPS, and ground-based instrumentation—has resulted in the growth of both a public and private information industry to support the needs of the DM. Communications and product dissemination options encompassing diverse electronic communications protocols—such as public networks and private networks —expand the effectiveness of the DM community in delivering its product. Analytical tools such as GISs and predictive models further expand the breadth of information services.

The changing state of technology has encouraged providers to become less autonomous and more interdependent. Products can be assembled using resources distributed among several organizations at various sites and disseminated to users via new information pathways. One only need examine the depth and variety of disaster-and crisis-related information available on the Internet to realize that the disaster community is operating within a new information paradigm.

These new capabilities transform the way business is conducted, placing a premium on information technology, training, and collaboration. Illustrations of the benefits of these changes are abundant. For example, classified satellite systems can now be tasked to add to information available through other sources. Instruments such as the Advanced Very High Resolution Radiometer (AVHRR) or Interfero-metric Synthetic Aperture Radar (IFSAR) can readily provide detailed synoptic representations of affected areas. Social and environmental data can be integrated with information on road and power infrastructure and then related to disaster risk. Data can be readily posted on Internet-based public bulletin boards to increase public awareness. Also, disaster managers can receive map-based damage assessments in minutes.

Technological opportunities bring new challenges to disaster information providers, who must respond to growing complexity and increased opportunities while satisfying their customers' needs within time and cost constraints. To do this, they need to:

— Understand the multiplicity of new data streams and formats.
— Manage data that seem to continually increase in volume, often outstripping the capacity of current communication bandwidths.
— Meet crisis requirements while maintaining appropriate baseline information and capability to support the needs of disaster mitigation and preparation.
— Maintain user awareness and understanding of ever-broadening capabilities.
— Integrate complex data into understandable thematic information products.
— Recognize interdependencies necessary to assemble products through formation and nurturing of relationships with other providers.
— Maintain awareness of technological and scientific advances in the fields of communications, measurement systems, modelling, and analysis.
— Ensure timely delivery of information to disaster managers despite the complexities of the production process.
— Maintain public awareness by exploiting and managing available communication options.

Current technology has made the disaster information management process even more complex. Yet, the potential exists to achieve unprecedented levels of performance in response to disaster management.

Existing and projected increases in the capacity for Earth observations from space and readily accessible in situ information—coupled with increased GIS use, model and simulation techniques, improved image processing, and information fusion—result in a potentially powerful and complementary set of tools for the DM community. Effective development and application of the observations through all phases of the DM cycle will depend on the ability of experts to adopt and adapt to the use of imagery and in situ data and its associated information.

The provider's ability to meet the needs of the DM community to turn data into useful information and the value of efforts in the pre-event phase to aid in the post-event phase of a disaster are best illustrated through the following example.

The Miller's Reach Fire #2, a fire that burned over 37,000 acres and destroyed 344 structures in Alaska in June 1996, was the worst urban/ wildfire in the state's history. Following are a few examples of identified needs, gleaned from the after-action report, that could have benefited from currently available exploitation tools. But when a team is not familiar with local conditions, be they weather, fuels, terrain, or politics, they need to be closely monitored.

The first is the local knowledge that "there were two different fuel types involved, mature birch with white spruce undergrowth and pure stands of black spruce. The black spruce was the primary carrier for the crown fire. This is a significant problem fuel in Alaska." After-the-fire analysis showed that indeed "burn patterns and eyewitness accounts indicate the fire spread by crowning and spotting" of black spruce cones, which are the primary source of spot fires. A mitigation strategy that created a species boundary and extent map would easily translate into fire characteristics for a team not familiar with local tree characteristics.

A comment on the information needed for the response phase was also noted: "The topography in the fire area is flat with low rolling hills. The fire burned with the wind, with influence from local topographic features." A GIS in which the local weather conditions were combined with accurate topographic data would be able to create a fire spread assessment useful to the DM team.

Functions of the Provider Community

The DM community would benefit from a mechanism to allow continuous dialogue between the field user and the community of practitioners that can provide actionable information. The DITF assembled a team to explore the opportunities for dialogue between these two communities. This team was tasked to assimilate the needs of the DM community and to assess the key provider functions in meeting the needs of end users. The following provider functions were identified in this process.

Data Acquisition

Process of capturing and transmitting the measurements, observations, and records that serve as the base materials used to meet DM community needs. Data immediately come to mind when one thinks of the provider community. Data within the context of DM includes a broad spectrum of measurements, observations, and records used to drive models, simulation tools, damage estimation and assessment algorithms, GIS databases, and the decision support tools enabling comprehensive disaster mitigation, preparedness, response, and recovery. In this context, data are not only raw baseline products captured by front-line collection systems but also processed information products used to drive models and as input for fusion techniques.

Requirements Satisfaction

Process of capturing, understanding, and responding to user needs. The provider must capture the DM community baseline requirements and understand community objectives in order to find creative new approaches to meet its needs. The interaction between the user and provider must be a dynamic one with its goal being the expansion of each other's base knowledge. In the Miller's Reach example above, such an effort would have been an effective contribution by the provider community in helping to meet the needs of the user community.

Documentation

Characterization of the data and information products available to the user. Metadata, or "data about data," is a key feature of data documentation and describes its content, quality, condition, and other characteristics. Metadata is one of the key features in the ability of the provider to meet the needs of the DM community. Metadata provides information to help the emergency manager determine what data are available, to evaluate its fitness, and ultimately to acquire, transfer, and process it. The order accessed and relative importance of metadata elements will vary by disaster type and phase. In addition, disaster managers with different objectives and working on different phases of a disaster may require the same information at different levels of abstraction.

Accessibility

The availability of data and information to users within the constraints of policy and confidentiality. User data/information requirements invariably address the issue of access. Knowledge of the existence of data/information, its availability, and the tools necessary to acquire it are key attributes of access. The disaster manager and the provider must identify the technical and other barriers limiting access and make a cooperative effort to surmount them.

Interoperability

Process that enables the inter-use of data/information products. Interoperability is a means to standardize the data to ensure connectivity between the disaster manager and the provider community. Key features of interoperability include symbology, formats, software, scale resolution, and frequency. In such cases where standards cannot be implemented, it is important to accommodate nonstandard data. This process, known as harmonization, is accomplished through software and other approaches.

Exploitation Tools

Management and enhancement of data into useful information products. A variety of tools is available to the provider community to exploit and turn data into useful information products. The provider can work in a geospatially referenced domain, generate images from satellite and other data sets, integrate and fuse the data into actionable information products, and use models and forecasts to aid the emergency manager. In the Miller's Reach example, enhanced exploitation tools could have been effectively used to delineate the burn characteristics to those unfamiliar with fire spread in Alaska.

Decision Support

Recommended course of action that the disaster manager should take. Decision support includes the following tools and techniques: modelling and simulation capabilities, data visualization and integration tools (particularly those supporting management of geospatial data objects), advanced data mining and core sampling applications, rapid damage assessment tools, logistics planning tools, groupware and collaboration technologies supporting real-time dissemination in distributed environments, and enabling technologies and methodologies supporting virtual expert forums.

Preservation

Maintenance, data integrity, management, and heritage of data/information. It is vital to preserve the data/information generated, usually at great expense and use of resources. Archives that do not manage data/information effectively over time are of little value to the DM community.

Quality

Value of information as represented in the context of user requirements. Quality refers to the data/information accuracy and precision, as well as the adequacy of crucial metadata describing the data or information set. GPSs have significantly improved the quality and utility of data by providing enhanced geospatial reference for use in GISs, models, and other analysis tools. Finally, an important attribute of data quality is its heritage, which relates directly back to its documentation. This increasingly complex suite of capabilities is technologically feasible and ready for exploitation by the provider to meet the needs of the DM community.

Information Generation

Federal, state, local, and private sector DM information users are amassing a variety of data types with differing formats and accuracy. In addition, new types of sensors are being developed, an increasing number of products are derived from classified sources, and improved hardware and software are coming into operational use. These advances, along with new integration and communication techniques, create new information-sharing opportunities during all phases of disaster support.

Data Acquisition

Data sources that are available to the disaster manager today include remotely sensed imagery, digital maps, and ancillary data. Imagery is an extremely powerful information tool, and its use is being demonstrated throughout a growing range of environmental support initiatives. Probably the two most widely recognized remote sensing capabilities that are used in support of disaster management are multispectral scanners and radar collection systems. The advantage of multispectral sensors is that they provide information from a variety of selective bands within the electromagnetic spectrum. This allows for the discrimination between feature types and is therefore useful for classifying various land and sea surface types. Products such as the Thematic Mapper and RADARSAT provide response and recovery teams with information on the extent of a disaster; they are also useful products for updating baseline information during the mitigation and preparedness phases. Radar tends to complement multispectral data by providing crisp representations of topography and drainage patterns and has a day-night, all-weather capability.

Digital maps are derived from a combination of imagery, hardcopy maps, and field surveys. They are available in many forms for various locations of the world at varying scales. Other ancillary data types that benefit the disaster management community include stream gauge data, meteorological/ climactic data, seismic readings, and census data. A challenge, therefore, to analysts using these various data types is not only determining which combination of these data types are available for their area of interest but deciding how they also might be best used.

The selective fusion of data sources allows for the generation of very sophisticated actionable information. Advances in other sensor types are also taking place, from microwave through thermal infrared; these sensors can be used to further support the varied requirements during both pre-and post-disaster phases.

Analysis

The key exploitation methodologies and resulting information products that provide support to emergency managers are image generation, data fusion/ integration, GIS-derived product generation, and modelling and simulation. Each of the following techniques normally requires specialists in the fields of photogrammetry, imagery interpretation, computer science, and GISs. A number of publications and curricula specialize in these areas of expertise.

Image generation

Once the imagery data have been collected, there are a number of additional steps needed to produce a product of use to the DM community. The collected data will need to be preprocessed, classified, field controlled, and checked for accuracy. In most cases these procedures will be performed by an intermediary who is trained in image processing, not the disaster manager. The disaster managers should be aware, however, of the quality and reliability of all source information under their purview.

Data fusion/integration

Normally no one source of information will meet the needs of the disaster manager. Individual images or elements of information often become much more meaningful when carefully combined with complementary data types. The fusion/integration of disparate information sources provides a disaster manager with a richer data set from which to create tailored products. Again, these are fairly sophisticated methodologies, many of which are still in their infancy, so a technically trained intermediary is needed to create these fused products.

Geographic Information System (GIS)

The GIS is one of the most important tools available to the disaster manager. The growth in geo-technologies has spurred the creation of GIS-based data sources, along with structures and standards that make relevant data more useful across the entire spectrum of GIS applications. GIS data sets naturally lend themselves to disaster reduction efforts. With a GIS infrastructure in place, additional disaster-specific information can be used in making informed decisions to help reduce the loss of life and property.

Pre-event information assembly activities—database development, automated analysis techniques, model incorporation, and system testing—are crucial to the success of disaster relief efforts. Field survey data can be combined with imagery and GPS technologies to yield information that can be produced in GIS-ready formats for use in disaster mitigation.

Data layers from various sources can be combined within a GIS environment to generate disaster support information. In this example a population density map is created to help planners and resource managers efficiently determine evacuation routes, calculate response times, predict resource distribution, and produce other tailored products for disaster management use.

Derived products

Products derived from National Technical Means often offer unique solutions to disaster information requirements. Derived products contain unclassified imagery and map products that have been derived from national systems. The intelligence community could provide various derived products to aid in both the pre-and post-disaster phases. Typically, NTM products supplement other sources through their ability to provide information in a timely manner, to provide data collected over hard-to-access areas, and to support detailed analyses (large-scale information).

The Imagery Derived Products (IDP) program provides a mechanism by which civilian agencies can acquire derived products. Currently, all derived products for the IDP program are generated at the U.S. Geological Survey's Advanced Systems Center (USGS/ASC). The program provides semiautomated techniques and capabilities for civilian agencies' derived products.

Modelling and simulation

Once an appropriate baseline data set is assembled, analysis can be performed for different disaster types. Combining digital products like FEMA's Q3 Flood Rate maps, USFS fire threat and drought data, and NOAA's storm surge models can delineate at-risk areas. These analyses can yield potential threat maps for different disaster types such as population and infrastructure susceptibility, dangers to aquatic and terrestrial ecosystems, and potential hazardous material effects. This process can be enhanced using expert systems. Such analyses could identify areas that should be rezoned or regulated because of their susceptibility to different disaster types.

Field simulation of communications equipment and GIS product generation under different disaster types and scenarios could aid future system development. Such simulations would also help disaster workers become more proficient and confident in using the GIS and other capabilities so that the whole system works smoothly in an actual disaster event. A sample of model output from the FEMA-sponsored Consequences Assessment Tool Set (CATS) is shown below. Under continual development and upgrade by the Defense Special Weapons Agency (DSWA) and in operation at FEMA and other Federal and state agencies, CATS estimates the potential impact from a threatening hurricane on population, facilities, and infrastructure.

Recent Changes

A fundamental change in the disaster information paradigm is occurring, fuelled by technological innovations. One of the fundamental characteristics of that paradigm is the greater dependency on information sharing, supported through communication systems such as the Internet. But this information revolution is still in its infancy, foretelling opportunities that will improve nation's ability to mitigate the impacts of natural disasters. Through the encouragement of broader collaboration among participants, in conjunction with the incorporation of new technologies into information-handling processes, the positive benefits can help to buffer the difficulties organizations experience in adapting to these new challenges.

New Data Sources

Providers can draw upon a growing array of space, airborne, and in situ instrumentation to measure terrestrial conditions and monitor a disaster event. Unmanned Aerial Vehicles (UAVs) are being evaluated to support collection of data under precarious conditions. Emerging technologies such as IFSAR enable the measurement of terrain details to millimeter levels of accuracy, with the added advantage of cloud penetration and day or night observation. Spaceborne hyperspectral instrumentation will enable scientists to examine a highly sophisticated spectral profile of surface feature to more fully characterize its condition. The selective use of derived products will provide added value to an expanded user community.

Improved Tool Set

There continue to be significant developments in the various techniques used to exploit data for the creation of disaster-related information products. Examples include: further advancement of GIS technology to provide both a platform for integrated display of a variety of geographic data and a means for manipulating data layers to explore alternative scenarios; formalization of image conditioning and exploitation techniques in user-friendly interfaces to provide access to complex algorithms formerly the domain of proprietary systems and experts; ongoing development of modelling and simulation tools that enable users to examine alternative scenarios and visualize the impacts of decision alternatives; and availability of more powerful computer platforms and visualization engines supporting the expanding need for manipulation of complex media.

Network Technology

Buoyed by the advancement of electronic publication technology such as the WWW, the Internet has become an important vehicle for data sharing, information dissemination, and public awareness. Broadcast technologies are enabling capabilities such as the Emergency Management Weather

Information Network (EMWIN), while NOAA Weatherwire relies on two-way satellite-based communi-cations.

Increasingly restricted information is conveyed through protected channels. The ERLink system, managed by the Office of the Manager, National Communications System (OMNCS), uses password protection; Intelnet provides a data communication channel for classified materials; and KG-75 FASTLANE technology enables multi-level network operation. E-mail provides connectivity for individuals over great distances, and the Emergency Information Infrastructure Partnership (EIIP) employs networked-based collaboration tools specifically to increase dialogue among those involved in disaster management. These technologies, which change the way information is created and distributed, demand increased bandwidth. ATM and satellite communications constellations of the future will offer a technological pathway to satisfy this growing demand.

Providers

The provider community is transforming as industry organizes to meet the challenges of new opportunities. Regional disaster information centers such as the Pacific Disaster Center (PDC), Alaska Volcano Center (AVC), and the proposed Western Disaster Center (WDC) have been formed to support the integration of information requirements and coordination of response to regional information. National exploitation centers such as the USGS-sponsored National Civil Application Program (NCAP) are designed to support integration of classified data sets. The National Imagery and Mapping Agency (NIMA) now provides classified imagery for disaster applications.

Users

The availability of advanced disaster information products has demanded that the user community become increasingly sophisticated and knowledgeable about new technological applications. This results in two expectations on the part of users. The first is that appropriate tools will be at their disposal to locate, acquire, and integrate information they need. The second is that providers meet more sophisticated demands for information; including better quality data and information products, models, predictions, and forecasts. The user expects to receive insights from the provider community on new ways to improve DM effectiveness.

Next Steps

In order to meet the ultimate objective of an improved capability in times of disaster, provider methodologies must be integrated into the DM life cycle. Providers must be responsive to needs of the DM community and effectively use dissemination community capabilities. They must accomplish their objectives using complex data sources, exploitation tools, and communication capabilities. As the DM community becomes more sophisticated and has increased access to improved technologies, it is demanding more and better products from the information provider.

Furnishing new information products by exploiting multiple measurement assets in response to user needs is a key challenge to the provider community. A pivotal need is for an effective operational infrastructure to enable information sharing within cost constraints. This requires that the user know what data are available and can access and use it. Also, the provider must be able to furnish data/ information products in a timely manner and, when appropriate, at the point-of-action. The provider community must ensure that the data/information is disseminated in a usable format. Customer satisfaction becomes a true measure of success, ensuring that the operational requirements are met.

To be most effective, the provider community must ensure that policies are in place to facilitate data/information sharing. Access to after-action reports, such as that produced for the Miller's Reach fire, will help the provider identify DM community requirements and also foster an environment of teaming and collaboration.

Identifying information deficiencies and making logical recommendations for overcoming them become a joint objective. It must also be recognized that this teaming must occur between Federal, state, and local experts and practitioners. Finally, establishing an effective integration of relevant research results into operational environments will cause both the user and provider communities to continually improve through the capture of new capabilities and technologies.

The collective action of various providers will ensure proper response to DM information needs. Such interaction is driven by the necessity to work as a team in a disaster event and by the fact that technological innovations force interdependencies. Today's disaster information management paradigm requires cooperation by providers. This occurs through developing common standards to facilitate data sharing; creating product catalogs, metadata, and software tool sets; collaborating on improved data integration technologies and expert systems for data search and retrieval; and using network-based collaboration and communication mechanisms. The key role of the GDIN is to stimulate, encourage, and support interagency and international cooperation to benefit the disaster management user community.

Disaster Information Infrastructure

Those responsible for emergency management learned long ago that their performance in such times of duress often was contingent upon being able to deal with critical and useful information, which in turn was dependent upon communication between key analysts utilizing the best 'systems' available including those drawing upon computer and communications technologies. The benefits of improved severe weather warning systems are strong evidence supporting this assertion. These systems depend on an array of sophisticated measurement capabilities deployed on the ground, in the air, and in space. Moreover, they require an information infrastructure to acquire, organize, distribute, and analyse the data and then to disseminate the results of analysis to the appropriate disaster managers. These managers depend on the infrastructure to instruct their support teams on necessary courses of action and to broadcast necessary details and advisories to the affected general public.

Today, the public is informed of weather and severe storm events through postings on the Internet, visually illustrated with storm track graphics and synoptic images taken from space; television advisories of weather developments; newspaper coverage of local, national, and worldwide events; and siren alarms alerting communities to the immediate danger of severe weather. At the same time, the supporting scientific infrastructure relies on computer technology to operate the models that perform the predictions, forecasts, and impact analyses and to communicate these in various ways. Today the technology base is available to support a robust disaster information infrastructure.

Elements of Disaster Information Infrastructure.

The three essential elements of a complete information infrastructure include the knowledge infrastructure, the interconnectivity infrastructure, and the integration infrastructure.

Knowledge Infrastructure

Encompasses the systems of measurement, methods of data visualization and exploitation, information analysis, event forecasting, knowledge modelling, and data and information management. These are often the purview of the information providers.

Interconnectivity Infrastructure

Encompasses the modes of communication employed to retrieve and distribute data, and to disseminate the information products, knowledge, and understanding developed within the knowledge infrastructure.

Integration Infrastructure

Encompasses the processes needed to ensure that the "mechanical" parts of the system are synchronized and that the "human" parts of the system are cooperating. Often ignored, or at best taken for granted, the integration infrastructure is key to an effective overall information infrastructure. The integration infrastructure addresses (1) the tracking of system performance to user requirements; (2) the definition of standards and protocols necessary to ensure system interfaces are understood; (3) the methods, processes, and procedures to ensure quality and reliability of the knowledge base; and (4) the training needed to ensure users can effectively use the system.

Information technology opportunities today are providing new ways for disaster managers to address needs. In Computing and Communications in the Extreme, the National Research Council recognized the opportunity and need to address crisis management and called for the establishment of crisis management test beds. As valuable as this would be in many respects, disaster managers are not waiting for a scholarly assessment.

The establishment in the past decade of the broad national network of Federal, state, and local (public and private) information providers is a clear indication of nation's ability to respond to the needs of disaster managers with innovative information products. It is neither optimized nor tuned to the needs of DM. This raises questions. How should disaster managers, scientists, and analysts access complex measurement data to assess a situation in time of crisis or otherwise develop contingency and mitigation plans? How can delivery of information be assured through robust channels? What is the best way for the community to share new knowledge about forecasting and prediction methods?

In many respects, tremendous progress in developing a disaster information infrastructure has been made since the Gatlinburg Symposium. Space remote-sensing assets—public and private, classified and unclassified—are routinely applied in DM applications. Communications technologies of every mode are exploited to deliver information to scientists, disaster managers, and the general public. Information providers are responding in growing numbers to user demands for understandable information products derived from increasingly complex sources. A disaster information infrastructure is indeed emerging. At this time, what is the best course of action needed to ensure a system that is responsive to the needs of DM?

Infrastructure Needs by Disaster Phase

The comprehensive DM cycle has been characterized as being composed of four overlapping phases: mitigation, preparedness, response, and recovery. A disaster-related information infrastructure needs to provide balanced support to each phase of activity. Each phase imposes unique requirements on the infrastructure, since data needs change according to the disaster phase and people involved. Mitigation and recovery phases have less urgent delivery needs and a broader audience but often cannot accommodate long delays. In its current state of evolution, the information infrastructure has been employed primarily for purposes of preparation and recovery, though other uses are evident. For example, the scientific community increasingly relies on the Internet for access to data and scientific collaboration supporting mitigation efforts. The requirements peculiar to each phase of disaster management and the implications to information systems and components employed are discussed below.

Mitigation Phase

Mitigation activities are pervasive both during and between times of crisis. They encompass activities necessary to reduce the impacts of disasters when they occur—such as the development and promulgation of zoning ordinances and building codes—and create the critical baseline data, analysis, and modelling capability needed to prepare for, respond to, and recover from a disaster event. The scientific community, business community, DM community, and disaster information provider community share in mitigation responsibilities. For the most part, however, these activities are not time critical but do impose other burdens on an information infrastructure.

Networking requirements to support the mitigation phase have key attributes, including the need to move large quantities of data/information, broad connectivity among a diverse group of organizations, and, in contrast to response and recovery, timeliness is generally not critical. Much of the data is GIS-based risk assessment, claims history, facility/resource identification, land use/zoning, and building code information. Use of modelling/prediction tools for trend and risk analysis is important. The data are largely archive-based, so several catalogued and linked repositories offered through good search engines or directory systems should permit better access by distributed users. Data providers are responsible for data quality (timeliness and accuracy), limiting redundancy, and updating catalog/directory information.

Preparedness Phase

Preparedness activities range from development of community training and logistical support, supply, and resource systems needed for disaster response to early warning and monitoring activities preceding disasters such as hurricanes, tornadoes, tsunamis, fires, or volcanic eruptions.

Network distribution of warning data during the preparedness phase is intense, and timeliness becomes a critical factor for some types of information dissemination. Public awareness through broadcast announcements and access to disaster web pages is key. Distance learning and other training activities making use of interactive video also fit into this category. Although disaster prediction accuracy and warning lead-times are improving, storm and earthquake alerts still require wide distribution in minutes or seconds. In remote areas, for example, full national coverage is a concern being addressed for the NOAA Weather Radio system.

Response Phase

Response to disaster events is time critical. Logistical options, damage surveys, baseline maps, equipment, human resources, and funds all need to be accessible. Communications among response teams and to the general public become critical.

Rapid, reliable, configurable, controlled-access communication is vital to efficient disaster response operations. Major challenges are presented by extreme conditions of facility destruction, traffic peaks, mobile users, and sensitive data. Intense management of property and casualty status, resource information, and response priorities require special access capabilities beyond normal commercial telephone/ Internet services. The Government Emergency Telecommunications Service (GETS) and Cellular Priority Access System (CPAS) from the National Communications System, Government and commercial "flyaway" systems, and private communication organizations address many of these needs, but incompatibility, cost, and complexity are widespread concerns.

Recovery Phase

The data needs during recovery include significant onsite data collection related to rebuilding, claims processing, and documentation of lessons learned. Feedback on the mitigation process and historical databases is important to prevent the same mistakes in the future. Timeliness concerns are relaxed in favour of efficiency, and the Internet is often ideal for such transfers.

The Internet is suitable for support to the recovery and mitigation phases, but urgent and life-critical communications during the preparation and response phases call for more robust systems. Currently, this need is being met by telecommunications providers who provide limited quick-response, mobile systems during emergencies. Much progress has been made in strengthening existing communication networks to survive catastrophes, but on-call recovery capabilities will continue to be important.

Clearly, system needs for access, privacy, and bandwidth vary among disaster phases. Today's disaster information infrastructure offers an eclectic mix of component technologies to respond to diverse requirements. Systems like the Internet are increasingly employed for purposes of mitigation, preparation, and recovery. Public and private telecommunications provide for quick response and real-time communication needs. Creative applications of broadcast technologies are being explored for warning and advisory systems.

Modes of Communication

Communication plays a vital role in transferring information between sensors, experts, archives, models, and key decision-makers involved in DM. As technology changes and disaster applications evolve, information distribution methods need to adapt. The design of an information infrastructure supporting comprehensive disaster management must weigh the relative merits of each mode in satisfying its specific requirements. The characteristics of each mode are described in this context. It is noted that while these are logical building blocks they are physically interwoven. For example, the physical manifestation of an "internet" depends on the public and private telecommunications. However, fax, phone, and pager technologies—all part of telecommunications mode—are useful alternatives because they conform to different sets of standards and provide different functionality. Today's incipient disaster-related information infrastructure relies in part on all these modes of communication; the future infrastructure, however, will need to address shortcomings present in its current manifestation.

Internet

The Internet is a global network of networks enabling computers of all kinds to directly and transparently communicate and share services throughout much of the world. It constitutes a shared global resource of information, knowledge, and means of collaboration among countless diverse communities. The Internet evolved from the DoD ARPANET project in the late 1960s and later research investments of the National Science Foundation. The Internet consists of more than one million network domains in more than 90 countries. Gateways that allow at least e-mail connectivity extend this reach to 160 countries. From its start in the late 1960s, the Internet has grown from 235 connected hosts to more than 20 million computers with an estimated total of over 100 million users. Network growth continues at around 10 percent per month. Data passing through the major network access points and metropolitan area exchanges exceed 700 terabytes of Internet traffic per month.

The most common Internet services are file transfer, WWW, e-mail, and remote computer access. Other popular services include information discovery services, real-time written interactions, audio and video conferencing, directory services to discover the addresses of people, or even multicasting of audio and video programs such as Internet Talk. Key characteristics include:

Decentralized

Very loose coordination among government, private sector, and academic organizations to develop standards and manage operations. No control of content or organization; anyone can publish what they want.

Widely deployed

Other than the telephone and TV/radio broadcasts, the Internet is available to more people than most other means of information delivery.

Best effort delivery

If bandwidth and end system capacity is available, delivery is made, but congestion and route failures can cause losses.

Local control/global knowledge

Subject-matter experts have control over posting data; it is then available for access by a worldwide audience.

Limited timeliness guarantee

Current protocols do not prioritize traffic or reserve bandwidth; thus, data may be delayed due to congestion.

No inherent security

Access control, authentication, data integrity, and confidentiality are added as needed.

Vulnerable to (Last Mile) Disruption

While routing around network link failures is automatic, the final connection to end systems is often a single point of failure.

Intranet

An intranet is a segregated community of network nodes with strictly controlled access, typically managed by a single organization. Access to and from the Internet is provided through security firewalls. It may also be called a virtual private network (VPN). Key characteristics include:

Strict control of access

Usually only members of the owning organization can have access. Internally, this occurs using userids and passwords. Firewalls limit external access to only specific subnets, protocols, and applications.

Traffic management

Since users are all from one entity, large traffic peaks can be identified and controlled more easily.

Security

Optional encryption prevents eavesdropping.

Wider Bandwidth

At a price, the net is scalable and the expeditious handling of large files on demand is enabled.

Robustness

If required, the net can be made resistant to interruption.

Extranet

An extranet is a specialized form of intranet that allows cross-organizational communications such as between a manufacturer and its suppliers. Access control may be at a finer resolution (i.e., at the directory, file, or record level). As discussed later, this type of network is highly suited to needs of the diverse DM community.

Wireless Broadcast

Broadcast includes mass media (TV, cable services [CATV], and radio) and special-purpose information systems (NOAA weather radio, EMWIN, etc.). Key characteristics include:

Broad coverage

Warnings through public/private alert system can reach the vast majority of citizens nationwide and worldwide.

One-way transmission

Broadcast media are not interactive.

Often wider bandwidth

Existing Disaster Information Broadcast Initiatives

Fixed Telecommunications

Fixed telecommunications include commercial and government voice, video, and data networks using cable, circuit, and packet switching. Key characteristics include:

Limited Priority Calling

GETS/TSP gives precedence for authorized priority users (military systems allow preemption of lower priority callers).

Dedicated Use Circuits

Give privacy, but do not permit cost sharing. Usually flat rate, distance-sensitive pricing.

Variable Bandwidth

Available at a price.

Documents

These include printed material, physical media (tape, floppy disks, video, etc.). Key characteristics are:

Archival features

Information can be retained indefinitely.

Slow delivery

Need to transport physically makes updates difficult.

Laborious to Catalog/Retrieve

Mostly sequential access and usually no on-line index.

High Capacity

Variable-volume, high-capacity media have historically been transmitted this way.

Capable of Reaching Large Audiences

One of the most common mechanisms for broad distribution (e.g., mass mailings, libraries, retail stores).

The interconnectivity infrastructure consists of much more than communication circuits and network hardware. Information search and browse tools, directory services, intelligent agents, and other emerging Web services are all part of matching a user's information need with a provider's data resource. Full integration among data organization, definitions, formats, and access tools is critical to efficiently making this match.

When comparing the features of the modes with the needs of providers and users of DM information, one finds that certain modes are better suited to particular scenarios and the needs of the specific disaster phase in question. For example, a researcher studying insurance claims records for recovery functions may need to plot data, layered on a dozen high-resolution images. If time is not critical and the images are over 100 MB each, transfer by 8mm tape may be best because of its large capacity and archival features. But the best use of analytic expertise may be via video conferencing, which dictates use of real-time, high-bandwidth systems. On the other hand, tornado or earthquake warnings generally need lower bandwidth and wide distribution in a short time. Both broadcast and fixed telecommunications provide wide coverage, but telephones are obviously unsuitable for rapid, mass warnings.

References

Drabek, Thomas E. (1991). *Microcomputers in Emergency Management.* Boulder, CO: Institute of Behavioral Science, University of Colorado.

Moore, Avagene, CEM, Sebring, Amy, et al. (1997). *Emergency* Information Infrastructure Partnership (EIIP) Strategic Plan. NCCEM, Falls Church, VA, September.

Sato, Kenji. (1996). *Map Database Construction in Disaster Information System.* Pasco Corporation, System Engineering Center, Tokyo, Japan.

UNDRO. (1991). *Mitigating Natural Disasters. Phenomena, Effects and Options*. United Nations Disaster Relief Co-ordinator, United Nations, New York, 164.

Wattegama, Chanuka. (2007). *ICT for Disaster Management e-Primers for the Information Economy, Society and Polity*, Asia-Pacific Development Information Programme.

Bibliography

Adams, S. & Crawford, A. (2000). *World War II.* First edition. Printed in association with the Imperial War Museum. Eyewitness Books series. New York, Doring Kindersley Limited.

Alexander, David (2002). *Principles of Emergency planning and Management.* Harpenden: Terra Publishing.

Alibek, K. and S. Handelman. (2000). *Biohazard: The Chilling True Story of the Largest Covert Biological Weapons Program in the World– Told from Inside by the Man Who Ran it.* Delta.

Appel, J. M. (2009). Is all fair in biological warfare? The controversy over genetically engineered biological weapons, *Journal of Medical Ethics*, Volume 35, pp. 429–432.

Arm, Stuart T. (2010). "Nuclear Energy: A Vital Component of Our Energy Future". *Chemical Engineering Progress*. New York, NY: American Institute of Chemical Engineers.

Barton A.H. (1969). *Communities in Disaster. A Sociological Analysis of Collective Stress Situations.* SI: Ward Lock

Beck, U. (2006). *Risk Society, towards a new modernity.* Buenos Aires, Paidos

Benjamin K. Sovacool (2011). *Contesting the Future of Nuclear Power: A Critical Global Assessment of Atomic Energy*, World Scientific, p. 192.

Bhushan, K.; G. Katyal. (2002). *Nuclear, Biological, and Chemical Warfare.* India: APH Publishing.

Borodzicz, Edward P. (2005). *Risk, Crisis and Security Management.* West Sussex, England: John Wiley and Sons Ltd.

Chaliand, Gerard. (2007). *The History of Terrorism: From Antiquity to al Qaeda.* Berkeley: University of California Press.

Chomsky, Noam. (2001). *Prospects for Peace in the Middle East*, page 2. Lecture.

Comfort, L. K., ed. (1988). *Managing Disaster: Strategies and Policy Perspectives.* Durham, NC: Duke University Press.

Constantine, G. Ted. (1995). *Intelligence Support to Humanitarian-Disaster Relief Operations, An Intelligence Monograph.* Washington, DC: CSI 95-005, December.

Cordette, Jessica, MPH. (2003). *Chemical Weapons of Mass Destruction*. Retrieved Nov. 29, 2004.

Croddy, Eric. (2001). *Chemical and Biological Warfare*, Copernicus.

Cuny, Fred C. (1983). *Disasters and Development*. Oxford: Oxford University Press.

Dezenhall, E.; Weber, J. (2007). *Damage control: Why everything you know about crisis management is wrong*. Portfolio Hardcover.

Drabek, Thomas E. (1986). *Human System Responses to Disaster*. New York: Springer-Verlag. p. 21.

Drabek, Thomas E. (1991). *Microcomputers in Emergency Management*. Boulder, CO: Institute of Behavioral Science, University of Colorado.

Eckerman, Ingrid (2001). *Chemical Industry and Public Health—Bhopal as an example*. Essay for MPH.

Erickson, Paul A. (2006). *Emergency Response Planning for Corporate and Municipal Managers* (2nd ed.). Burlington, MA: Elsevier, Inc..

Garshnek, Victoria and Burkle, Frederick M., Jr. (1999). Applications of Telemedicine and Telecommunications to Disaster Medicine: Historical and Future Perspectives, *J Am Med Inform Assoc,* Jan-Feb 6(1): 26–37. 7.

Haddow, George D.; Jane A Bullock (2003). *Introduction to emergency management*. Amsterdam: Butterworth-Heinemann.

Hoffman, Bruce. *(1988). Inside Terrorism*. New York: Columbia University Press.

Hugh Gusterson (16 March 2011). "The lessons of Fukushima". *Bulletin of the Atomic Scientists*.

James C. Oskins, Michael H. Maggelet (2008). *Broken Arrow — The Declassified History of U.S. Nuclear Weapons Accidents*. lulu.com. I

Johnston, Robert (September 23, 2007). "Deadliest radiation accidents and other events causing radiation casualties". Database of Radiological Incidents and Related Events.

Kahneman, D. y Tversky, A. (1984). "Choices, Values and frames". *American Psychologist* 39 (4): 341-350.

Mikiso Hane. (2001). *Modern Japan: A Historical Survey*. Westview Press.

Mileti, D. and Fitzpatrick, C. (1992). "The causal sequence of Risk communication in the Parkfield Earthquake Prediction experiment". *Risk Analysis*. Vol. 12: 393-400.

Mitroff, Ian I.; Gus Anagnos (2000). *Managing Crises Before They Happen: What Every Executive Needs to Know About Crisis Management*. New York: AMACOM.

Moore, Avagene, CEM, Sebring, Amy, et al. (1997). *Emergency* Information Infrastructure Partnership (EIIP) Strategic Plan. NCCEM, Falls Church, VA, September.

Phillips, B. D. (2005). "Disaster as a Discipline: The Status of Emergency Management Education in the US ". *International Journal of Mass-Emergencies and Disasters*. Vol. 23 (1): 111-140.

Quarantelli, E.L.. "Emergencies, Disasters, and Catastrophes are Different Phenomena". *Preliminary Papers*. University of Delaware Disaster Research Center. Retrieved September 26, 2011.

Sato, Kenji. (1996). *Map Database Construction in Disaster Information System.* Pasco Corporation, System Engineering Center, Tokyo, Japan.

Shrishti (2002). *Toxic present—toxic future. A report on Human and Environmental Chemical Contamination around the Bhopal disaster site.* Delhi: The Other Media.

Smart, Jeffery K., M.A. (1997). *History of Biological and Chemical Warfare.* Retrieved Nov. 24, 2004.

Smith, Larry; Dan Millar, PhD (2002). *Crisis Management and Communication; How to Gain and Maintain Control* (2nd ed.). San Francisco, CA: International Association of Business Communicators.

Staff, IAEA, AEN/NEA (in Technical English). *International Nuclear and Radiological Events Scale Users' Manual, 2008 Edition*. Vienna, Austria: International Atomic Energy Agency. p. 184. Retrieved 2010-07-26.

Sublette, Carey. (2007). "Types of nuclear weapons". *FAQ*. The Nuclear Weapon Archive. Retrieved 2010-02-13.

Ulmer, R. R.; Sellnow, T. L., & Seeger, M. W. (2006). *Effective crisis communication: Moving from crisis to opportunity*. Thousand Oaks, CA: Sage Publications.

UNDRO. (1991). *Mitigating Natural Disasters. Phenomena, Effects and Options*. United Nations Disaster Relief Co-ordinator, United Nations, New York, 164.

Wattegama, Chanuka. (2007). *ICT for Disaster Management e-Primers for the Information Economy, Society and Polity*, Asia-Pacific Development Information Programme.

Weir D (1987). *The Bhopal Syndrome: Pesticides, Environment and Health.* San Francisco: Sierra Club Books

Wong, James, Robinson, Cassandra et al. (2004). *Urban Search and Rescue Technology Needs: Identification of Needs*. Savannah River National Laboratory, November.